Foreign Policy and Congress

Foreign Policy and Congress

An International Relations Perspective

Marie T. Henehan

Ann Arbor

THE UNIVERSITY OF MICHIGAN PRESS

Copyright © by the University of Michigan 2000
All rights reserved
Published in the United States of America by
The University of Michigan Press
Manufactured in the United States of America
⊗ Printed on acid-free paper

2003   2002   2001   2000   4   3   2   1

A CIP catalog record for this book is available from the British Library.

Library of Congress Cataloging-in-Publication Data

Henehan, Marie T.
    Foreign policy and congress : an international relations perspective /
Marie T. Henehan.
        p.   cm.
    Includes bibliographical references and index.
    ISBN 0-472-11102-7 (cloth : alk. paper)
    1. United States—Foreign relations—1993–   2. United States.
Congress—Decision making.   I. Title.

JZ1480 .H46   2000
328.73'0746—dc21   00-028706

To my son, Sean,
whose death taught me more about life and love
than I had bargained for.

To my daughter, Elyse,
whose life has given me such joy
in the dark period between A.B.D. and A.B.P.*

For John

*All but Published

Contents

Figures

Tables

Preface

In 1966, Aaron Wildavsky (1966, 8) declared, "In the realm of foreign policy, there has not been a single major issue (since 1930) on which Presidents, when they were serious and determined, have failed." Despite the significant defeats handed to the president by Congress regarding Vietnam and the war power in the 1970s, Wildavsky's classic statement has remained a compelling undercurrent in thinking on the role of Congress, or lack thereof, in foreign policy.

Thirty-five years later, with the benefit of historical perspective, it is possible to perceive a much more complex picture of congressional involvement in foreign policy than at any previous time. Woodrow Wilson saw congressional government. Wildavsky saw two presidencies. Arthur Schlesinger labeled the presidency "imperial." After Vietnam, some perceived an imperial Congress, and others predicted a return to business as usual. Congressional behavior in the 1990s indicated that the foreign policy president has been weakened but not eliminated and that the resurgent Congress has backed down but not gone away. The decade's culmination in the impeachment of the president does not directly affect foreign policy but will affect the relationship between the two branches.

What is more striking than the differences in perspectives over time is the wide disagreement within the literature over the nature of congressional behavior on foreign policy. This disagreement results from two flaws: much of the work is theoretically deficient, and a great deal of it is time bound. This book will address the theoretical problem by applying an international relations perspective to the analysis of congressional behavior on foreign policy. It will avoid being time bound by covering 88 years.

An international relations perspective reverses the typical notion that domestic politics shapes a nation's foreign policy and posits that the international system has an impact on the domestic politics that produce the nation's foreign policy. The theoretical thrust of this book that distinguishes it from studies of Congress within American politics is that it looks at changes in congressional behavior on foreign policy over time as the product of the international environment's introduction onto the U.S. foreign policy agenda of critical foreign policy issues. The theory proposed is based on the argument that congressional activism on foreign policy rises and falls in a curvilinear pattern driven by the rise and resolution of critical foreign policy issues, whose provenance is the international system. This theory is tested by measuring and observing indicators of activity on and disagreement over foreign policy in the U.S. Senate from 1897 to 1984. These indicators confirm that the critical issue pattern characterizes the Senate's behavior on foreign policy.

The study of Congress's role in foreign policy has generally been dominated by the American politics field, and as a result the role of the international arena has been largely ignored. This research has been undertaken in the conviction that Congress has an important role in shaping the content of American foreign policy and that international relations theory has a role in explaining such policy. The evidence uncovered here shows that even though significant congressional input may occur only at long intervals, that input sets the limits and tone of the most important U.S. foreign policy decisions.

Like many authors' first scholarly books, this one is based on a dissertation. In the process of researching and writing that dissertation, I incurred many debts. The deepest is to my adviser, Ross Baker. He was always enthusiastic about my work, helpful with problems, and patient when needed. I am very grateful to him.

For help with data acquisition and analysis, I thank Diana Owen, Gert Lewis, Chris Jarocha-Ernst, and Mary Dietrich. Richard Tucker read the segment on impact analysis and generously offered many valuable comments. In particular, I thank economist Junsoo Lee for help in conducting the time-series impact analysis. His patient instruction and persistence in searching for optimal procedures greatly aided in completing the analysis. I am indebted to him.

For reading the text, suggesting improvements, and saving me from errors, I thank Steve Salmore, Roy Licklider, Lloyd Gardner, Irwin Gertzog, Jim McCormick, and anonymous reviewers for the University of Michigan Press. John Vasquez did more than read the manuscript more than once. His input pushed me to improve both prose and argument again and again until the manuscript was really my very best. At the University of Michigan Press, Colin Day was encouraging from the start, and Chuck Myers was patient and helpful above and beyond the call for an acquisitions editor. Kevin Rennells and the staff at the University of Michigan Press have been professional and helpful. I thank the copyeditor for finding errors and tightening up my prose.

My students in a seminar on Congress, the president, and foreign policy at Vanderbilt have constantly challenged me to clarify my ideas and to integrate my work into the bigger picture.

My closest friend, Chris Nevin-Woods, listened to endless discourses on pitfalls and stumbling blocks. She lent all of the types of support a friend can provide, even (in desperation) a good-luck charm!

As someone who did not come from a privileged background, I am acutely aware of just how much certain cultural advantages contribute to future success. Despite severe economic constraints, my parents fostered an atmosphere where education was highly valued, and they provided me with skills that have served me well in writing this book. My mother is a stickler for proper grammar and bequeathed to me a drive to use the English language correctly. When my siblings and I were young and asked all the classic questions about how the world works, my father would always say "Let's look it up" and take us to the encyclopedia. He is gone now, but I am still "looking it up."

The person who has provided the most support for this work is my husband, John Vasquez. He was my first professor in international relations, and I anticipated doing a dissertation under his direction. He then proceeded to disqualify himself by falling in love with me, but I have been living with the shadow director ever since. The extent of his guidance and support gives more than the usual meaning to the phrase "I couldn't have done it without him." That should have been enough, but he has had to carry us both through tragedy and illness that could have wrecked the life of a woman married to a lesser man. Through thick and thin, he has hung in there, and I am deeply grateful to him.

The last acknowledgment is to the person who paid the highest price exacted by my work—my daughter, Elyse. Conceived at the same time as the dissertation, she has had to compete for my attention and endure the fallout of missed deadlines. I wish I could have gotten my work done faster and spent more time with her.

Introduction: Congress and Foreign Policy from an International Relations Perspective

This book is an analysis of congressional behavior on foreign policy from an international relations perspective. An international relations perspective consists of looking at Congress and foreign policy in terms of the effects the international system and external relations have on both the direction of foreign policy and the type of behavior exhibited by Congress on foreign policy. The international system is seen as an environment within which issues arise, are contended over by nation-states and nongovernmental actors, and are resolved. An international relations perspective can provide additional insight into why the level of involvement of Congress in foreign policy varies over time because the international system gives rise to the issues to which the country needs to respond. The issues on the global agenda give rise to the critical issues in American foreign policy, and this book argues that critical foreign policy issues are the key variable in explaining why the level of congressional activity on foreign policy changes over time.

The field of Congress and foreign policy has profited little from the insights one might gain from looking at the impact of the international system on congressional behavior on foreign policy, while the field of international relations has largely neglected the internal workings of domestic institutions. International relations analyses tend to see foreign policy mainly as the reaction to external phenomena, especially external threats (Morgenthau 1948; Waltz 1959). Domestic political considerations may play an important role (Putnam 1988; Rosecrance and Stein 1993), but external relations are seen as the primary factors that shape the goals, objectives, and strategies of foreign policy options and the domestic debates over them. The field of American politics tends to see the actions of Congress as the sum of members' votes as influenced by such domestic factors as constituents, district interests, interest groups, members' ideologies, political parties, and the president (Kingdon 1989; Poole and Rosenthal 1997). As a result, the field of Congress and foreign policy remains in something of a no-man's-land with much of the emphasis on the advantage of the president in foreign policy (Wildavsky 1966) and the effects of domestic variables on members' votes (Carter 1986a). Yet there is a body of work on the impact of the international system on domestic politics from which one can derive a starting point for explaining Congress's behavior on foreign policy in terms of the international environment.

Empirical findings show that war and global depression have major impacts on domestic politics and even domestic structures. Rasler (1986) finds that global war affects domestic political coalitions, profoundly affecting what policies are pursued. According to Stein (1980), wartime mobilization can disrupt society and decrease domestic cohesion. Rasler and Thompson (1985) demonstrate that global war produces permanent increases in both taxes and governmental expenditures and thereby increases the power and centralization of the state. Such economic and structural impacts of war cannot fail to affect the options available to and favored by domestic actors. This body of evidence serves to elaborate Hintze's (1975) idea that war has a tremendous impact on the nature of the state and Tilly's (1975, 42) formulation that "war made the state and the state made war" (see also Tilly 1990). While war helps the state expand, other external phenomena, such as the global economy and especially depressions, constrain the options of domestic decision makers (Gourevitch 1986).

In an article reversing the second image of Waltz (1959), Gourevitch (1978) argues that it is incomplete to look at only domestic sources of foreign policies, pointing out that there are many ways in which the international system can affect the internal workings of the nation-state. Building on Gourevitch, Peterson (1994a) makes a case for applying international relations theory to the two-presidencies thesis, arguing that the president has an advantage in foreign policy because of the dangers posed by the anarchic international system.

The present analysis brings the focus down further to the subnational actor of the Congress. Bringing an international relations perspective to the study of Congress and foreign policy means looking at the effects of the international system on both the content of foreign policy and what actions Congress takes on foreign policy. What is new in this perspective is the proposition that changes in the international system have a direct impact on what Congress does in the area of foreign policy.

The reason an international perspective is needed is that the explanations currently offered for changes in congressional behavior appear to be incomplete. Until 1971, there was near consensus, with some exceptions, that the role of Congress was in decline and the executive was ascendant. The activism of the 1970s spawned more attention to an apparent change in Congress's role. Now, the question many asked was whether the new activism was an exception or the beginning of a new trend. By the 1980s, the literature on Congress was replete with varied and contradictory conclusions about where Congress was headed. Some scholars said that congressional behavior in this period was merely an anomaly in an otherwise downward trend in congressional influence. Others felt that the 1970s had ushered in a new era of increased congressional participation, ending the executive dominance of the 1950s and 1960s. Still others argued that the 1970s were simply part of a natural cycle of ups and downs in congressional activism. Finally, a fourth perspective produced arguments that congressional behavior on foreign policy is neither linear nor cyclical but that changes in behavior are triggered by certain factors, such as wars, issues, or characteristics of presidents, producing an irregular, curvilinear pattern.

There are three key reasons for this very wide range of disagreement in the literature. First, many works on Congress focus on a short time period characterized by a small number of extraordinary events. It is little wonder that conclusions generalized from the observation of unusual circumstances do not hold up for long periods.[1] Second, there is a lack of systematic theorizing about changes in congressional activity. There is a great deal of normative commentary, and recent years have brought an increase in descriptive analyses, some with lists of reasons for increased congressional activity, but rarely is the question engaged of why Congress behaves as it does and why this behavior changes over time.[2] The third stumbling block to reaching a consensus in this field is the lack of empirical evidence. What little effort is devoted to general theorizing is hardly ever followed up by data-based tests.[3] Without evidence on which to build, the research in this area cannot be cumulative.

The 1990s have witnessed a dramatic change in research on Congress and foreign policy. While the pre-Vietnam period was characterized by near neglect of the topic, the field has now settled into the task of analyzing the burgeoning amount of congressional activity on foreign policy. In other words, as Congress has institutionalized a new and larger role for itself in foreign policy, the field has institutionalized a place for the study of this phenomenon. For example, while most volumes on Congress or on the president and Congress have just one or two chapters on foreign policy (e.g., Dodd and Oppenheimer 1981, 1985, 1989, 1993), Spitzer's (1993) book on the president and Congress devotes fully 50 percent of its pages to foreign policy and the other 50 percent to domestic policy. More typical is the edited volume on Congress and foreign policy, of which there has been an increasing number in recent years (Mann 1990b; Ripley and Lindsay 1993a; Peterson 1994b; Adler and George 1996 [on the Constitution and foreign policy]). This scholarship would seem to indicate that a type of normal science stage has been reached, with more and more specialization and detail in the studies that are emerging.

While this is useful for the storehouse of descriptive knowledge on Congress, the subfield has skipped a crucial stage. There is nearly no theoretical foundation for much of this work. With the end of the Cold War, there is some sense of having been engaged in describing how Congress behaved during the Cold War and how it is behaving after the Cold War, but there is a glaring lack of a theoretical and historical framework into which the various stages of congressional behavior of foreign policy fit. One can see hints of theoretical concerns, for example, in the introduction to Ripley and Lindsay (1993a). This volume is rich in research, findings, description, and analysis. In the introduction, the editors assign themselves the task of summarizing the main contributions of the diverse studies. The first generalization they draw is that "Congress continually changes" (1993b, 11). Such a statement is too general, though. Ripley and Lindsay then list some of the chapters' explanatory variables for the changes, one of which is "a decline in external threats to American security." Stockton's (1993) chapter on defense policy focuses on the changes in the Soviet Union, but only a couple of other chapters mention this variable and then only in the conclusions. By far the majority of the book's substance consists of descriptions of internal changes in committees, constituency influence, legislative behavior, budgetary constraints, and interest groups. Lindsay and Ripley's (1993) chapter specifies on which types of issues Congress is likely to have the most influence, but not how attempts at influence vary over time. Stating that congressional behavior has changed and describing the changes is not enough—it must be determined how, how much, when, and, most importantly, why the changes occur.

A few analysts explain the variations in this behavior over the long term, and dozens of analyses review reasons why Congress has been more assertive, or at least active, after Vietnam than before. But of what was Vietnam an instance? How can an explanation of these changes be expressed in more generalizable terms? Vietnam was not just a trauma. It was a failure of a major policy (containment) that was designed to respond to the critical issue of the era (communism), which came onto the American foreign policy agenda from an international environment with particular characteristics.

The application of an international relations perspective is promising because it has the potential to resolve some of the contradictions in this literature. For example, why do some authors say that the increase in congressional activity after Vietnam was temporary and others say it is permanent? Why do some perceive cycles while others see linear trends? Why do some find that the current era is not even characterized by much activity or conflict? Why do some see Congress as imperial and others see it as impotent? Claims and counterclaims abound, and yet taking an international relations perspective would put many of them to rest by explaining why congressional activity is higher at some times than others. All of these questions will be addressed by the analysis contained in this volume.

In this book, it will be argued that in the area of Congress and foreign policy, the search for a stronger theory will not succeed as long as the search remains confined to internal U.S. politics. The way congressional behavior on foreign policy varies over time can be explained fully only by looking at the rise and resolution of critical issues in foreign policy, which in turn originate in the international system. Following Gourevitch (1978), this analysis holds that the international system has an impact on the internal workings of the nation-state. Critical issues arise in the global arena, and nation-states feel obliged to respond to them. These issues in turn shape the foreign policy agenda of the state. As one issue begins to emerge as more important than any other, responses emerge from domestic actors.

This study argues that an underlying pattern shaping congressional behavior on foreign policy is formed by the rise and resolution of these critical foreign policy issues. When a critical foreign policy issue arises, congressional activity and attempts to influence foreign policy increase. Once the debate is resolved and one side wins, a consensus emerges, and Congress settles into a more passive role. As long as the chosen policy works, this passivity continues until a new issue arises. If the policy fails, Congress can be expected to reassert itself. This pattern of behavior should predominate because it revolves around the most important issue, and the pattern will be curvilinear and irregular because it depends on when the critical issue arises. Furthermore, since the critical issue shapes overall behavior, this book also hypothesizes that behavior will vary by issue area. For example, congressional activity on the tariff issue has decreased since the 1930s (see Lowi 1979, 94–104; Hayes 1981, 28), while foreign aid is an issue that has increased congressional participation in foreign policy (see Crabb 1965, 91; R. Moe and Teel 1971, 48–49).

The basic task in investigating the questions raised and the explanation proposed here is to delineate empirically exactly what pattern congressional behavior on foreign policy follows. The use of a longitudinal design will make it possible to move beyond time-bound analyses, and the international relations perspective will aid in constructing a long-term explanation for variations in congressional behavior. Data based on all of the roll-call votes on foreign policy issues taken by the Senate from 1897 to 1984 will be used to generate indicators of congressional behavior that will be observed over time. Two aspects of congressional behavior will be operationalized: activity on foreign policy and disagreement over foreign policy. If the critical issue explanation is correct, both activity and disagreement should rise after a new critical issue comes onto the agenda. A time-series impact analysis will be performed on the data to assess the extent and duration of the impact of the critical issues on the amount of activity. Furthermore, each roll-call vote will be coded for issue area to see whether congressional behavior on foreign policy varies by issue area. If the evidence supports the explanation presented here, many of the contradictions in the literature will be resolved. The critical issue explanation will account for why behavior changes when it does and why it changes as an issue develops.

This explanation was derived as a result of examining the literature in both American politics and international relations and attempting to reconcile the contradictions and inadequacies in the literature in terms of explaining long-term trends in congressional behavior on foreign policy. The first chapter takes on two tasks: it presents a literature review organized around four different perspectives taken by studies of Congress and foreign policy, and it derives from the contributions and limitations of that literature a new theory that explains congressional activity on foreign policy over time.

The second chapter elucidates many of the problems in operationalizing concepts such as influence, assertiveness, and success and moves toward the scientific explanation of behavior. The chapter then lays out the study's research design.

The third chapter presents the findings on the Senate's activity on foreign policy over time. Data based on all of the roll-call votes on foreign policy issues taken by the Senate from 1897 to 1984 are used to generate indicators of congressional behavior that are observed over time. Two aspects of congressional behavior are operationalized—activity on foreign policy and disagreement over foreign policy—and are examined for long-term patterns. A time-series impact analysis is then performed on the data to assess the extent and duration of the impact of the critical issues on the amount of activity.

Since the critical-issue theory is based largely on the concept of contention, it is expected that much of the increased activity observed should be in the nature of disagreement. Chapter 4 presents findings on close votes and on votes on amendments and procedural votes as indicators of disagreement.

It is also hypothesized that behavior will vary by issue area. Thus, each roll-call vote will be coded for issue area to see whether congressional behavior on foreign policy varies by issue area. These results, along with how they relate to the critical issue patterns, are presented in chapter 5.

The last chapter demonstrates how the findings fit into the literature, assesses alternate explanations, and points the direction for future research in the post–Cold War era. To the extent the evidence supports the explanation presented here, many of the contradictions in the literature will be resolved. The critical issue explanation will have accounted for why behavior changes when it does and why it changes as an issue develops.

CHAPTER 1

The Study of Congressional Behavior over Time

A search of the literature on Congress and foreign policy for insights on how congressional behavior varies over time reveals that there are very few works that combine theoretical rigor, a longitudinal perspective, and adequate evidence. There are, however, many competing claims regarding congressional behavior on foreign policy, and a number of them implicitly or explicitly indicate how that behavior has changed over time, or at least what recent trends are. Such views can be usefully divided into four perspectives.

The first perspective is that certain presumably irreversible changes that took place when the United States emerged as a global leader and the increased importance of secrecy and access to information have given the executive a growing advantage in the making of foreign policy that causes a concomitant decline in the role of Congress. The second perspective recognizes the changes in the executive during the twentieth century but argues that with those changes, the role of Congress has grown, not declined. The third perspective posits a cyclical pattern and often uses a pendulum analogy, stating that Congress is very active at one point, then the activism fades and it becomes acquiescent, until, tired of executive usurpations, it asserts itself again. The fourth perspective has the most explanatory potential. This conception identifies certain factors or variables that co-occur with changes in congressional behavior. Identification of such factors is potentially very useful because therein could lie an explanation of why the changes occurred. Such factors include war, national mood, and the explanatory variable in this analysis, critical issues.

I. The First Perspective: Executive Dominance

The first perspective, that the executive has become dominant at the expense of Congress, enjoyed widespread acceptance up until the Vietnam era. Since then, this perspective has lost its hegemony but has remained a resilient aspect of the debate. It has its normative foundations in the Supreme Court

7

decision written by Justice Sutherland holding that the president has powers in foreign policy that he does not have in domestic affairs (*United States v. Curtiss-Wright*, in J. Smith 1989, 7) and in commentary arguing that Congress has lost its ability to initiate or influence foreign policy. Members' time is spent on constituent service, oversight, power struggles within their chambers, and parochial matters, leaving little time or inclination to formulate national-level policy (Huntington 1971, 30; Dodd 1981, 406–10; Lehman 1992).

Even in the post-Vietnam era, many analyses show that the executive continues to dominate. Labeled "skeptics" by Lindsay (1994b, 3), they argue that the executive will dominate regardless of Congress's attempts to assert itself. Their conclusions range from asserting that the president has the dominant role in war making (Adler 1988, 2; Ely 1993) to the lament that the struggle between the president and Congress over war-making power is over and the president won (Rourke and Farnen 1988); from showing why the president "(almost) always wins" (Koh 1986) to the startling conclusion that the president has gained ground as a result of the increased use of the legislative veto: because the Supreme Court struck down the legislative veto in *Chadha* but let the provisions delegating authority to the president stand, Congress has given the president more authority than he previously had (Silverstein 1994, 25).

Evidence of executive dominance can be found in a handful of classic empirical works, most of which predate Vietnam, and in more recent refinements of the earlier arguments. In his 1946 study of the previous fifty years of legislation, Chamberlain (1946, 11) observes the increasing importance of the president in the initiation and formulation of public policy. He cites the area of national defense as most particularly the domain of the president and his appointed representatives (456). The only trend upon which Chamberlain (454) remarks is that, during the decade of the 1930s, the influence of Congress relative to the president was beginning to decline. Of the 23 laws in his study that were passed between 1932 and 1938, Congress is credited with preponderant influence for only two (454). He does not speculate on what the future trend will be, but Robinson (1962, 9) argues that an extension of Chamberlain's study would reveal virtually exclusive initiation by the executive.

A few years after Chamberlain's study, Dahl (1950) observed increases in the resources available to the executive branch coupled with a lack of leadership and party responsibility in Congress. Given these disadvantages of Congress, the executive is often able to dominate in foreign policy, leading the author to conclude that it is not much of an exaggeration to say that "the President proposes, and the Congress disposes," and Congress often does not even have the chance to dispose (58). Carroll's (1966, 368) study of the House of Representatives and foreign affairs concurs, finding that the House's major tool is the power of the purse but that it is not very useful in shaping foreign policy. He then recommends that the House "develop more effective procedures" to increase its participation to "arrest its decline."[1]

The classic study offering empirical findings to support the arguments behind the executive dominance perspective is Robinson (1962). Examining 22 foreign policy decisions between 1933 and 1961, Robinson indicates among other things whether congressional involvement was high or low, whether Congress or the executive initiated the policy, and whether the executive's or Congress's position won (65, 68). The major finding is that the executive won on 16 of the 19 cases it initiated, and Congress won on the three cases it initiated (65). This finding implies that the branch that initiates is likely to win and shows that the executive initiates most policies. The preponderant instance of executive initiation in this study probably results from the fact that Robinson chose for his sample cases on which studies had been published, so they are the most important ones. Thus, the executive is likely to initiate most important foreign policy proposals and is likely to get its desired outcome on most of them. To tell whether this conclusion is valid for all foreign policy proposals, one would have to look at the universe of cases or at least a random sample of all cases.

In later chapters, Robinson looks in more detail at congressional initiative in foreign policy and legislative-executive relations. Most of his findings indicate that the executive branch has a privileged position over Congress in foreign affairs. Congress's role has largely shifted away from initiation of policies and toward legitimation and amendment of policies drawn up by the executive branch (Robinson 1962, 191). He assumes that this finding will come as no surprise in this field, pointing out that, since the making of mid-twentieth-century foreign policy requires a great deal of technical information, speed, and money, most of the advantage belongs to the executive (192). The only power Congress has that is relevant to these needs is the power of the purse, which is not helpful in initiating and formulating policies (192). Little did he know how well, one decade later, Congress would learn to use that power to shape foreign policy.

Throughout the 1960s, Robinson's findings seemed consistent with congressional behavior, but then that behavior changed. Congressional assertiveness in the 1970s challenged the generalizability of his conclusion. In light of those changes, it seems that three decades may not be a long enough period of time to demonstrate the full range of congressional behavior. In fact, of Robinson's 22 cases, 21 take place within only the two decades from 1941 to 1961 (Robinson 1962, 65). The other case is the neutrality legislation of the

1930s (24–27). Interestingly, this case does not even fit the generalization that executive-initiated proposals will produce the outcome desired by the executive (65). Robinson acknowledges that Congress actively struggled with President Roosevelt, handing him a defeat early in his first term, a period otherwise characterized by presidential victories in Congress (25). Between 1935 and 1939, Congress maintained its position against administration opposition (26). This apparently single anomalous case is really an eight-year struggle involving numerous proposals and several pieces of legislation. Is this one anomaly in otherwise executive-dominated foreign policy or a decade that is only the last stage in an earlier era of congressional influence? The resurgence of Congress in the 1970s makes this question even more compelling, because it is important to determine whether that decade constituted an exception or a return to a level of congressional influence that had been experienced previously. To find out, a longer-term view would be needed, with many more cases from which to generalize.

One study that addresses these questions by taking a long-term perspective is Sundquist (1981). Covering more than 200 years of American legislative experience, this work traces the evolution of the U.S. president's role toward greater leadership as well as Congress's periodic attempts to reassert itself. For Sundquist, the balance sheet shows an overwhelming advantage for the executive for a number of reasons. First, even the recent advances in legislative assertiveness are no match for the president's dominance because of the size and capabilities of the executive branch, its access to secret information, the speed with which the president can act, and the fact that the public has come to expect and demand that the president act as the country's spokesperson abroad (30–35). Second, not only did Congress acquiesce in its own decline relative to the president, but it also passed the legislation that created many aspects of the modern presidency (30–36). Third, even though the 1970s showed evidence that Congress will assert itself under certain conditions, such periods appear only as aberrations in the overall picture (456–59).

The reason, or "chain of causation" as Sundquist calls it, for Congress's lack of initiative is the ironic effect of the principle of representation (1981, 456–57). Because members of Congress represent only small sections of the country, they will not be willing to take responsibility for national policy (of which foreign policy is certainly an example). They want to take credit for what they can do for their constituents but are unwilling to risk anything going wrong on a national policy, when the payoff, even in the best case, is negligible in terms of their constituents and reelection (446–54).[2] Thus, only when a president is especially weak or malevolent is Congress forced to take a role in national policy matters. Sundquist predicted (457–58) that as "the memory of Nixon and his 'usurpations' fades, and congressmen live with presidents they respect and trust," the old pattern of giving up responsibility to the executive will reappear (for the opposite view in the same year, see Destler 1981a, 175). In 1988 Shepsle (482) expressed a similar notion: "representative impulses inside the legislature conflict with the legislature's ability to maintain its separateness, its independence, and hence its influence in the larger political system." This perspective implies that congressional assertiveness is but a rare anomaly and fails to see any permanent change in Congress's role stemming from the Watergate/Vietnam trauma.

A separate but related strand in the executive-dominance literature is the two-presidencies school founded by Wildavsky. The important contributions of his 1966 article are that it attempts to generalize about the presidency and is data-based, although it is limited by the fact that it covers only 17 years (1948–65). Wildavsky argues that the United States has two presidencies, one for domestic policy and one for foreign and defense policy. Using *Congressional Quarterly*'s box scores of support for and opposition to the president within Congress, he finds that congressional approval of presidential proposals on foreign policy exclusive of immigration and refugees is about 70 percent, compared to a 40 percent approval rate for domestic proposals (Wildavsky 1966, 9). This portrayal of executive dominance remained very widely accepted during the 1960s. As late as 1973, Rieselbach (1973, 179) asserted that Congress had been "unable to mount a serious challenge to executive hegemony in the making of American policy in the international sphere," citing the usual reasons of executive advantage in informational resources and technical expertise.

Congress's assertive behavior in the 1970s caused many, including Wildavsky himself (Oldfield and Wildavsky 1989), to conclude that the two-presidencies thesis is time bound. However, several studies have been conducted to show that there is a core of accuracy in the thesis and that it applies beyond the early Cold War era. Extending the two-presidencies thesis back in time, Cohen (1991) looks at State of the Union messages and records of legislation from 1861 to 1970 and finds that the president had an advantage in foreign policy compared to domestic policy long before World War II. Fleisher and Bond (1988) find that the thesis holds for Republican presidents through Reagan, more strongly in the Senate, and only when looking at all conflictual votes, not just important issues. This phenomenon may result from the fact that the responsibility for governing rests more heavily on the majority party, which for much of the post–World War II era was the Democratic Party, so its members may have been more willing for that reason to support the president and present a united front to the world. However, Democrats were more likely to take a partisan stand on the more visible, important issues (Fleisher and Bond 1988, 762–64, 766).

These results are somewhat unsatisfying, since one can easily conjure up anecdotal evidence that even Democratic presidents (Johnson on the Gulf of Tonkin Resolution) and recent presidents (Bush on Panama and the Persian Gulf War [Rohde 1994b, 101]; Clinton on Bosnia [Fisher 1995, 157–61], Iraq, the bombings of terrorist targets in Sudan and Afghanistan, and the NATO war on Serbia)[3] seem to have advantages in foreign policy that they do not have in domestic policy. Rohde (1994b, 101) points out that most studies of the two presidencies continue to find a presidential advantage on foreign policy, but it does decline over time. Using innovative data on the House of Representatives, Rohde presents evidence that there is increasing distance between the president and representatives because of changes in their electoral coalitions and that the reforms of the 1970s have increased the distance between the committees and the membership on the floor. As agreement between the president and committees decreased and the gap between committees and the membership increased, presidential success decreased even when he was supported by committees (Rohde 1994b, 102).

Rohde's findings differ from those of Fleisher and Bond because Rohde looks at the foreign policy committees and because he separates foreign policy from defense policy. He finds that the president still has an advantage in the Kennedy-Johnson years because of the strength of committees and the degree to which the committees would support the president. In the Nixon-Ford years, the advantage was lost in defense issues but remained for foreign policy. Carter had more difficulty with defense than with foreign policy, and Reagan had the advantage only on defense, at least until the Democrats became more united (Rohde 1994b, 126).

This literature is clearly plagued by inconsistent findings due to differences in the data used. It is not surprising that this school should be examined for the implications that the measures have for the findings. Lindsay and Steger (1993; see also Covington 1986; Van Doren 1990; Sullivan 1991; Bond et al. 1991) provide a critique of the measures used in this research and recommendations for improving them. In its current state, Lindsay and Steger argue, the research on the two presidencies thesis cannot really determine whether the two presidencies exist. By using examples of aspects of congressional and presidential influence that roll calls cannot tap, these authors show that the president may well be either more or less influential on foreign policy than was previously thought. For example, when a committee slashes a presidential request but then shepherds its bill through the floor vote, roll call measures find a victory for the president, although he lost in committee (Lindsay and Steger 1993, 107). Conversely, a president may be able to derail a challenge without a floor fight (108). In this way, roll-call votes both overestimate and underestimate presidential influence. Lindsay and Steger recommend refining roll-call analysis by excluding minor votes and multiple votes on the same issue and controlling for issue area, moving beyond roll-call analysis by attempting to measure presidential influence through executive orders and other unilateral acts, and building on past arguments to construct a more sophisticated theory to explain why or why not the two presidencies exist (109–13).

What would be even more to the point would be a theoretical explanation beyond that of Fleisher and Bond (1988) for variations in the amount of congressional assertiveness over time. The critical-issue theory uses international relations theory to aid in construction of such an explanation. Rarely has international relations theory been brought to bear in this literature, but there is one case. Peterson (1994a) suggests a new direction for theory in this field that is closely related to the theoretical perspective of this study. Suggesting that conflict between Congress and the president has not really increased, he argues that this conflict is kept to a minimum and that the president has an advantage in foreign policy that he does not enjoy in domestic policy because "the international system places certain constraints on the foreign policy making of the United States government" (6). Building on Gourevitch's (1978) article on the effects of the international system on domestic politics, Peterson argues that the American presidency grew in direct proportion to the increase in American international responsibilities. Since the international system in which the United States was becoming more involved is dangerous, Congress was constrained from challenging the president as much as it might desire because of fears that the national interest might be damaged in the process. Thus, the more pressure exerted by the international system, the more accurate is the two-presidencies conception.

In the post-1970s environment, most executive-dominance school analyses recognize that Congress has reasserted itself but insist that the executive still retains significant advantages. Destler, Gelb, and Lake (1984) indicate that congressional assertiveness is not all it seems. Peterson and Greene (1994b) suggest that there is only the perception that there is a high level of conflict between the executive and Congress: these authors' data show that the level of conflict has in fact been decreasing, even in the presence of increased activity. Even Lindsay and Ripley's chapter on how Congress influences foreign policy begins with the reminder that the president is the most important actor in the process (1993, 18), and Lindsay (1993, 280) asserts that the president has advantages that Congress cannot begin to match.

Hinckley (1994) goes even further, arguing that one need not even address the question of congressional assertiveness because the assertive Congress is a myth. In fact, Hinckley rejects both sides of the debate: it is neither the case that an active executive is dominating Congress nor that an assertive Congress is reining in the executive. However, two other logical possibilities remain: an inactive president faces an active Congress (the Whig-style president Sundquist describes), and the "default pattern," where neither the president nor Congress is innovative and both support past programs or fail to enact anything (Hinckley 1994, 11). Hinckley maintains that we are closer to the default model. Congress's making of foreign policy can be expected to be the exception rather than the rule, and problems caused by the budget will probably serve only to decrease the influence of Congress in some areas (Hinckley 1994, 13, 19; see also LeLoup 1993).

In one test of her thesis, Hinckley uses the number of bills each chamber considers on foreign policy. By this measure, the level of activity is not generally up. It increased in the 1970s but fell again in the 1980s. The most that can be said for any increase in congressional activity is that the number of symbolic resolutions is up sharply. Not only are these resolutions not representative of substantive legislation, she argues, but many of them are trivial. Her analysis of foreign aid is particularly telling. She shows that Congress was most assertive on this issue in the Kennedy-Johnson years, very compliant by the end of the Carter years, and while not always in agreement with Reagan, seriously constrained against authorizing aid in the 1980s because of concerns about the budget. Thus, "since foreign aid had been the congressional strong point [in influencing foreign policy in general], the net result was to weaken the Congress in foreign policy making" (Hinckley 1994, 124).

In the end, she finds only two examples of what she would call genuine congressional assertiveness: the War Powers debate in 1973 and the debate over Lebanon in 1983. The 1993 debate over Somalia was a real debate, but Hinckley stresses that the ground rules were set in advance, so that the debate was not as much of a confrontation with the president as were the other two incidents. Thus, perhaps "real" debate can be expected only every ten years (Hinckley 1994, 202–3). In the interim, Congress and the president cultivate the impression of being locked in a struggle by engaging in symbolic battles, but in the real battle of avoiding tough issues, they are partners (79; see also Weissman 1995).

As an overall perspective on the respective roles of Congress and the president, the executive-dominance literature captures aspects of the presidency built into the office by the Constitution but exaggerates them by peering through the normative lens of distaste for congressional involvement in foreign policy. This literature then turns this lens on a particular historical era—the early Cold War. This focus on a period in which Congress was not very active produces a picture that is, from a historical point of view, incomplete at best and distorted at worst. Such a perspective does not help explain why congressional behavior changes when it does because this view does not expect or desire such change.

Vietnam changed everything or nothing, depending on one's perspective, showing that theorizing to this point was insufficiently general to account for the changes. The changes exhibited by Congress in the 1970s prompted more attention to its role, but even before then, some analysts saw a significant role for Congress in foreign policy. Their works make up the second perspective, which holds that Congress is and has been an important actor in the making of foreign policy.

II. The Second Perspective: Congress as a Major Actor in Foreign Policy

The second perspective consists of arguments that the role of Congress either has been greater than recognized or has increased, whether since 1945 or 1973. Some authors see Congress as more important than the president, others concede that the president is more influential, but all agree that congressional participation on foreign policy is significant.

If the second perspective were the opposite of the first perspective, it would say that Congress is dominant and that the executive is at a disadvantage. Only two types of analysis have made that strong a statement. The first is a classic and was written in an era that differed substantially from the twentieth century. Wilson (1885) saw congressional dominance of government as the product of a century-long evolution of the American system. Only with the candidacy of Grover Cleveland, just before the book was published, did Wilson (15–16) begin to see the possibility that the presidency might regain some of its power. The fact that Wilson almost fell into the trap of concluding that the rise of congressional government was a permanent change in the American system can serve as a reminder to contemporary students of Congress and the executive that it is necessary to take a long view to avoid time-bound analyses. Naturally, this problem plagued the earliest speculations on the congressional resurgence of the 1970s. Nevertheless, several analyses in this perspective go back at least to World War II, and some recent works on the post-Vietnam era have more of a historical perspective than many of the early Cold War analyses.

The other type of analysis that indicates that Congress has become dominant at the expense of a beleaguered executive is typified by the following titles: *The Growing Power of Congress* (Abshire and Nurnberger 1981), *The Imperial Congress* (Jones and Marini 1988), *The Fettered Presidency* (Crovitz and Rabkin 1989), and *The Tethered Presidency* (Franck 1981b). Abshire and

Nurnberger (1981) include the section heading "Neocongressional Government," indicating that we are back to the system Wilson described—and decried. These works are characterized much more by normative concerns about protecting presidential prerogatives than by empirical analysis. Put off by congressional assertiveness and determined to thwart it if possible, these analysts are labeled "irreconcilables" by Lindsay (1994b, 2–3).[4]

Typically, however, works in the second perspective do not argue that Congress is dominant.[5] In fact, many normative arguments counter the irreconcilables' worries with exhortations of Congress to increase its influence in the face of continuing usurpations by the executive, especially in the area of war powers (e.g., Wormuth and Firmage 1986). Rourke (1993) claims that presidential war making is a threat to democracy, Glennon (1990) and Katzmann (1990) respectively propose reforms to the War Powers Resolution to increase the likelihood that presidents would abide by it and Congress would invoke it, and Rourke and Farnen (1988, 518–20) are so dismayed by entrenched executive dominance that they recommend an amendment to the Constitution to force other elected officials besides the president to participate in war-making decisions.

Proposing an amendment to the Constitution assumes that the president has powers that need to be curtailed, but such is not the case. It is the president's behavior that needs to be constrained. Ely (1993) points out that it is already unconstitutional for the president to make war on his own, and in fact the most serious flaw in the War Powers Resolution is that it indicates that the president can make war for 60 days without congressional authorization. Ely's proposed Combat Authorization Act (appendix A) would reform the legislation to restrict the president's prerogatives to real emergencies and a very short period of time.[6] As Adler (1988, 3) points out, "the authority to initiate hostilities . . . is vested solely and exclusively in Congress. The president has only the power to repel invasions."

Based on a foundation of constitutional powers for Congress, including senatorial advice and consent to treaties and nominations, the power to declare war, power over appropriations, the implied power to investigate, and powers of oversight (Fisher 1987), analysts in the second perspective find considerable evidence of a significant, and often growing, congressional role in foreign policy.[7] Empirical studies of the rise of Congress range from the qualitative to quantitative, from longitudinal to contemporaneous commentary.

Analyses of the rise of congressional involvement in foreign policy have been common in the past 20 years, but they were not nonexistent before 1973. Even during the heyday of the "imperial presidency" (Schlesinger 1973), there were several works that argued that the power of Congress was growing at the same time. In the mid-1960s, Crabb (1965, 91) writes that

[a] striking phenomenon associated with the control of foreign relations in recent American history is the expanded role of Congress in virtually all phases of external affairs.

Since 1945, there has been tremendous growth in areas of foreign policy on which Congress has an impact by virtue of its constitutional power over appropriations. These arenas include foreign aid, foreign trade, cultural exchange programs, participation in the United Nations and other international organizations, and peacetime development of atomic power (Crabb 1965, 91).

R. Moe and Teel (1971) make a similar but more elaborate argument. Disturbed by what they see as an uncritical acceptance of the assumptions of executive dominance, they embark on what they call "a necessary reappraisal" (32). They begin by asserting that, contrary to what most authors say, Congress has provided more initiative and leadership historically than has the president. Moe and Teel reinterpret Chamberlain's (1946) findings, showing that they indicate that the president shapes less than half of the legislation on national security. They feel that, in the 25 years between the two studies, there has been a chronic tendency to exaggerate congressional impotence.

R. Moe and Teel (1971) examine the role of Congress in each of the policy areas that Chamberlain covered. In three of four issue areas, they find a significant or growing role for Congress. In the area of immigration policy, they cite the clear pattern of congressional dominance documented by Chamberlain (1946, 352–74) and confirm that this dominance continues (R. Moe and Teel 1971, 44). Congressional participation in national defense policy-making, they find, has been marked by wide oscillations that depend largely on the role the secretary of defense chooses to take (47). An increase in congressional influence can be found in a fourth category called "foreign policy exclusive of tariff, national defense, and immigration." Only in the area of tariff policy do they find a decrease in the role of Congress, which gave up much of its role to the executive branch, but these authors point out that Congress still sets limits on executive discretion in trade policy (38–39). Moe and Teel acknowledge the aggrandizement of presidential power in foreign affairs since World War II but do not see it as occurring at the expense of Congress: "Quite the contrary: both the president and Congress have found their powers and responsibilities increased" (48).

The Vietnam era produced a large amount of work focusing on what seemed to be a new role for Congress in foreign policy, whether ephemeral or permanent. An early depiction of the rise of congressional involvement in foreign policy in terms of its negative effects on policy and on the executive branch is that of Franck and Weisband (1979). Their argument deals with more than just congressional opposition to the executive; it asserts that Congress has actually taken over the making of foreign policy. They characterize the resurgence of the 1970s as a genuine revolution in which a new class, Congress, overthrows the ancien régime, the executive. The major tool of Congress in this revolution is, of course, legislation. The authors see problems with this new mode, because legislation can set the means and ends of policy in stone, effectively preventing the kind of flexibility and maneuvering that only the president can provide. Franck and Weisband plead that Congress abandon the use of legislated foreign policy and allow the executive to deal with unforeseen situations (see also Purvis and Baker 1984).[8] Although the level of congressional activity has abated somewhat since the 1970s (Hinckley 1994, 27), Sinclair (1989, 138) shows that the Senate has undergone a fundamental transformation, concluding that it is a much more active body than it was in the 1950s or 1960s.

With the observation that the role of Congress has increased in foreign policy, the two-presidencies thesis has been reexamined and found to be time bound. In an analysis performed eight years after Wildavsky's, Peppers (1975, 463) points out that the thesis has been weakened by changes such as the loss of the sense of urgency of the Cold War, the reaction to Vietnam, and the passage of the War Powers Act. Arguing that Wildavsky's findings were exaggerated by the inclusion of many trivial decisions, Sigelman (1979) examines only the more controversial issues in both the domestic and foreign spheres and finds that presidents receive only 1 percent more support on foreign policy issues than on domestic issues from 1957 to 1972 and 3 percent more from 1973 to 1978. This finding indicates not only that the president was less dominant in the earlier period than previously thought but also that the 1970s were not very different from the earlier period.

Even a replication using the same type of data found that the success rate for the president in foreign policy was falling toward that for domestic policy. LeLoup and Shull (1979, 712) show that presidential success in foreign and defense policy declined from 70 percent (1948–64) to 55 percent (1965–75). In fact, for the later period, the presidential success rate for foreign policy issues (without defense) was only 50 percent, which is no better than the success rate for social welfare proposals (50 percent) and agricultural policy (49 percent).[9] In the face of this evidence, Oldfield and Wildavsky (1989) characterize the two-presidencies thesis as time bound and culture bound.

Edwards (1980, 13–14) examines *Congressional Quarterly* data on the percentage of legislative requests made by presidents that were enacted into law between 1953 and 1975. In only four of the twenty-three years was this success rate above 50 percent, and in three years it was below 30 percent. He asserts that presidential influence has declined in the area of foreign affairs, citing as examples the Case Act and the War Powers Act (16–18).

If the point of the two-presidencies thesis is to assess the influence of the president on foreign policy compared to domestic policy, then it must be asked where that additional support comes from and how much greater the support is for foreign policy than for domestic policy. In a later book, by disaggregating data by party, Edwards (1989) finds that additional presidential support in foreign policy comes from the opposition and that Eisenhower got the most extra support. Edwards concludes from the fact that the two-presidencies effect erodes over time that the larger success rate in foreign policy that Wildavsky observed is not a constant inherent in the constitutional powers of the president but a function of policy agreement on a liberal internationalist posture between a Republican president and a largely Democratic Congress (1989, 65–69). The two-presidencies thesis declined because later Republican presidents offered hawkish foreign policies that were increasingly opposed by northern Democrats. If a president fails to offer a foreign policy that appeals to a substantial portion of the opposition party, the apparent two-presidencies phenomenon disappears: "There is less to the two presidencies than meets the eye," concludes Edwards (1989, 69). By implication, there has been more to Congress all along.[10] Even if its influence is only at the margins, they are, according to Frye (1971, 121), frequently the "vital edges, and Congress's ability to shape them is of real importance."

Evidence to that effect can be found as early as Chamberlain (1946). He finds that out of 90 cases, the president was credited with preponderant influence in only 19, compared with 35 for Congress (450–52). Furthermore, he points out that fully 77 of the 90 bills were originally initiated in Congress before the president took a position on them (454). Recognizing these legislative roots, Polsby (1971, 7) confirms that the policies a president chooses to support often were initiated years or even decades earlier in Congress. Even when the executive does initiate policy, Briggs (1994, 179) concludes on the basis of nine case studies of president-Congress relations in the making of foreign policy that "the congressional power to propose, delay, and shape such policy remains substantial."

Rourke (1983) argues that there is little new in the "new" role of Congress in making foreign policy. Through a historical examination of the making of foreign policy from Truman to Reagan with a focus on congressional influence, Rourke (xiv) argues that Congress was "never as weak as it was usually portrayed in the past nor is it as powerful as contemporary commentary often pictures it." Looking at the large number of trade bills reported and passed into law in the House between 1967 and 1984, O'Halloran (1993,

286–87) shows that congressional activity on trade has been significant even after 1934 and before the Vietnam era.

The argument that Congress has been assertive all along has been submitted to quantitative tests by Carter (1986a). The dependent variable described in the first part is a measurement of congressional foreign policy behavior based on 668 cases drawn from the *Congressional Quarterly Almanac* between 1946 and 1982. The cases are coded as "compliant," "resistant," "rejection," or "independent." Carter finds that for 65 percent of the cases, Congress is compliant or resistant and that in 35 percent of the cases, Congress rejects the administration's request or initiates its own policy. Although a 65 percent success rate indicates considerable presidential influence, the fact that Congress rejects the administration's proposals or initiates its own policies the other 35 percent of the time implies that the executive-dominance school has given Congress short shrift.

Although Carter finds more assertive behavior after 1968 (43 percent) than before (29 percent), he points out that congressional assertiveness is not unique to the Vietnam era: "independent" behavior has comprised 25 percent of congressional foreign policy behavior since the 1950s, leading him to conclude that the overall pattern of congressional foreign policy behavior is basically the same for the 1960s as it is for the 1970s and early 1980s (1986a, 352). However, it is unlikely that the level of assertiveness is virtually constant. The analysis presented in this study suggests that it is not. If the time periods were instead 1946–50, 1951–68, 1968–75, and 1976–82, perhaps the findings would be more revealing; at least the "Vietnam era" would be more distinct. The contribution made by the measurement of assertiveness over a fairly long period of time is limited by the lack of a theoretical framework to suggest why assertiveness may be higher at some times than others.[11]

In the second part of his article, Carter presents the findings of a regression analysis that uses as its dependent variable whether the president's position is supported. Because his findings appear to be consonant with Kingdon's (1989), Carter concludes that the president is not very influential and that foreign policy-making is more similar to domestic policy-making than different. However, the two sets of findings are not that comparable. Carter does not measure success on domestic policy, and the success rate on foreign policy he finds is 65 percent, which is much closer to Wildavsky's (1966) finding of a 70 percent success rate for foreign policy than to Wildavsky's 40 percent success rate for domestic policy. Moreover, his independent variable of presidential involvement does not measure influence. It is not that the more involved the president gets, the more influence he has. The negative correlation between presidential involvement and congressional assertiveness implies that the president gets more involved on issues on which Congress is not countering him and backs off on issues on which Congress is assertive (see Lindsay and Steger 1993 on anticipated reactions). Also, whereas King-don's dependent variable is the member's voting decision, Carter's depen-dent variable is congressional assertiveness. What is needed is a theory to explain why congressional assertiveness exists where it does, increases when it does, or varies over time. Such a theory would lend precision to claims about whether Congress is more assertive than previously thought or more assertive at one time than another.

The 1990s have seen a spate of analyses of congressional behavior in the foreign policy realm. They are generally not concerned with explaining long-term variations in that behavior but rather take as a given what one author calls the "resurgent Congress thesis" (S. Smith 1994, 130–31), a bundle of explanations for why and how Congress has asserted itself since the 1970s.[12] As Emery and Deering (1995, 1) state, a "post-reform Congress's resurgent role in foreign policy making" is assumed: "the question is not whether Con-gress 'influences' foreign policy but rather 'How?' and 'How much?'"

Although such rich descriptions are finally taking the subfield beyond the "backwater" status that Lindsay (1994b, 2) ascribes to it and moving it toward normal science, they are usually not longitudinal and do not offer explanations for why congressional behavior varies across time. Their utility for this study is mainly in indicating how congressional behavior on foreign policy has changed since Vietnam.

Among the changes in behavior are the increased use of procedural leg-islation (Lindsay 1994a; 1994b, chap. 5), which, though no more common than substantive legislation (which has also increased), has become more complex, detailed, specific, and aggressive (Emery and Deering 1995, 13–14). The Supreme Court struck down a major type of procedural provision, the legislative veto, (*INS v. Chadha*), but this approach continues to be favored by Congress and accepted by the executive (Mezey 1989).[13] In the area of trade policy, where Congress has been seen as reluctant to take an active role since 1934 (Sundquist 1981; Destler 1986; Pastor 1980), O'Halloran (1993, 284) argues that congressional delegation to the executive is not abdication but rather delegation with built-in "procedures by which [Congress] can limit, modify, or veto executive actions."

A major aspect of the resurgent Congress is its increased willingness to use the power of the purse to shape policy (Burgin 1993a; Tierney 1994). For-eign policy is no longer the domain of just the Senate Foreign Relations Com-mittee: power has spread to the House Foreign Affairs Committee, its sub-committees, and the Armed Services Committees as well as to the Foreign Operations Subcommittees of the House and Senate Appropriations Com-mittees (McCormick 1993; White 1993). In arms-control policy, this shift can be seen in the tendency to go beyond consent to treaties and use of hearings and reports to broader use of the power of the purse and legislative innovations (Blechman 1990, 112; Frye 1994, 185–91, 202). Perhaps the most significant example of the use of the purse strings was the legislation to bring the Vietnam War to an end (Franck and Weisband 1979, chap. 1; Smyrl 1988, 14–17).

Tierney (1994) names several other sources of activism, including offering amendments on the floor and increased participation in the growing number of committees, subcommittees that handle foreign policy especially on oversight, direct diplomacy such as House Speaker Jim Wright's meeting with Nicaraguan leaders and Contras (also known as "Lone Ranger" diplomacy [Lindsay 1993, 262]), and going public. Perhaps the most important area of increased oversight is intelligence. Johnson (1994, 69–70) shows that congressional participation has risen markedly and has increased conflict with the executive.

In observing questioning of executive officials by congressional committees, Peterson and Greene (1994a, 75) find not an increase in congressional-executive conflict since Vietnam but an increase in activity that they call "enhanced interbranch collaboration," which is similar to Lindsay's (1994b, 6–8) concept of cooperation in contrast to deference. More criticism of the president is found on the floor than in committees, however. Rohde (1994a, 85) finds stronger support for the president in the foreign policy–relevant committees in the House, which was one of the impetuses to reform in the 1970s and which endured into the 1980s. During the Reagan years, the bipartisan cooperation that typified the early Cold War years did not disappear, but much of it was supplanted by confrontation, institutional competition, and constructive compromises (Jentleson 1990, 146–47). Observation of such increases in contention generally imply that Congress has seized back certain aspects of its role that it will not relinquish again.

To a certain extent, some analyses of the second perspective are just as time bound as those of the first. Instead of looking to the past for insights on a longer perspective, as the critical-issue theory does, the second perspective looks at how Congress behaves "now" as opposed to before Vietnam. For some analysts, the increase in contention since the 1970s has raised the question of whether such increases have occurred in the past and recur in cyclical fashion. Analyses of this type comprise the third perspective.

III. The Third Perspective: Cycles in Congressional Involvement

The third perspective proposes a cyclical or pendulum model. In some works, it is only implied that cycles exist in congressional behavior; in others, cycles are only part of the explanation; and in a few works, cycles are used to conceptualize the total picture. Binkley (1962) is an example of an analysis that implies that congressional behavior is cyclical. This historical treatment revolves around a theme of executive encroachments followed by congressional attempts to assert itself, followed in turn by rebuffs when a strong president comes to power. The implication is that weak presidents invite congressional activism, and it takes a strong president to put Congress back in its place. The word *cycle* is never used, but it seems that strong presidents alternate with weak ones, creating a sort of pendulum effect in the behavior of Congress.

Sundquist (1981) combines a cyclical perspective with an argument about the long-term decline of Congress. In a chapter called "Two Centuries of Ups and Downs" (15–36), he traces the early struggles and subsequent developments in the decline and resurgence of Congress. Following a "golden age of congressional ascendency" (25–29) that stretched from the administration of Andrew Johnson to that of William McKinley, Congress was instrumental in creating the modern presidency, which Sundquist sees as congressional acquiescence in its own decline (30–35). In acknowledgment of the resurgence of the 1970s, Sundquist (294) entitles that section "The Pendulum Swings Back—Part Way." A synthesis of the two parts to his argument would be that congressional assertiveness swings back and forth, but with each swing in the twentieth century, the executive gains a little more and Congress loses a little more.

In a similar fashion, Lindsay (1994b, 24–32) places the post-Vietnam increase in assertiveness in historical perspective by showing how the current era resembles the pre–World War II situation. He indicates that Congress's great deference to the president during the late 1950s and most of the 1960s was merely a brief period during which members of Congress felt that it would serve the national interest to allow the president to dominate. Thus, while Sundquist sees occasional surges of activism in an overall pattern of decline, Lindsay has painted a picture of an anomalous period of acquiescence followed by both a return to historical levels of activism and a permanent increase in the breadth of congressional impact.

A more explicit argument of the cyclical type is found in the work of Crabb and Holt (1992). Borrowing Corwin's phrase that the Constitution presents Congress and the president with an "invitation to struggle" (1948, 171) for the privilege of directing foreign policy, Crabb and Holt outline the extremes to which Congress can go in assertiveness and acquiescence. This formulation implies a pendulum effect, with the Constitution acting as the force of gravity. The theoretical rationale is that Congress and the president take turns pulling as far as they can until one uses its constitutional powers to pull the other back. In the last chapter, these authors state that congressional assertiveness in foreign relations has been a "cyclical occurrence" at least since the War of 1812 (286). With the lament that no single theory accounts for this phenomenon, they refer the reader to Klingberg's (1952) theory of mood swings in the American public.

Klingberg (1952) does not specifically explain congressional behavior. He does say that at any given time, a dominant mood encompasses the administration and Congress as well as the electorate (239). What is most important about his analysis is that it attempts to explain long-term cycles in political behavior. The mood of the public on foreign policy through history alternates between isolationist (introvert) and internationalist (extrovert) tendencies. The reasons for this alternation are the different value orientations of successive generations and how they interpret political events.

Holmes (1985) follows up Klingberg's theory, updating and testing it with new data. Holmes and Elder (1983) correlate Klingberg's mood cycles with type of president. These authors find that activist presidents are elected at the end of introvert periods and at the beginning and end of extrovert periods. More passive presidents are chosen in the middle of extrovert periods and at the beginning of introvert periods (p. iii). If there are longitudinal patterns linking the type of president to public moods, then mood cycles may be linked to congressional behavior the extent to which congressional behavior varies according to type of president à la Binkley.

In his 1985 book, Holmes devotes considerable attention to the role of Congress, although there is no fully developed theory of congressional behavior. He asserts that Congress becomes quite strong by the end of an extrovert phase and that during introvert phases, Congress actively challenges the president. As a consequence of these challenges, there are usually Supreme Court cases to resolve the interbranch disputes, which, Holmes points out, usually reaffirm the primacy of the executive branch.

Two points can be derived from this work that are relevant to this study. First, even if the Supreme Court does favor the executive branch, the existence of suits brought by Congress is an indicator of congressional assertiveness. If such cases occur more often in introvert phases, then congressional assertiveness can be said to be greater during those times. Second, as long as the president's actions are in harmony with the public's dominant mood, Congress will be fairly quiescent. During the 1930s, an isolationist Congress was very active in pursuing neutrality legislation. When the president attempts to pursue a policy in the opposite direction from the dominant mood, the people will push their representatives to oppose the president's program and to try to pass legislation in the other direction.[14] This can account for an assertive Congress in the isolationist 1930s resisting a more internationalist president who was ahead of his time (see Klingberg 1952, 248–49). As internationalism replaced isolationism after World War II, Congress became more passive, and the executive took the lead in pursuing an extrovert policy. If congressional behavior is found to be cyclical, it will be interesting to see whether it correlates with the Klingberg-Holmes mood swings.

Roskin (1974) applies a cyclical perspective that focuses on generations rather than moods. He argues that rare major events or catastrophes in foreign policy, such as Pearl Harbor and Vietnam, shape the foreign policy beliefs of an entire generation. The periods he identifies are 1870–90, 1890–1919, 1919–41, and 1941–Vietnam era, finding that Congress is most active at the beginning of noninterventionist periods. Within just one of Roskin's cycles (1943–76), Bax (1977) sees five successive stages in congressional-executive relations: accommodation (1943–51), antagonism (1951–55), acquiescence (1955–66), ambiguity (1967–70), and acrimony (1970–76), and recommends a new style of legislative-executive competition for the future.

Although Rourke (1983, 302) concludes that the executive generally dominates on foreign policy and that Congress plays a secondary but important role, he also sees a cyclical pattern in post–World War II congressional activism. The Truman years were marked by increased congressional activity together with a strong institutional ego on the part of Congress, executive weakness, and lack of consensus. The Eisenhower, Kennedy, and Johnson administrations and Nixon's first term were marked by congressional quiescence. Nixon's second term brought a return to increased congressional activity. Finally, Rourke perceives in 1983 the potential for a new stage of executive assertiveness.

Hinckley (1994, 27) presents some evidence that there is a cycle in the number of bills on foreign policy from 1961 to 1991. Although the overall thrust of her study is that levels of activity are generally low and no higher in the 1980s than in the 1960s, she finds a curve that shows an average of about ten bills per year in the House in the 1960s, doubling to twenty in the 1970s, and then returning to the earlier level in the 1980s. The same pattern appears in the number of substantive bills (those bills left after subtracting authorization and appropriation bills). The pattern in the Senate is the same, with smaller absolute numbers (eight to twelve back to eight). She also finds three periods in intelligence oversight: World War II–1974: hands off, 1974–80: moderate but restrained oversight, 1980–present: a step back (50–57). These three periods are similar to Johnson's (1989) eras: benign neglect, skepticism, and uneasy partnership. In the process of demonstrating that the 1980s are not significantly more active than the 1960s, Hinckley has found that with the increases of the 1970s interposed between the other two decades, there is a curve in some areas of congressional foreign policy activity.

It is quite common to find in the literature references to cycles or pendulum swings in congressional assertiveness. For example, Cronin (1983, 342) notes that a theory of "cyclical relations between the president and Congress has long been fashionable." Bert A. Rockman (cited in C. Jones 1995) finds three cycles important to the analysis of any president, one of which is the cycle of congressional activism and passivity.[15] Warburg (1989, xxiii) points out that much commentary misses the basic fact that legislative-executive contests in foreign policy are not new. He applies Klingberg's (1952) and Schlesinger's (1986) cycles to congressional-presidential relations, finding that Congress tends to be ascendant during introvert periods and that the executive prevails during extrovert periods (Warburg 1989, 18–22). What is changing is that new weapons have been developed and the cycles are coming more rapidly, so the conflict can become more intense.

What is generally lacking in the cyclical perspectives is a comprehensive theoretical explanation for why such behavior should be cyclical and more precise specification of how long the cycles can be expected to be. The Constitution may indeed be acting as the force of gravity acts on a pendulum, but why does the pendulum move? The Constitution could act as a constant, as indeed Wilson perceived the situation in the nineteenth century to be. The Constitution gave Congress the advantage; Congress took that advantage and held onto it. Yet that situation did not endure, so it is necessary to look at what factors besides the Constitution trigger swings in the pendulum, affect how far it swings, and explain when the brakes are put on. The examination of such factors is found in works under the fourth perspective.

IV. The Fourth Perspective: Variables Affecting Congressional Activism

The fourth perspective consists of arguments that identify certain factors that trigger shifts in congressional behavior. The advantage of the fourth perspective over the third perspective is that it offers explanatory variables that can be measured. The triggering variables or events are not necessarily likely to occur at equal intervals, so the patterns predicted in the fourth perspective are not likely to be exactly cyclical, but they should be curvilinear, reflecting an increase and then decrease in congressional involvement. The possibility exists, however, that the triggering factor could be cyclical.

There are very few works on Congress and foreign policy that posit variables to explain why congressional behavior changes over the long term. In the foreword to Crabb and Holt's book, Robert L. Peabody briefly states that congressional assertiveness usually follows aggressive administrations or major wars (Crabb and Holt 1992, v). Binkley (1962, 207, 383) does not explicitly identify variables, but he implies that presidential incompetence invites congressional activism and that Congress asserts itself when presidents are weak and is more passive when the president is strong, and at the end of the book he remarks that healthy economic conditions can produce passive Whig-style presidents who leave policy-making to Congress. A more explicit but idiographic specification comes from C. Jones, who states that congressional-presidential relations "depend substantially on how each judges the legitimacy and competency of the other" on particular issues (1995, 105). Finally, Rosenau (1971a, 439) hypothesizes that the more domestic resources a foreign policy commands, the more involved Congress and the public will become.

Gregorian (1984) looks at the long term and specifies variables that trigger congressional assertiveness. Although he lists no fewer than sixteen variables as relevant, the key explanatory variable is war. Congressional assertiveness occurs after war as a reaction to executive dominance during the conduct of the war. The bipartisanship immediately following World War II, which was commonly taken to characterize a new era, was actually an exception to the general rule (97–98) resulting from the emergence of superpower rivalry and the attendant wartime mentality of the Cold War. The data set examined in the present study covers a span of time in which the United States was involved in five wars, and it finds that there appears to be some kind of relationship between congressional activism and war, but it is more complicated than Gregorian's hypothesis.

Several other factors also have emerged in the literature. On the basis of his study of the making of foreign policy from 1945 to 1982, Rourke (1983, 304) finds that the following congressional values deter Congress (and can be used by the executive to deter Congress) from asserting itself: parochialism, congressional belief in the legitimacy of executive dominance, desire for national unity, and the loyalty of those of the president's party. Meanwhile, the executive has at its disposal the symbolic power of the commander in chief, persuasive power of the president, support for members' favored projects, and partisan appeal (304–6). Certain variables make for exceptional cases of congressional activism: issues that cost domestic resources (see also Rosenau 1971a), the rise of major innovative policies, an increased activity of interest groups (especially ethnic groups), a rise in constituent interest in a foreign policy issue, a challenge to Congress's institutional prerogatives, and executive weakness (Rourke 1983, 306–8). Under these kinds of conditions, Congress can use the means at its disposal—formal means such as veto overrides or the power of the purse and informal means such as generating debate and holding hearings—to assert itself. When it does, the executive may be responsive because of the value it places on consensus and avoiding a loss (Rourke 1983, 308–10).

What is unusual about Rourke's book is that he looks at a fairly long period of time (1945–82) in the search for patterns in congressional behavior. Very few works take this approach. Sundquist (1981) is indeed one of the few. He explains the decline of Congress over time in terms of how representation replaces national policy-making, but he does not adequately explain why Congress asserts itself when it does. Hinckley (1994) takes a fairly long view (30 years), but her purpose is not to explain changes over time; rather, she presents evidence in the context of demonstrating continuity rather than change and default rather than activism and explains these phenomena in terms of the two branches' political motives.

Far more common are analyses of the increases in Congress's role in foreign policy over the past 20 years. The "resurgent Congress" literature offers a plethora of explanations for the recent increases in Congress's role in foreign policy. Lindsay (1994b, 24–29) provides a summary of the major factors that have "push[ed] executive-legislative relations on foreign policy back toward historical norms": the Vietnam War (see also Carter 1994), a larger gap in executive-legislative preferences (see also Rohde 1994b), the internal congressional reforms of the 1970s (see also Whalen 1982), and the increase in interest-group activity (see also Tierney 1993; Wayman 1985, 1995). Lindsay (1994b, 29–31) adds to these factors three developments that make the current situation different from the pre–World War II situation and will tend to make congressional activism persist. The first is that there is a much wider range of foreign policies in which the United States is involved, giving Congress more programs to shape and oversee; the second is that the power of the purse has replaced advice and consent on treaties as the major means of congressional input (see also Blechman 1990); and the third is the larger role of the House of Representatives that attends the increased significance of the power of the purse.

Impetuses behind the increased role for Congress have come from the executive branch, from the international environment, from within Congress, and from society at large. It has been claimed that executive malevolence (Sundquist 1981) or weakness (Binkley 1962; Rourke 1983) can force Congress to assert itself. Franck (1981a) shows that Congress became involved in micromanaging human-rights policy only when the executive effectively engaged in impoundment by refusing to implement congressional mandates. Congress will also become more involved when there is a policy vacuum, as when President Bush was perceived as failing to respond appropriately to the end of the Cold War (Stockton 1993). With divided government (the White House controlled by one party and one or both houses of Congress controlled by the other) more the rule than the exception, it has become easier and more likely for Congress to overrule the president. For one thing, the minority party has less incentive to take responsibility for governing (as Fleisher and Bond [1988] hypothesize) and institutionalizes partisan critiques of foreign policy. Mann (1990a, 2) asserts that interbranch conflict will increase when there is greater policy disagreement and when constraints on institutional assertiveness are weakened. Changes in the electoral coalitions of the president and the House of Representatives have created a gap in their policy preferences that increases conflict, and this phenomenon is augmented by the change in the relationship between the committees and the membership on the floor subsequent to the reforms of the 1970s (Rohde 1994b).

The international system has changed its demands on U.S. foreign policy in a way that affects Congress. The increase in global interdependence makes for more similarity between foreign and domestic policy (Deese 1994). Rockman (1994) points out that exogenous changes in the world system with the end of the Cold War have reduced the need for centralized decision making and presidential prerogative, thus increasing congressional activity. Finally, Peterson (1994a) indicates that the less the threat from the international system, the more room there is for congressional involvement. Peterson and Greene (1994a) find that threats from the international system affect the foreign policy committees' questioning of executive officials: conflictual questioning increases as the perceived level of threat increases.

Contention within Congress, particularly divisions within the Democratic Party in the House (Rohde 1994b, 106–7) spawned reform, which in turn gave rise to the expression of more contention. Ironically, however, the reforms have also made it more difficult to present a united front in a struggle with the executive (Whalen 1982). Nevertheless, as members have gained more expertise, they have become more skeptical, more self-confident, and better equipped to counter executive mistakes and excesses (Frye 1994, 181–83). Tierney (1994, 124) points out that the nature of the foreign policy elite has been transformed from an anonymous, homogeneous group sharing a consensus on the U.S. role in the world to a diverse, publicity-seeking, career advancing, polarized, and politicized cadre of foreign policy professionals. Sinclair (1989, chap. 4) shows that changes in the Washington policy community have led to a dramatic increase in the extent of the international involvement agenda. From the eighty-fourth to the ninety-ninth Congresses

(1955 to 1986), international involvement, together with government management of the economy, dominated the Senate's contested floor agenda (as indicated by roll calls) (Sinclair 1989, 117).

This increase in activity is just one aspect of the transformation of the Senate over the past 40 years. According to Sinclair (1989, 5), this transformation was driven by the advent of new liberal northern Democrats and by changes in the policy system that included an increased number of groups, a change in the issue agenda, and the increased importance of the media. The number, type, and influence of interest groups related to foreign policy have increased greatly in the past 20 years, opening avenues from the public to Congress and increasing contention both within Congress and between Congress and the executive (Tierney 1993, 1994; Wayman 1995). Public opinion on foreign policy became more mobilized in the 1970s, a major influence on the behavior of Congress (Mann 1990a). When the administration is out of step with the public or refuses to modify its policy in the face of opposition, Congress will become more assertive (Blechman 1990).

The increase in partisanship is a major theme in much of this literature. Sinclair (1993) and S. Smith (1994) both study a largely overlooked set of actors in this literature, the party leaders in Congress. Smith finds that party leaders are now more active as party spokesmen, more partisan in their support for the president and in consulting with him, and more active on foreign policy in their leadership positions in Congress (154–55). Sinclair (230) points out that party leaders are more active, involved, and visible on foreign and defense policy, but their impact depends a great deal on the degree of consensus with an also active membership. Rohde (1994a, 98) relates the increase in assertiveness on defense and foreign policy to the increase in partisanship, which stems from changes in electoral behavior and voter loyalty. Thus, the parties have become more homogeneous internally and more different from each other on foreign policy. In the presence of divided government, a more cohesive and partisan opposition party can succeed in passing legislation over the objections of the president.

Some of these explanations are more generalizable than others. For example, factors such as the reforms of the 1970s, changes in the foreign policy elite, and the increase in the gap between executive and legislative preferences are fairly idiographic. Under what conditions do these variables operate? If these changes are attributable to Vietnam, what is its theoretical significance? This explanatory problem will be addressed at length later in this analysis.

More generalizable are variables such as weakness of the executive, the executive being out of step with the public, the level of threat from the international environment, and level of activity of interest groups. Also, some of the other factors could be recast as general explanations. For example, how and why does the gap between executive and legislative preferences widen and narrow over time? What other conditions co-occur with these changes? Have shifts from bipartisanship to partisanship occurred in the past? Under what conditions? Were they related to congressional assertiveness? However, factors that change with time cannot be rendered generalizable unless a much longer time frame than 20 (or even 30 or 40) years is used. The framework for the analysis in this book falls within the fourth perspective in that it identifies variables that explain why congressional behavior on foreign policy varies as it does, and it examines a long enough time frame to overcome problems of being time bound and idiographic.

V. Foreign Policy Issues and Issue Areas

It is now clear that research on change in congressional behavior has produced quite contradictory conclusions. They cannot possibly all be correct. In fact, this study assumes that none of them are both correct and complete and proposes instead a thesis based on the role of issues in shaping foreign policy behavior. Many political scientists have found issues to be important to understanding politics, but the role of issues in long-term congressional behavior on foreign policy has yet to be thoroughly elaborated.

Dahl (1961) provides early evidence that political behavior varies by issue in his study of New Haven, Connecticut. He finds that different elites arise for each of three different issues. Lowi (1964) takes a different tack, making a very influential theoretical argument that different types of issues, depending on the disaggregatability of the stakes involved, produce different policy processes (see also Ripley and Franklin 1991). Hayes (1981, 19) applies the general notion of different issue types to the study of interest groups and Congress, arguing that the role of interest groups will depend on the type of issue. Adding one category, constituent-type issues, to Lowi's three categories of distributive, regulatory, and redistributive issues, Spitzer (1983) suggests that there are four presidencies—that is, that the president has a different level of influence for each of the four types of issues.

In the area of foreign policy, Rosenau (1971b, 134) argues that the nature of the issue is crucial in determining who becomes involved, what their motives are, and what kind of interaction evolves as the issue is resolved. Clausen (1973) and Clausen and Van Horn (1977) find that although members' votes are consistent in four areas of domestic policy, the votes shift in the area of foreign policy when the party of the president changes. This implies that the president can more successfully influence members in the area of foreign policy than in domestic policy, a finding corroborated by Edwards (1980, 65–66).

The assumption that the role of Congress in foreign policy varies by issue area is implicit in every book that has separate chapters on war powers, trade, arms control, defense, and foreign aid (Mann 1990b; Crabb and Holt 1992; Ripley and Lindsay 1993a; Peterson 1994b). For example, Destler (1981b) finds that multilateral trade agreements are characterized by success-ful interaction between the branches, whereas interbranch relations resulted in stalemate on the SALT II Treaty. Destler (1994) finds trade policy generally to be characterized by more continuity than change in interbranch relations. Peterson (1994a, 11) contrasts Destler's conclusions with Carter's (1994) findings on defense that show that conflict over expenditures has increased greatly because of Congress's advantage in the power of the purse. Rohde's (1994b, 114) findings confirm his argument that defense policy needs to be considered separately from the rest of foreign policy. When controlling for issue in this way, he finds that some presidents have an advantage in foreign policy but not defense policy, and others experience the opposite. Also, con-gressional support on roll calls the president favored declined greatly in defense but were fairly static in foreign policy.

Several works have hypothesized or identified different modes of con-gressional behavior depending on the issue. As noted earlier, R. Moe and Teel (1971) find that Congress has given up its role in tariff policy, has occasional input to defense policy, dominates immigration policy, and has a growing role in the remainder of foreign policy. In a similar type of analysis, Hinckley (1978, chap. 8) rank orders types of foreign policy from least to most input by Congress. On questions of war, the president dominates; in making peace, especially by treaty, Congress begins to play a role. In defense, Congress is still likely to defer to the executive on questions regarding responses to external threats but becomes more involved in the "real estate" questions of funding bases. Finally, in foreign aid, Congress "appears to know what it is—an inde-pendent branch of government," frequently saying no to the executive branch (Hinckley 1978, 183–84). Since she wrote, of course, congressional assertive-ness on defense has increased (Carter 1994). Rockman (1994, 60–64) offers a more recent rank ordering, listing six foreign policy issue areas in declining order of amenity to presidential prerogative: intelligence operations and assessments, strategic policy, trade issues, foreign assistance, ethnic interven-tions, and human-rights issues.

Rosati (1984) also uses issue area as a key to his historical analysis of executive-congressional relations on foreign policy. Borrowing from Ripley (1975), Rosati posits three different models of executive-congressional rela-tions: executive dominance, congressional dominance, and codetermination.

He finds that executive dominance fits war powers and informal international agreements, while codetermination is the rule in formal international agreements, foreign assistance and sales, and foreign economic policy (Rosati 1984, 327).[16]

Following Huntington (1961), Lowi (1967), and Ripley and Franklin (1991), Lindsay and Ripley (1993, 18–22) differentiate among three different types of policy within foreign and defense policy. In crisis policy, the president tends to dominate; on strategic policy, the president still has the advantage in initiation, although in some areas, Congress must approve the policy; and in structural policy, Congress plays its largest role, mostly because of the power of the purse (see also Lindsay 1994b, chap. 7).

Data-based findings are scarcer than assertions that behavior varies by issue. Carter (1986b) finds differences between national security versus non-national security issues. Carter (1985) investigates the variations in congressional assertiveness across issue types for five different typologies. He finds that congressional assertiveness is more likely as issues become more controversial or as the process becomes more regulative or redistributive and that congressional compliance is more likely on routine issues or political-diplomatic, protective-interactive, or status-type issues. Congressional amendation is most likely on distributive issues and those involving human resources (Carter 1985, 33–36). In another paper, Carter (1986b, 22–23) finds that party leaders and domestic pressures are more important for national security issues than for non–national security issues. Congress is less assertive on national security than on non–national security issues, but it does regularly modify administration proposals on national security.

An issue-area perspective could help clear up some of the disagreement among those who have "reassessed" Wildavsky's two-presidencies thesis. Hinckley (1978) raises the question of whether, if there are two presidencies, there are also two Congresses. In fact, she identifies four different Congresses within foreign policy, corresponding to the four different issue areas of war, peace, defense, and foreign aid. Despite finding that the president's success rate is nearly as low in foreign policy as it is in domestic policy, LeLoup and Shull (1979, 707, 715) conclude that Wildavsky (1966) is still partially correct about the existence of a foreign policy presidency. LeLoup and Shull caution that there is no single monolithic dominance as implied by Wildavsky, but there are two different modes of presidential foreign policy making. The president still dominates in high-level diplomacy and military and national security questions that are never even submitted to Congress. "Foreign aid, trade, and general defense and national security issues" (717) are more similar to domestic policy-making, involving shared power. These latter issues usually require appropriations or have other domestic implications. Their later work indicates that as the system has moved from presidential dominance to a system of tandem institutions sharing power, there are four patterns in presidential-congressional relations, depending on the type of issue (1999, 7–19, 130–43).

Rourke (1987) reports some suggestive findings in this area. His replications of Sigelman's (1979) and Wildavsky's (1966) analyses for the first Reagan administration show support for both of their arguments: presidential success on foreign policy is no higher than for domestic policy when only key votes are used, but presidential success is higher for foreign policy than for domestic policy when all votes on which the president takes a position are used (Rourke 1987, 9–11). However, while Wildavsky found the president to be about 30 percent more successful in foreign policy, Rourke (1987, 11) found Reagan only 13 percent more successful in foreign policy than in domestic policy.

Rourke finds stronger support for the Wildavsky thesis by dividing foreign policy into "intermestic" policy and "pure" foreign policy, based on whether Congress perceives a foreign policy issue as having a strong domestic dimension or as purely foreign policy. When key votes and all votes on which the president takes a position are divided into three categories instead of two, the president is found to be significantly more successful on pure foreign policy than on domestic policy, especially after the honeymoon period and especially in the Democratic-controlled House, where the difference reaches 30 percent, which is comparable to Wildavsky's findings.[17] Although there is much less of a difference between the two areas in the Senate, such is not the case because approval of foreign policy is low. The approval rate for foreign policy in the Senate is actually higher (89 percent) than in the House, but the approval rate for domestic policy is also very high (84 percent). These high success rates lead Rourke to conclude that the Wildavsky thesis is generally supported except when all levels of success are very high.[18] A somewhat different interpretation would be that Wildavsky's second presidency has survived in so-called pure foreign policy but has expired in the intermestic area. This finding would mean that the role of Congress has grown—that it has chipped away at executive supremacy in the area of intermestic policy. Shull (1997) provides more detailed findings across both issue area and over time by introducing three new variables—presidential position taking, controversy over congressional votes, and executive order issuance—and combining them with the more traditional variable of legislative support.

These studies offer some evidence that patterns of behavior differ by issue. It can also be observed from the different findings at different times that a given issue area can change over time (e.g., defense), and that new issues can arise to increase Congress's role (e.g., human rights). For this analysis, patterns in congressional behavior will be traced over time in several issue areas. However, it remains to be seen just what it is about issues that shapes overall behavior across time.

VI.   The International System, Critical Issues, and Long-Term Patterns in Congressional Behavior

When behavior on all of the issues is aggregated, what kind of pattern characterizes overall congressional behavior on foreign policy? This is the question most of the authors reviewed in this chapter were trying to answer. However, most of them encountered difficulty because the pattern they found fit only a certain period of time. Wilson's "congressional government" gave way to the executive-dominance school of the early twentieth century. Then the congressional revolt of the 1970s again challenged the conventional wisdom. However, the new era of legislated foreign policy was not permanent. Each author captured a segment of the history of Congress, but none seemed to adequately describe the long term.

One can derive a long-term picture by combining the cyclical and linear elements of Sundquist's (1981) analysis. From McKinley on, Congress is generally on the decline, but within this large pattern is a smaller cyclical or curvilinear pattern made up of occasional spurts of activism followed by longer periods of submission to the executive. The cyclical analyses can also be adapted to fit this model. The problem with this synthesis is that it does not explain the smaller pattern. There is still a need to explain why Congress is generally assertive at one time and more passive at another.

The explanation offered here has roots in both international relations and American politics. On the international relations side, it draws on an elaboration of the levels-of-analysis literature; from American politics, it borrows the notion of critical issues.

Gourevitch (1978) offers a review of both international relations and comparative politics approaches to the study of foreign policy that makes the point that not only does domestic politics affect foreign policy but the international system also affects domestic politics. Although he does not analyze Congress systematically in this article, his reversal of Waltz's (1959) second image suggests an innovative approach to the study of congressional behavior: an examination of the effect of global politics on the behavior of domestic institutions.[19]

In his review of the literature, Gourevitch criticizes the tendency of some studies to focus on internal process and institutional arrangement to explain foreign policy behavior (1978, 901–2). The example he uses is directly relevant to this study. He cites the argument that, as protectionist interests in the United States were strong in Congress and free trade interests stronger in the executive, the shift from protection to free trade after World War II was possible because of the shift in institutional power from Congress to the president. Gourevitch sees this argument as spurious and suggests that it is less likely that the policy change was caused by the shifting balance of institutional power than that both changes were symptoms of something else—that is, changes in the international system.

An example of such an application would be that, instead of asking what domestic regime factors (democracy, dictatorship, capitalism) lead states to go to war, we should look more closely at Hintze's (1975) argument that war (or its absence) affects the way states organize themselves internally (see Gourevitch 1978, 896). Although some studies have looked at the growth of the state as a result of war (e.g., Rasler and Thompson 1985, 1989), when it comes to looking inside the state at the behavior of particular institutions, the tendency is to focus on domestic sources of that behavior. This book uses the Gourevitch thesis as a basis for arguing that the international environment has an important and measurable impact on the content and range of behavior of domestic institutions.

This statement should not be very controversial, yet much of the literature on American institutions fails to look beyond the borders for explanations of their behavior. While policy choices on domestic issues may well be determined internally, in the area of foreign policy, at least, there is insufficient attention to questions of how the agenda is set and what constrains policy choice. Specifically, the debate over the relative impact of the legislative and executive branches on foreign policy has been prone to ascribe too much autonomy to the two branches, without considering the simultaneous impact of the international environment on both of them.

Crabb and Holt (1992) organize their study around the notion that the Constitution is an invitation to struggle to the two branches; yet, although the Constitution limits the power of each branch, it does not explain why a branch's behavior changes when it does. Sundquist (1981) examines how the political tradition of Whig-style presidents is replaced by a more activist presidency and documents the role of the Congress in creating the modern activist presidency. He acknowledges the role of the change in the U.S. role in the world in this shift in institutional power, but variations in the relationship are seen as swings of a pendulum that are more or less undetermined. Even though Klingberg's (1952, 1983; see also Holmes 1985) mood swings offer better explanations of variations in foreign policy, the causes are all domestic, rooted in public preferences and the American political tradition. In general, this type of analysis leaves a gap by ignoring the extent of the impact of the international system on both branches.

Peterson (1994a) indicates that Americanists are beginning to look at international relations theory. Peterson draws on international relations theory (as articulated by Morgenthau [1948], Waltz [1979], Keohane [1984], and Krasner [1978]) to argue that national interest is the major constraint in the formation of foreign policy. Peterson then challenges this theoretical assumption to move one logical step forward: "if the international system constrains the policies of nations, so also must it influence the way in which nation-states deliberate upon and decide these policies" (1994a, 19). To move in this direction, Peterson then cites Gourevitch's (1978) article on reversing the second image as a basis for looking at how the international system affects domestic politics. Peterson goes beyond Gourevitch by applying this insight explicitly to the operation and development of domestic political institutions—the American presidency grew in direct proportion to the increase in American international responsibilities.

According to Peterson (1994a, 21), the executive has retained the advantage in foreign policy, and committees protect and support presidential requests because members are more aware of the constraints of the anarchic international system. When Congress does override the executive, Peterson argues, it does so because the executive's assessment of U.S. long-term interests were dubious and Congress had a better grasp of the national interest (see also Frye 1994; Pastor 1994). This conception of international relations theory is solidly in the conventional "realist" or "neorealist" school. Realism holds that all nations are continually locked in a struggle for power, that the international system is a dangerous place, and that nations ignore the importance of power at their peril. If anarchy and the struggle for power are constants, however, then the constraints imposed by the international system are also fairly constant (although the level of external threat may vary over time). Thus, Peterson's perspective would imply that as long as the United States is involved in the world and as long as the world is anarchic, Congress will be constrained and the executive will have the advantage. Such a constant, however, cannot explain why congressional involvement varies over time.[20]

There are several other problems with the assumptions underlying an analysis based on conventional realism. First, the international environment is not completely anarchic. It has many characteristics of an orderly society and exhibits cooperative as well as contentious behavior (Bull 1977; Burton 1984; Vasquez 1993). Second, the struggle for power does indeed exist, but power is not the only thing over which nations contend. Various other issues produce a variety of different behaviors (Coplin 1974; Dean and Vasquez

1976; O'Leary 1976; Mansbach and Vasquez 1981; Vasquez 1985). Third, a realist analysis based on national interest assumes that the nation-state is a rational unitary actor, whereas there is considerable evidence that governments frequently act in ways that are at variance with policies deduced to be in the national interest (Allison 1971; Mansbach, Ferguson, and Lampert 1976). Fourth, a realist perspective generally makes such stringent assumptions about national interest and national policy that there is little room for considering the input of domestic institutions such as Congress. It is ironic that a treatment of Congress and foreign policy should take a realist perspective while the field of international relations is dissecting realism and proposing alternatives to it (Vasquez 1983a; Kegley 1995 [especially Doyle 1995; Zacher and Matthew 1995]; Moravcsik 1997; Vasquez 1998). For example, Rosecrance and Stein (1993) explicitly demonstrate that realism does not account for the domestic sources of grand strategy. In fact, Putnam (1988, 460) goes beyond both the "second image" and the "second image reversed" by showing that decision makers are involved in a "two-level game" in which they must respond to both domestic and international pressures at the same time.

Finally, it is common to find politicians talking about the national interest, but the literature shows that it is probably impossible to accurately derive what the national interest is (Wolfers 1952). Thus it would be difficult to explain interbranch relations in terms of which branch better assessed the national interest. Rohde (1994b) points out that it is not feasible to specify objectively the national interest and identify who more accurately assessed it. Rather, "disagreements about what is in the national interest and what is a realistic assessment of the world situation have become the stuff of partisan political conflict—within the Congress and in the country at large" (128).

Even without looking at partisan conflict per se, one can see that there is frequently internal disagreement over even the most basic foreign policy postures on issues of national security and grand strategy. Evangelista (1993, 161–62) argues that if the international system were truly a determinant of the foreign policy behavior of decision makers (as Waltz [1979] argues), then there should be consensus within the polity over what policy to pursue. Instead, Evangelista shows for the Soviet case that there is disagreement between hard-liners and moderates over what course to follow, an argument that is easily applied to the United States (Vasquez 1985; 1993, chap. 6). The policy outcome has more to do with who is in power than with a rational national interest dictated by the international environment.

An alternative to the realist theory of international relations is to conceive of states as contending over various issues (Coplin, Mills, and O'Leary 1973; Coplin 1974; Keohane and Nye 1977; Mansbach and Vasquez 1981;

Vasquez 1985; Randle 1987). A shift from the realist paradigm to an issue paradigm will help elucidate why congressional behavior varies as it does over time. Congressional behavior changes as a function of the pattern in how issues arise and are resolved. Important issues on the global agenda capture the attention of both branches and produce conflict both within and between them. This study maintains that the amount of activity and disagreement on foreign policy exhibited by Congress is governed by the rise and resolution of critical issues that arise in the global arena.

The notion of a critical issue as an explanatory variable was inspired by the work of V. O. Key (1955) and others on critical elections and party realignment in American politics. Prior to Key's work, it had been observed that voter turnout varies from one election to another and that the distinctions between parties are sometimes blurred and sometimes very sharp. These variations, however, were not explained. Then Key developed the theory of critical elections to show how the rise of a salient, crosscutting issue causes a realignment of the parties, a sharper distinction between the two major parties, and a higher voter turnout. Likewise, variations in congressional behavior and ups and downs in congressional-executive relations have long been observed but not adequately explained. It is hypothesized here that there is a dynamic in the relationship between the most important foreign policy issue and congressional behavior that is similar to that between a critical election and voting behavior in domestic politics.

According to Key (1955), some issues in American history have been so salient that they cause people to participate in politics more than usual. Some members of the electorate become more involved in the party to which they belong, some switch parties because of their positions on the new issue, and others join a political party for the first time because of the new issue (see also Sundquist 1973). As Sundquist (1973, 28–36) summarized and elaborated, these elections are seen as resulting from the rise of a particularly salient issue around which debate revolves, such as slavery, populism, and the Great Depression. This phenomenon accounts for the higher voter turnout and the clear distinctions between the parties. The electorate chooses one of the parties and gives it the chance to implement its chosen solution (see Ginsberg 1976; Brady 1988). As the issue is resolved, participation and heated debate decrease, the general climate becomes more apathetic, and the distinctions between the parties start to blur (see also Burnham 1970).

Sundquist's definition of this "critical issue" has been elaborated and applied to the global environment by Vasquez and Mansbach (1981, 261; see also Vasquez 1985), who contend that such issues as revolution, imperialism, fascism, and communism shape the global agenda and define or change the alignment of global political actors. These "global critical issues" then shape internal debate on foreign policy. The theoretical utility of this approach for explaining American voting behavior (turnout and direction of vote) and global friendship and enmity suggests that critical issues in American foreign policy may help explain the amount and type of behavior on foreign policy exhibited by the U.S. Congress.

It is hypothesized that the rise and subsequent resolution of a salient foreign policy issue has a major effect on congressional participation in foreign policy and relations with the executive branch. Global critical issues draw the attention of the nation-state members of the international system. In the case of the United States, which has been a major player in that system for approximately the past hundred years, responding to the global critical issue of the time has been an integral part of developing a grand strategy. Thus, the aspect of the global critical issue to which American foreign policy responds becomes the critical foreign policy issue of that era. While there may exist a global critical issue for a previous time, the issue does not become a critical foreign policy issue until it is highly important to American foreign policy decision makers. For example, the issue of Germany's expansionism was a critical issue of global scale from the time World War I broke out in 1914. However, the issue of becoming involved in that war did not become critical to U.S. foreign policy until 1916.

The rise of a critical foreign policy issue causes contention over what policy options to choose as a response to the issue. Because there is much at stake, the critical issue produces increased conflict and debate between Congress and the executive and increased disagreement within Congress. The prediction is that, with the rise of a new critical foreign policy issue, the amount of attention devoted by Congress to foreign policy and disagreement among its members on foreign policy questions will be at its height. When the debate is resolved in favor of one side (because some legislators change their minds, votes are taken that shape a policy, and some people are replaced through turnover in elections), attention to and disagreement over foreign policy will decrease. This period after the resolution of the new issue is what Sundquist (1981) and others characterize as congressional "abdication," but within this theoretical perspective, it is more accurately seen as a time in which, having participated in shaping the broad outlines of policy, Congress allows the executive to implement it. This relative passivity will continue until one of two things happens. If a new critical foreign policy issue arises, the process will start over with a fresh debate. A second possibility is that the solution for the original issue begins to fail. Such a failure would again raise the level of disagreement in Congress as a new solution is sought.

Testing this critical-issue explanation is this book's major task. As this theory is quite different from those already in the literature, a new and original data set will be generated for the task. In the process of testing the theory, many of the contradictions that were highlighted in the preceding literature review will be resolved. Before the behavior can be observed, however, some conceptual problems must be resolved. The next chapter addresses these conceptual problems and sets out the research design for the analysis.

CHAPTER 2

Conceptualizing, Explaining, and Measuring Congressional Behavior

The literature review has shown that there are many contradictory claims made about Congress. The diversity of methods and assumptions behind these studies' conclusions makes it difficult to compare their conclusions to each other or to make progress in the cumulation of knowledge. As Rosati (1984, 313) points out, much of the work done on congressional behavior lacks a conceptual framework for organizing the data or information analyzed. Fifteen years after Rosati wrote, there is more data analysis, but there is still little in the way of a framework for explaining long-term trends in congressional behavior. Sundquist (1981) is longitudinal and theoretical but not data based. Cohen (1991) has extraordinary historical data but insufficient theory. Hinckley (1994) makes a point with some innovative data, but 30 years is more medium term than long term, and there is no theory of the long term. Carter's (1986a, 1994) data set is rich but also medium term. It highlights the effects of Vietnam, but the analysis is rather atheoretical, and the presidential-involvement variable is misspecified.

This chapter will begin by examining the concepts normally used to analyze congressional behavior in light of what kinds of theories they produce (or fail to produce) and will then present a conceptual framework for describing and explaining the U.S. Senate's behavior on foreign policy. Next, the longitudinal design will be described and justified. Two indicators of senatorial behavior, activity and disagreement, will be operationalized and critical issues and issue areas will be specified. Box-Tiao impact analysis will be performed on the series produced by the activity indicator. The chapter concludes with predictions of what will be found in the data and a preliminary validity test.

I. Conceptualizing Congressional Behavior

The U.S. Congress receives a great deal of attention because of the role it plays in policy-making. Scholars, journalists, and politicians are all interested in determining how much influence Congress has, both in absolute terms and relative to the president. Although the question of congressional influence has provoked a great deal of discussion, the answers are far from straightforward and may in fact be unattainable. There are sufficient problems with trying to measure influence to justify measuring behavior instead.

The Concept of Influence in the Study of Congress

The most frequently used concept in this literature is that of influence. Although seemingly straightforward, influence is a multidimensional concept that is extremely difficult to measure precisely. Influence can be over content or over passage; it can be conceived of as changing someone's mind or as winning a vote. One approach is to identify the most important actor in shaping a bill, as Chamberlain (1946) does.

Chamberlain (1946, 453) recognized the complexities in assigning influence; he often found that assigning preponderant influence to the president on a particular bill failed to take into account the role of Congress in the formulation of the policy. R. Moe and Teel (1971, 35) discuss this problem, pointing out that there is a difference between influence over content and influence over passage. While a bill may get its content from members of Congress, presidential endorsement gets it passed. Rosati (1984) looks at influence over initiation and implementation as well as formulation (content) and approval (passage). The executive has the advantage in initiation (Robinson 1962) and implementation, although Congress occasionally becomes involved in these stages. As a result, each branch may have influence on the initiation, content, passage, or implementation of a law. To complicate the process further, in addition to the president and Congress, interest groups and the bureaucracy may also have an impact. As R. Moe and Teel (1971, 34) point out, it may well be impossible to determine exactly how much influence each factor contributes.

The second main approach is to identify who wins on a particular bill. Robinson (1962) takes this approach when he identifies the positions of the president and of the congressional sponsors of a bill and assigns "win" or "lose" to each. Most works in the two-presidencies literature use the concept of winning. Regardless of how much or little influence the president exerts over members of Congress, Wildavsky's (1966, 8) original thesis was that "[i]n the realm of foreign policy there has not been a single major issue . . . on which Presidents, when they were serious and determined, have failed." Clearly, this is about winning.

One of the problems with inferring influence from victory is the widely recognized phenomenon of anticipated reactions (Friedrich 1941; Lindsay and Steger 1993). When the president favors passage of a bill and it passes, it is assumed that the president had preponderant influence on the outcome. However, if the president's request is shaped according to what will pass Congress, then Congress had an influence on the president. As O'Halloran (1993, 303) points out, if the president anticipates what Congress will accept, the outcome when the president dominates will be "observationally equivalent" to an outcome influenced by Congress.

Lindsay and Steger (1993, 107–8, 114) elaborate on this point. Besides looking at whether the president wins, one would also need to know how the president shaped the proposal, how willing the president was to accommodate Congress, how much risk the president was willing to take, and whether the president was more concerned about congressional reactions or a potential loss in one type of issue than another. For example, a confrontational president, a president who compromises with Congress, and a president who happens to agree with a majority of Congress could all get success scores of 75 percent, but they would exercise very different levels of influence.

Fleisher and Bond (1988) find that the two presidencies holds only for Republicans, but the difference is not so much that Republicans do better on foreign policy than Democrats. They do about the same, but Republicans do much worse in domestic policy, so the difference is greater. The two-presidencies phenomenon is produced not so much by an advantage in foreign policy as by a disadvantage in domestic policy among Republicans. The real advantage is held by Democratic presidents in domestic policy as long as the Democrats control Congress.

Edwards (1989, 16) draws a sharp distinction between presidential influence over Congress and success in obtaining passage of legislation. In measuring success, the literature has erred in using aggregate measures of success. Edwards uses measures that disaggregate level of support and source of support by party. He finds that the extra support comes from the opposition party, so that "when the appeal of a president's foreign policies to the opposition diminishes, so do the two presidencies" (262). Probably the most telling aspect of his critique of the two-presidencies thesis is his finding that Eisenhower had the greatest two-presidencies effect, which Edwards explains as resulting from Democratic agreement with Eisenhower's foreign policy but disagreement with his domestic policies. If a president has greater success in Congress on foreign policy than on domestic policy because of policy agreement, then little in the way of influence is occurring.

Pritchard (1986) criticizes the use of the presidential support scores generated by *Congressional Quarterly* (*CQ*) to indicate influence when influence is defined, as Edwards says, as "the ability of the president to move congressmen to support him when they otherwise would not" (quoted in Pritchard 1986, 481). Pritchard uses more sophisticated data to show that members' votes can result from constituent preferences or the member's party rather than the president. Since presidential support scores do not reveal why members vote the same way as the president, she concludes, they do not indicate presidential influence.

A major problem in assessing assertiveness with *CQ* support scores is that compromises are not included. When Rourke (1987) attempted to identify instances of "intermestic" policy in the *CQ* data, he ran into the problem that many of the cases of intermestic policy ended in compromise, leaving a very small number of cases for him to analyze. This outcome is frustrating, since the intermestic area, as noted in chapter 1, may be the area in which Congress has made the greatest inroads.

Another problem with assessing victory or defeat for the president and Congress is that it often implies a zero-sum game. A victory for the president is not necessarily a defeat for Congress. Victory and defeat can be identified for the president when he specifies his position before the vote. However, there is rarely an analogous "congressional" position on which one could base a judgment of victory or defeat for that body. The closest thing to a congressional defeat would be a presidential veto, and an override could be seen as a congressional victory over the president. Also, considering that all votes in Congress have some members on one side and some on the other, it is not clear how a vote by the majority could be considered a defeat for the body (see also Lindsay 1994b; Ripley and Lindsay 1993b, 18; Shepsle 1992). The only way such an argument can be made is to specify when the institutional interests of Congress are at stake and call it a defeat for Congress when a majority of members vote against their own institution's interests. Determining congressional interests is controversial, however, so finding objective measures could prove difficult.

The most important drawback in using *CQ* data is the lack of scientific rigor used in their collection. The editors of *CQ* themselves have stressed this shortcoming, pointing out that there are no systematic coding rules, that judgment calls are quite subjective, and that there is a lack of data reliability because of turnover in personnel in a situation where only one person is responsible for identifying foreign policy votes.[1] The presidential box scores used by Wildavsky (1966) were abandoned altogether after claims were made regarding President Carter's success in getting his legislative program passed (*Congressional Quarterly Weekly Report* 1982, 18). Presidential support scores are still generated and are still vulnerable to some of these criticisms, although Eugene R. Wittkopf and James M. McCormick (1998) are among a handful of scholars using them profitably (also McCormick, Wittkopf, and Danna 1997).

Determining which institution succeeds in getting its proposals passed is an interesting question politically because of the importance of the role of representatives in democratic ideology. However, predicting success as a dependent variable is not necessarily of scientific significance. Stating who had the preponderant influence tells who won in a particular case but does not explain why the outcome occurred. The problem is similar to that experienced in the literature of American politics before *The People's Choice* (Lazarsfeld, Berelson, and Gaudet 1944) and *The American Voter* (Campbell, Converse, Miller, and Stokes 1960). Lazarsfeld, Berelson, and Gaudet pointed out that earlier electoral studies had been of the horse-race type—predicting who would win and offering explanations of why they won such as "because he carried New York." A description of success is not an explanation of why that person got the votes he needed in New York and elsewhere. As Niemi and Weisberg (1976, 7–8) put it, Harris and Gallup polls try to predict who will win, while political scientists try to explain why the victor won.

Likewise, tracing the success of the president or Congress in getting laws passed does not explain the actors' behavior. A president may win a vote without exerting influence or exert a great deal of influence and still lose. The fact that one vote can mean the difference between victory and defeat means that the same behavior may be exhibited prior to two opposite outcomes. Success is of course what is important politically, but for the advancement of knowledge, explaining behavior is more important. Predicting success is like cancer researchers trying to predict who will live and who will die—an important question to the patients and their relatives, but less important to the scientific goals of understanding the disease.

Attempting to study the phenomenon of influence will always be a frustrating experience because it entails making an empirical comparison between an observed fact and a counterfactual (Tetlock and Belkin 1996). If influence means one party getting another party to do something it otherwise would not have done, then to "prove" influence means doing a controlled experiment to see what the second party would have done in the absence of the first party's action. Of course, this inability to prove is endemic to the study of human behavior, and it is rare that controlled experiments can be studied, but that does not mean that the scientific endeavor should be abandoned.

In international relations, there has been for three decades an argument that not enough is known about the phenomena we study to construct theories about them. J. David Singer and Melvin Small founded the Correlates of

War project to collect data and identify the empirical patterns associated with war before attempting to explain it. Opponents of that approach argued that the project was too inductive and atheoretical (Waltz 1979), preferring to theorize without data. Which approach has been more fruitful? This question is certainly controversial, but those who have theorized without reference to data-based research are now under attack for being engaged in a degenerating research program (Vasquez 1997), while the Correlates of War project is preparing a volume that presents and integrates the findings of the project in a synthesis that will move the cumulation of knowledge forward (Geller and Singer 1998).

Sullivan (1991) finds a very similar epistemological problem in the two-presidencies literature. Distinguishing between "fact" (that which is observable qualitatively or in data) and "conjecture" (theoretical explanation), he shows that both pieces of the puzzle have suffered. Conjecture proceeds apace, revising and reformulating without using more appropriate data as in Oldfield and Wildavsky (1989), and data collection follows the same assumptions, merely updating, as in LeLoup and Shull (1979) (Sullivan 1991, 144).

Sullivan (1991) measures success and influence separately: success as votes going the president's way and influence as head counts and movement of members toward or away from the president's position. The latter variable, labeled "sway," gets at some of the key questions for the two-presidencies thesis by looking at what are often small numbers of members in terms of changing positions. This approach overcomes several of the problems of earlier studies, but it does not deal with Pritchard's (1986) point about other possible influences on members' votes. Interestingly, Sullivan (1991, 155) concludes that the two-presidencies effect may result from the existence of two Congresses, one for domestic policy and one for foreign policy. Copeland (in Bond, et al. 1991, 197) sees the two Congresses as follows: one for which all politics is local that acts in a partisan and constituent-sensitive manner on domestic policies and foreign policies with domestic costs (intermestic), and another for issues of national security around which a consensus forms. This consensus is not so much a product of presidential influence as a reflection of shared values on what is good for the country.

Congressional assertiveness is an alternate conception to influence. It is more easily measurable than influence because it does not entail making any inferences about changing anyone's mind or about impact on policy. Carter's project on "congressional foreign policy behavior" codes instances of behavior as varying degrees of either compliant or assertive. Carter (1994) finds more assertiveness after the Tet Offensive than before, which is consonant with the conventional wisdom. Such a measure, however, depends again on

CQ data on the president's position, so the lack of data prior to World War II remains the major stumbling block impeding longer-term analysis.

Assertiveness does not have as severe measurement problems as influence but can nevertheless be difficult to observe. Hinckley (1994, 8) offers an interesting angle on congressional assertiveness: "The notion of an assertive Congress is itself an assertion—stated as fact and not investigated." Her statement is also an assertion, of course. It highlights the extent of contradiction and disagreement in interpreting what has been observed in this subfield. An example of the type of evidence of assertiveness generally offered is the War Powers Resolution, which undoubtedly was an expression of assertiveness. However, Hinckley (1994, 90) points out that the key provision of the 60-day clock is virtually unused. Thus, it could be invalid to measure congressional assertiveness in terms of legislation if Congress itself refuses to assert itself and use the legislation. Similarly, Lindsay (1993, 280) warns the observer not to confuse activism with influence, as Congress may become more activist without changing the president's behavior.

Many attempts have been made to assess congressional influence and assertiveness. A most useful description of the various ways in which Congress influences foreign policy is Lindsay and Ripley (1993). They point out that substantive legislation is the most obvious but is only one of four principal means of exerting influence. The other three are anticipated reactions, procedural legislation, and framing of opinion. While such an approach moves the field forward toward more empirical observation, the emphasis on influence stems more from political interest than from a scientific concern for objectively observable behavior. There still remains the logically prior task of describing and explaining the changes in behavior over time. The study of Congress and foreign policy can benefit from more systematic observation of what Congress does in the foreign policy realm.[2]

From Assessing Influence to Measuring Behavior

Given these pitfalls in assessing influence and assertiveness, it is appropriate at this stage of inquiry to attempt to identify dependent variables that are more amenable to measurement and that can be explained theoretically. The way this problem was surmounted in American politics was to ask the prior question of what explains the behavior that leads to the success or victory of a candidate. That behavior is each citizen's vote. Once the vote replaced success as the dependent variable, significant theoretical advances were made, and predictions of the vote became very accurate. Out of these findings, of course, came an ability to predict which candidate would win, but this development is merely a politically interesting bonus that was quite separate from the scientific breakthrough of explaining and predicting individuals' votes.

Similarly, there are analyses of how members of Congress vote. Identifying the factors that influence how members vote (Kingdon 1989), how their voting varies by issue area (Clausen 1973), the role of ideology in shaping votes (Schneider 1979), or the formation of coalitions (Collie 1987) is much more generalizable and scientifically more fruitful than is some of the congressional-executive relations literature. However, there are limitations to both the *American Voter*–type analyses and the Kingdon-type analyses. Since many voting studies are cross sections at one point in time, they do not reveal how behavior changes over time.[3] Once voting studies had been done for a number of years, questions were raised about why the behavior changed over time. Poole and Rosenthal (1997) have produced a major study mapping the roll-call behavior of members over the entire history of the U.S. Congress, finding remarkable stability in a unidimensional model of the ideological space members occupy. While this study is a breakthrough in the long-term analysis of congressional voting behavior, it does not address the question investigated here of why the amount and type of behavior on foreign policy vary over time.

In the field of voting behavior, Key made the conceptual breakthrough of looking at how voting behavior changes over time. Although he was concerned with how individuals vote, his contribution was a reconceptualization of how policy changes come about over the long term. Less important than why individuals vote the way they do is Key's explanation for why party distinctions become sharp every thirty years or so, producing a realignment and a fundamental shift in policy.

This study's focus is similar in that it centers on identifying and explaining actions taken by Congress on questions of foreign policy. As Van Doren (1986, 7) cogently puts it in an analysis of congressional decisions, "Do we really care why Bill Bradley supports tax reform while Russell Long does not, or is the more important question why did Congress fundamentally change the tax code in 1986 despite the failure of similar reform attempts in the past?" (see also Van Doren 1991, 90). This study will avoid questions of winning and losing and analyses of individual voting decisions in favor of observing the behavior of Congress as an institution on foreign policy issues.

The dependent variable will be the behavior of Congress on foreign policy issues. Before specifying more precisely what congressional behavior on foreign policy issues is, it might be useful to say what it is not. It will not be called here congressional foreign policy behavior (cf. Carter 1986a), because foreign policy behavior is usually conceptualized as one nation's actions toward another (Hermann 1978). In this sense, there is no such thing as "congressional foreign policy behavior," since Congress does not normally formulate and carry out U.S. foreign policy. Congressional behavior on foreign policy is also not foreign policy decision making. This concept typically refers to individuals, groups, or bureaucratic actors, generally in the executive branch, who formulate foreign policy and decide how to carry it out (see Paige 1968; Allison 1971; Janis 1972). Thus, the word *issues* is added to the phrase congressional behavior on foreign policy to stress further that the term does not refer only to legislated foreign policy but to all activity on foreign policy issues that come before Congress. In contrast to Van Doren's (1986, 1990) analysis, the dependent variable will not be decisions to pass particular policies into law, although the findings will be relevant to an understanding of historical trends in the content of foreign policy.

This study focuses on what Congress as an institution does in the area of foreign policy. It seeks a picture of congressional activity on and disagreement over foreign policy—the amount and nature of its output in this area as it changes over time. In an article on studying Congress longitudinally, Cooper and Brady (1981, 999) distinguish between outputs and outcomes. They see the products of legislation, such as bills and resolutions, as outputs; role relationships, such as the congressional-executive relationship, are outcomes. While most of the literature reviewed in chapter 1 concerned outcomes, this study will focus on the output of Congress as an institution. Once this activity is identified, it could be used as a variable in a study designed to explain congressional-executive relations. Also, once the patterns in this activity are described and explained, it will probably be easier to predict when and whether Congress will score any victories over the executive.

This study's design is inspired by the conviction that many studies of Congress and foreign policy have drawn conclusions based on an inadequate empirical and theoretical foundation. The research that has been done is useful, but a great deal of it is atheoretical and/or time bound. This analysis looks at the questions that are logically prior to questions of influence and assertiveness. It asks how active Congress is on foreign policy, how much disagreement exists within Congress, and most important, how this behavior has varied over time.

II. Spatial-Temporal Domain

The Senate will be the focus of this investigation of how congressional behavior on foreign policy varies over time. The Senate has a distinct role in foreign policy under the Constitution in giving advice and consent to treaties and nominations. Also, because of this role, senators are more likely to be competent in foreign policy, to spend more time on it, and to try to affect it.[4] Not only do many senators have a personal preference for dealing with national-level policy and international issues, but there is "an institutional bias in the Senate in favor of large, visible, and often controversial issues," according to Baker (1989, 123). This penchant for controversy means that it should be easier to tap foreign policy disagreement within the Senate than within the House.[5] An analysis of just the Senate will be both sufficiently rich to be intrinsically interesting and adequately representative of congressional behavior to advance our knowledge.

To overcome the time-bound nature of many works in this area, the Senate will be observed over an 88-year period. Taking this longer view will not only resolve some of the controversies, it will also make it more feasible to develop a long-term theory of congressional behavior. The main problem in the literature has been inaccurate predictions based on 10 to 30 years of experience. For instance, what Franck and Weisband (1979) see as a revolution when they compare the 1970s to the 1960s seems much less extraordinary when viewed alongside the post–Civil War era or even the 1920s and 1930s. A longitudinal design will allow a comparison among these different eras that will lend greater precision to descriptions and explanations of congressional behavior.

One logical approach to doing a longitudinal study of U.S. foreign policy is to cover its entire history, since it is relatively short. However, the key to the validity of a longitudinal study is comparability among the different time periods covered (see Clausen 1967, 1020). It is clear that there are significant differences between the foreign policies of the new nation at the end of the eighteenth century and beginning of the nineteenth century and the policies of the world power of the twentieth century. But where can that line be drawn, and how many really different eras of American history are there?

This study identifies 1898 as the beginning of the era of the United States as a major state. Since the Congress that was in session at that time was elected in 1896 and came into office in 1897, the data collection will begin with 1897. This starting date can be justified by looking at the diplomatic history, American politics, and international relations literatures.

With regard to foreign policy, many historians and political scientists argue that there are fundamental differences between the foreign policies of industrialized and nonindustrialized states (Rosenau 1971b; East 1973; Wilkenfeld et al. 1980, 215). Thus, one can expect to find that the United States had very different policies when it was an agrarian nation from those it has pursued since it industrialized. Another common distinction in international relations is that between major states ("great powers") and others.[6] For the U.S., becoming industrialized and emerging as a major state occurred in the late nineteenth century.

Gardner, LaFeber, and McCormick (1976, 214–18) offer a persuasive case for dividing the history of American diplomacy into two periods. These authors point out that after the Civil War, continental expansion was complete and that commercialism was revivified in a new form (188, 191–93). Between 1861 and 1893, a gradual shift occurred from the nation-building phenomenon of acquiring new territory on the continent (formal empire) to the quest for overseas markets without acquiring territories in the formal political sense (informal empire). The shift from agrarian economy to industrial economy meant a change from exporting raw materials at little profit to exporting surplus manufactured goods at occasionally huge profits, which aided the capital formation that turned the United States from a debtor nation to a creditor to a growing portion of the world.[7] In its early stages, however, industrialization was very painful, because the overproduction it triggered caused unprecedented economic downturns. The Panic of 1873, the downturn in the mid-1880s, and the Panic of 1893 set business leaders and politicians searching for a solution to the recurrent crises that seemed to characterize industrialization. According to Gardner, LaFeber, and McCormick (1976, xxiii, 217), the shift to an industrial economy is crucial to foreign policy because of the solution that was found to overproduction. Between the Panic of 1893 and the Spanish-American War in 1898, a consensus emerged that the way to economic stability was to export the surplus to overseas markets. To have secure and stable access to such markets, America developed an increasingly broad world role, in which the war with Spain was only the most extreme thrust.

The focus on the United States as an industrial state can be seen in much of the political science literature. The emergence of the United States as a major state has inspired many of the hypotheses on congressional behavior and congressional-executive relations. With the exception of works such as Sundquist (1981), which covers the entire span of congressional history, analyses of Congress and foreign policy generally are not concerned with explaining congressional behavior in the agrarian, nation-forming America of the first century after the Constitution (e.g., Robinson 1962; Dahl 1950; Ripley and Lindsay 1993a; Crabb and Holt 1992; Mann 1990b; Peterson 1994b). In fact, during the early years of the republic, foreign policy was largely dominated by trade and tariff policy, which involved a larger role for the House of Representatives. With U.S. emergence as a world power, policy shifted to wider use of treaties, giving the Senate a new advantage over the House (Baker 1989, 41).

In the international relations literature, twentieth-century U.S. foreign policy behavior is seen as that of a new major state. Traditional realist explanations emphasize power as a key variable affecting behavior and foreign policy. Major states are thought to occupy a special place in the international system and are distinguished from other kinds of states (see Morgenthau 1948; Organski 1958). Behavioralists have followed this tradition. For example, Singer, Bremer, and Stuckey (1972) establish dates of entry to the major state system on the assumption that these states behave differently. Levy (1983) does the same, referring to such states as "major states." Small and Singer (1982, 42) argue that the United States became a major state in 1898, after the Spanish-American War. A number of empirical studies have found that major states do in fact behave differently from minor states (see Vasquez 1993, 127, 168, 191, 235–36, 242–43).

Some international relations scholars have gone further and have posited not only a pecking order of major states but also a hegemonic leader (Gilpin 1981) or global leader (Modelski and Thompson 1989). Gilpin sees the hegemonic leader emerging out of its dominance of the international political economy. In the modern period he sees Britain and the Pax Britannica as one period of hegemony, subsequently replaced by the United States and a Pax Americana starting around the 1890s. History is seen in terms of the rise and decline of hegemonic leaders. This perspective has produced explanations of foreign policy that focus on the policy of a hegemon in periods of decline (e.g., Friedberg [1988] for Britain, and Keohane [1984] and Skidmore [1996] for the United States).

Others criticize the concept of hegemon, preferring the term *global leader* (Modelski and Thompson 1989). They see the history of the system in terms of long cycles in which different global leaders based primarily on naval superiority (but also on economic innovation) rise and fall. From this perspective there have been four leaders in modern times: Portugal, the Netherlands, Britain (leader for two cycles), and the United States (Modelski 1978). Like Gilpin, these authors see the economic foundation of U.S. global leadership becoming ascendant around the 1890s (Bremer 1980, 64; Kugler and Organski 1989, 181; Kennedy 1987).

This time period has one final advantage. While the entire period has the shared characteristic of industrialization, economic hegemony, and the U.S. rise as a global leader, this era also provides enough variation in congressional behavior to make it possible to identify periods of low levels of activity and high levels of activity. The time frame begins with the period during which Congress heavily pressured McKinley, includes the consensual stage in the Cold War that culminated with what Sundquist (1981, 4) calls the nadir of congressional influence as well as the "revolution" of the 1970s and its aftermath, and ends in the waning years of the Cold War.[8] Thus, it is clear from the start that significant changes have occurred, and the task remains to specify when, in what direction, and why.

III. Operationalizing the Variables

Foreign Policy

In their quantitative analysis of foreign policy behavior, Wilkenfeld et al. (1980, 110) define foreign policy as consisting of "those official actions (and reactions) which sovereign states initiate (or receive and subsequently react to) for the purpose of altering or creating a condition (or problem) outside their territorial-sovereign boundaries." This definition will be used to determine which actions pertain to foreign policy. If a vote in the Senate has any mention of an actor outside U.S. boundaries, or if the vote concerns problems of international origin such as immigration, tariff, or national defense, it will be included.

The only potential problem with using this definition is the authors' reliance on identifying the purpose of an action. Naturally, senators may have differing ideas of the purpose of their acts on certain policies (Lindblom 1959). Therefore, two criteria will be used for determining whether an instance of behavior belongs in the foreign policy category. First, the policy should be seen as a policy of the United States as a whole, not a goal of an individual senator. For example, even if a senator is seeking to protect constituents from foreign competition, the overall purpose of U.S. trade policy is to regulate trade relations with other countries. Second, when determining the purpose of the policy, the focus should be on the primary purpose. For instance, one purpose of initiating arms talks with the Soviet Union may be to defuse domestic protest, but the primary purpose of the talks would be to seek an agreement with a foreign state.

While it has always been true that certain foreign policies could have domestic ramifications (see Rosenau 1971a, 411), some have more of an impact than others. The recognition of this link reached new heights in the 1970s when American citizens found themselves in lines at gas stations because of U.S. policy in the Middle East. Manning (1977) coined the term *intermestic* to refer to issues in foreign policy that have a significant domestic component. Foreign policy concerns can thus be seen along a continuum from most purely foreign to the most intimately linked with domestic issues (see Rourke 1987).

At the purely foreign end of the spectrum would be policies the reason for which and the target of which are external, such as statements denouncing state-sponsored terrorism, the imposition of sanctions against Yugoslavia, or the U.S. commitment to securing Iraqi cooperation with United Nations weapons inspectors. The target is clear and the impetus for the policy comes from the external situation. In the middle are policies the need for which comes from outside U.S. borders but with very important domestic sources and effects. Immigration policy may have specific targets or general aims, but it always affects who from outside the United States can enter. Of course this policy has the domestic impact of changing or maintaining the population's makeup. Finally, at what might be seen as the interface between domestic and foreign policy are certain aspects of defense and trade policy. Defense spending is deeply influenced by domestic politics, is not always directed toward a particular target (especially since the Cold War has ended), has a tremendous impact on domestic industry, and comprises a large percentage of the national budget. However, the reason for a defense policy is the existence of powerful and potentially threatening foreign nations, and arguments in favor of the defense budget in the United States are based on assessments of growth in the military capability of rivals and on commitments to friends and allies. Similarly, trade policy is heavily tied to the domestic economy and is often seen as an important issue for American labor and industry. Nevertheless, the basic reason for a trade policy is the existence of foreign trade partners.

Although all cases of votes on foreign policy will be included regardless of their domestic implications, there will be some recognition of variation among the votes by coding for issue area to see if different patterns of behavior emerge, as discussed later in this section. There are two reasons to expect different patterns of behavior. The first is that there may be characteristics intrinsic to different issues that produce different behavior. For example, because of the large expenditures entailed in defense spending, congressional activity in this area can be expected to be higher than on, for example, U.S. policy on the Soviet Union during the Cold War or on Iraq in the post–Cold War era, which can be carried out through declarations and diplomacy that may not require appropriations. The other way that behavior might vary is between two different policies in the same issue area. For example, within the general area of defense, the president can make a declaratory statement in support of an ally without any congressional involvement, but getting the defense budget passed requires congressional approval because of the power of the purse. These are two policies in one area that involve different arrangements of constitutional powers.

For the purposes of data collection and coding for this study, foreign policy will be taken to include any policy that is directed toward any place in the world outside U.S. borders, any policy that deals with people or things that come into the United States from abroad, and any policy that is made internally but the reason for which is the existence or perception of an external threat.[9] To operationalize foreign policy behavior in the Senate, the roll calls taken on the Senate floor will be read and coded as either foreign or domestic policy. The next section presents a description of the roll-call data as well as coding rules and reliability tests.

The Dependent Variable: Conceptualizing and Measuring the Senate's Behavior on Foreign Policy

Once foreign policy is distinguished from domestic policy, it is necessary to operationalize the Senate's behavior on foreign policy. Two aspects of this behavior will be measured: activity on foreign policy issues and disagreement over foreign policy.

Activity on Foreign Policy

A straightforward way to conceptualize congressional behavior can be found in the answer to the question "What does Congress do?" It does not make foreign policy, but it engages in a variety of activities that are related to the formulation of foreign policy as well as investigation of, oversight of, and implementation of foreign policy. Activity is a useful concept to examine because speculation on change in the role of Congress over time frequently observes or predicts that Congress is more active at some times than at others (see, e.g., Crabb and Holt 1992, chap. 9; Sundquist 1981, chap. 2). Using a measurement of the amount of activity, this study will explore answers to the questions of whether and how senatorial activity on foreign policy varies over time and why the variations occur when they do.

A measurement of activity can also give an indirect indication of the extent to which members see a role for Congress in foreign policy. While some congressional activity will result from policy disagreement with the administration or from increases in workload, if the members of Congress believe in taking an active role, it will show up in a high level of activity. Conversely, a Congress whose members largely believe that the body has little proper role in foreign affairs will not be active, regardless of whether they disagree with the administration.

The concept of congressional activity on foreign policy can be defined as actions that Congress (or, in this study, the Senate) takes in the attempt to influence and shape foreign policy. This is similar to Verba and Nie's (1976, 45) definition of political participation by citizens: "an instrumental activity through which citizens attempt to influence the government to act in ways the citizens prefer." Notice in each case that the emphasis is on the attempt to influence, not on the success of influence itself.[10]

There are numerous ways that members of Congress can become active on foreign policy. They can speak to or be consulted by members of the executive branch, meet with fellow members of Congress and lobbyists, and speak to their constituents, the press, and foreign audiences. Members of Congress can travel abroad, and they occasionally participate in international negotiations. They can introduce bills and resolutions, conduct hearings in committees, present reports to the full chamber, speak in committee or on the floor, and, finally, vote on a bill, resolution, treaty, or appointment. In terms of output of the institution as a whole, votes on the floor are one of the most widely used indicators. For this study, the indicator of activity will be the number of roll-call votes on foreign policy matters taken by the Senate.

There are two important validity arguments for the use of roll-call votes as the indicator of activity. First, the consideration and passage or defeat of legislation is the major function that Congress as a body performs. The number of votes gives an indication of how much attention Congress as a body pays to foreign policy matters. This measure does not give a complete picture of the range of congressional activity, but where there are other aspects of activity on foreign policy, there is likely also to be legislation. For example, although investigations will not be measured, they usually either come about because of prior legislation (e.g., the Iran-Contra hearings) or lead to new legislation.

Although legislation is the key to tapping the behavior of Congress, a focus on voting would leave certain cases out. One can get an idea of both the extent and the limitation of the ability of legislation to get at important foreign policy cases by examining the role of legislation in Robinson's (1962) foreign policy decisions. Each of the 22 cases had been the subject of a case study, which means that they were among the most important foreign policy decisions of the three decades that were covered. Of these cases, 17 resulted from the passage of laws or resolutions or involved formal approval of a treaty or a nomination (66), and one involved an unsuccessful attempt at legislation. Two other cases had no congressional involvement at all.

There remain only two cases in which there was congressional activity but no votes that would be picked up by the indicator used here. The first is the Bay of Pigs decision, in which Senator Fulbright was called in for his reaction to a decision that the executive had already made. Looking at roll calls certainly would not pick up this case, but the case had little or no role for Congress. In 21 of the 22 cases, looking at legislation to describe the activity of Congress on foreign policy would paint a fairly complete picture.

The second case is the Indochina decision of 1954. Not only was this foreign policy decision characterized by meaningful consultation of congressional leaders, but the position of the legislators carried the day.[11] These leaders were acting as representatives of their institution, and their influence can be seen as a congressional influence on that policy. Even though this kind of consultation is not routine, it is obviously very important to a complete understanding of congressional activity in foreign policy. A statistical analysis of roll-call votes can give a representative picture of congressional activity, but for a complete picture, it would be necessary to supplement it with case studies of the rare instances of real consultation. Even so, the Indochina case involved no act of Congress as a body, while this study has self-consciously concerned itself with the behavior of Congress as an institution. Therefore, it seems reasonable to assert that roll-call votes are valid indicators of the behavior of the institution as a whole.

The second validity argument is that this indicator is appropriate for drawing the inferences this study is designed to explore. It is not necessary to measure every aspect of activity to discover which pattern characterizes congressional behavior on foreign policy over time. There is no need for an absolute measure of that activity, only for a representative measure that will allow for observations of changes in the relative level of activity. If congressional behavior does vary over time, the variation will show up in counts of votes.

Three caveats should be noted regarding the utility of roll-call votes. Van Doren (1990, 328–29) finds that the factors affecting members' voting decisions differ for decisions made in committees, for voice votes, and for roll calls (see also Van Doren 1991, 94). For example, the influence of interest groups and of the minority party are much stronger on voice votes than on roll-call votes (Van Doren 1986, 12–14). As a result, an assessment of the impact of these variables on policy or of the factors in members' voting decisions using just roll calls would be incomplete. This is an important critique of conventional roll-call analysis, but this study is not concerned with assessing the influences on members' votes. Rather, it is concerned with observing how the amount and type of behavior of the institution as a whole vary over time and with testing whether the pattern conforms to the predictions of the critical-issue explanation. It can be safely assumed that, as a representative of the Senate's behavior, the number of roll-call votes will vary over time in a pattern that will provide information about overall senatorial behavior. It needs only to be remembered that this is but one aspect of that behavior.

The second caveat concerns the role of voice votes in foreign policy. The omission of voice votes could be problematic if one were interested in studying, for example, the formation of a consensus. An increase in the number of voice votes would be a strong indication of a growing consensus within Congress.[12] This study, however, relies much more heavily on the indicators' ability to tap dissension. As disagreement increases and voice votes are not feasible, the number of roll-call votes should increase. Therefore, a rise and decline in the number of roll-call votes can give a valid picture of variations in the amount of contention. These changes cannot by themselves give an accurate measure of the absolute amount of consensus. A year with very few roll calls may also have very few voice votes or many voice votes. Such a year may be marked by either great consensus or simply inactivity—without looking at voice votes, one cannot tell. One can tell from roll calls that a year with many roll calls is more active and more contentious than a year with very few roll calls.

The third caveat is that proposals that do not receive approval from committees do not even reach the floor for a vote, so roll-call votes would not include this aspect of congressional activity. For studies of congressional opposition to the president, it would be important to look at these failed proposals as well as at votes. Van Doren (1986) finds it essential to look at proposals, both successful and unsuccessful, because he is interested in policy outcomes. A long-term study of congressional workload, as Cooper and Brady (1981, 1001) suggest, should also look at proposals considered. However, roll-call votes have been used for indications of congressional assertiveness (e.g., Carter 1986a) and presidential influence (e.g., Edwards 1980).

Given that this study seeks to cover a long period of time and to produce generalizable findings, it is important to use data that, as Edwards (1980, 51) puts it, are the only systematic data on congressional decisions, cover a wide range of issues, and include a large proportion of all votes. In fact, Schneider (1979, 93), after listing all of their shortcomings, still concludes that roll-call data are the "sole hope of attaining valid and reliable generalizations." Rohde (1994b) makes valid use of roll calls in his assessment of presidential success by distinguishing between bills and primary amendments. In the key book on the transformation of the Senate since the 1950s, Sinclair (1989) uses amendment activity as an indicator of a member's activism. Although Van Doren (1990) points out that roll-call voting taps only a part of congressional activity because so many important decisions are made in committees, Poole and Rosenthal (1997, 56–57) show that there is a sufficiently wide range of issues on which roll-call votes are taken to tap the full range of members' voting behavior.

While most studies use roll-call votes to investigate the behavior of individual members, this study uses the actual roll calls as the indicator of the institution's behavior, or output. Hinckley (1994) is one of the few who takes such an approach. She counts the number of bills on foreign policy as an indicator of just how much (or little) Congress does on foreign policy. Thus, while there are limitations to roll calls as an indicator, there is still much that can be learned from them if they are used appropriately.

It must be pointed out that these measures will not be absolute but, rather, relative. One cannot say how much activity the Senate exhibited in a given year the way one can say that a particular container holds a quart of milk. However, one can observe the rise and fall in relative amounts of activity. It will be possible to say, for example, the Senate was more active on foreign policy issues in one year than in another, but less active than in a third.

Also, there is no way to assess the significance of the activity by looking solely at frequency. All that will be shown is whether activity and disagreement increase or decrease. To assess the significance of this activity, it is necessary to use a historical method and to make value judgments. Naturally, one vote to cut off funds for Cambodia is more important than 10 votes on general foreign aid bills. A quantitative study can only indicate how much behavior, and only relatively speaking, the Senate exhibits.

This study assumes that the Senate's roll calls on foreign policy, while indicating neither all of its behavior on foreign policy nor even the entire breadth of its voting activity (i.e., voice votes), is a dependent variable that is worthy of study in its own right. Even if roll-call voting does not reveal every instance of consensus or reflect the influence of interest groups, it does not matter because this analysis is not concerned with these phenomena. Looking at roll-call votes may make the Senate appear more contentious than it actually is, but if so, it is not a problem as long as the study is looking at relative levels of contention and not attempting to assess in absolute terms the amount of consensus.

It would seem a simple matter to examine all roll-call votes on foreign policy, but such data are not readily available. The data that do exist on roll-call voting are organized according to member of Congress and are collected with a view to explaining why members vote as they do. Most studies are concerned with the act of voting as a decision-making process, whereas this study will analyze votes: the output of Congress.

The most widely known roll-call data are collected by the Inter-University Consortium for Political and Social Research (ICPSR) in a file called "Congressional Roll Call Records 1787–" in which the unit of analysis is how the member votes and the main independent variable is the member's party. The analysis envisioned here does not attempt to explain the member's vote, but rather to measure the behavior of the institution as a whole. Therefore, a new data set had to be generated to indicate aspects of that behavior. The ICPSR data set does not include the subject matter of the roll call votes and the number of yeas and nays on each in its data set, but this information can be found in the codebooks. Therefore, the codebooks were used as the source of the data, and each roll-call vote in the codebook became a case in the new data set. For the 1897–1984 period, there are over 19,000 roll calls. From these, it was possible to produce a data set of *every* roll-call vote on foreign policy from 1897 to 1984. First, the roll calls were read and assigned to either the domestic or foreign policy category according to the coding rules, since the ICPSR does not classify votes (see appendix A). This produced a data set of 6,556 cases of foreign policy roll-call votes. Then the number of roll calls in the foreign policy category were counted for each year. The number of foreign policy roll call votes in a year ranged from only 7 (1903) to 382 (1922). Coding reliability for distinguishing roll calls on foreign policy from those on domestic policy was 92 percent.

To compare years to each other in terms of more or less activity and disagreement, a second data set was created from the 6,556 cases in which the year was the unit of analysis, producing 88 cases. The ICPSR data are organized by Congress (fifty-fifth to ninety-eighth), which is appropriate for the study of members' behavior, since changes in membership occur only every two years and most studies of members' voting decisions concern party and ideology. This analysis, however, is concerned with the effects of global events and foreign policy issues, which are normally identified by the year in which they occurred (e.g., the 1914 crisis), making the use of the year as unit of analysis the appropriate choice for a study with an international relations perspective. Each year was coded for the total number of foreign policy votes. The amount of activity in a year is thus operationalized as the number of foreign policy roll calls taken by the Senate in that year.

Raw numbers will be used (as opposed to percentages) to measure the amount of activity.[13] The numbers for each year will be plotted on a line graph so that the longitudinal trends can be observed. This measure will give an indication of both the numbers of foreign policy issues the Senate handles and the amount of attention devoted to them. This time series will be used for the impact analysis (see section V).

Disagreement over Foreign Policy
The other aspect of congressional behavior on foreign policy that will be measured is disagreement within the Senate over foreign policy. This measure is an indicator of contention over foreign policy. Critical foreign policy issues produce widespread debate, both within the branches of government and between them. The concept of disagreement within the Senate has the virtue of being more objective and complete than the concept of assertiveness toward the president, both because it does not suffer from the deficiencies of the *CQ* measures and because it does not rely on any of the assumptions

about winning, prevailing, or influence that hinder measurements of the congressional-executive relationship. One can accurately describe the amount of disagreement within the Senate and then use that information for further analyses.

The theoretical utility of the concept of disagreement within the Senate derives from the critical-issue explanation, which holds that debate produces increases in activity, so increases in activity that are associated with the critical issue should be accompanied by increases in some indicator of debate. Increases in activity that are not related to the critical issue (such as that posited by R. Moe and Teel [1971]) should be unrelated to disagreement.

Measuring disagreement within the Senate does not directly tap disagreement between the Senate and the executive, although there is a relationship. In a case where there is a solid consensus within the Senate that opposes the president, this measure would not tap it. In fact, in a case where there is that much opposition to the president, his proposal would not even make it out of the committee, so no floor activity would even take place. Any inferences drawn from this study's data regarding opposition to the president would have to be very tentative, and they would depend on how the data analysis compares to what we know about the historical record. One way to draw these inferences would be to follow Rohde (1994b). He points out that the president makes proposals to committees, and if the committee opposes the president, the proposal gets killed. If the bill is reported out of committee and is passed on the floor, it can be seen as an indirect indicator of support for the president. If, however, there are many secondary amendments proposed and passed, it would indicate more opposition to the president. In general, measuring the amount of contention within Congress can give an indirect indication of disagreement between Congress and the executive, because the president's position is likely to be represented by one of the sides in the congressional debate, but assessing the relative influence of the two branches would have to be the subject of a separate study.

There are two measures of disagreement: closeness of the margin of victory and whether the vote is on an amendment or a bill. As each foreign policy roll call was entered into the data set from the ICPSR codebook, it was coded for the number of yeas and nays on each vote and for whether it was a bill, an amendment, a conference report, or a procedural vote.

The first measure, which is based on the margin of victory for each vote, indicates where a vote lies on a continuum ranging from a tied vote to a unanimous one. The formula for the measure when there are more yeas than nays is:

margin = $y/(y + n)$

and when there are more nays than yeas or an equal number of each:

$$\text{margin} = n/(y + n)$$

where

y = the number of yea votes

n = the number of nay votes.

This produces a fraction ranging from .50 to 1.00. Close votes—those for which one side receives 50–55 percent of the vote (e.g., a 10-vote margin in the post-1959 Senate)—will produce a score between .50 and .55. The number of close votes in a year indicates the amount of disagreement.[14] Unanimous and near-unanimous votes, which are often operationalized as votes to which 10 percent or fewer votes are opposed (Schneider 1979, 111), will have a score of .90 to 1.00. Looking at the number of unanimous votes each year will give an idea of whether consensus varies over time.

The second measure is a nominal measure that codes each roll call as an amendment, procedural vote, bill, resolution, nomination, or conference report.[15] This measure assumes that passing bills, resolutions, nominations, and conference reports is the normal business of the Senate when consensus reigns. Disagreement among senators is reflected, among other places, in the attempt to pass amendments to modify the proposed legislation and in procedural motions to table amendments or refer bills to committees. This indicator is especially appropriate when the focus is on disagreement within the Senate. Senate opposition to the administration can result in bills and particularly in resolutions, but contention among members is reflected in struggles over legislation using parliamentary procedure and amendment as weapons. Thus, amendments and procedural votes are a valid indicator of contention.

In the data set with the 88 years as the cases, each year is coded for the number of close votes, unanimous votes, amendments and procedural votes, and bills and conference reports in that year, so that the amount of disagreement is operationalized as the number of close votes and the number of amendments and procedural votes. This data set is also used for calculating measures of association between the indicator of activity and the indicators of disagreement.

Defining the Issue Variables

The role of issues is key to this study. Thus, it is appropriate to begin with a definition of *issue*.[16] Mansbach and Vasquez (1981, 59) state that "an issue consists of contention among actors over proposals for the disposition of stakes among them." This definition is useful for a study of Congress because bills, resolutions, and treaties can be seen as proposals, and votes on them are part of the process of disposing of stakes.[17] This section will discuss critical issues and issue areas. Critical issues are highly important issues that tend to overwhelm, shape, or push off the agenda more minor issues. They have the characteristics of being potentially threatening to the perceived national interest and thus become linked to a grand strategy that dominates policy over a fairly long period (20–40 years). Issue areas, conversely, are broad and are more like topics than like issues in that they are not susceptible to resolution. They are categories in a classification scheme in which the members of each category have something significant in common with each other.

The two major hypotheses of this study are that critical issues produce contention within the Senate and that activity and disagreement vary by issue area. To test these hypotheses, each of the 6,556 foreign policy roll-call votes was coded as an instance of either one of the critical issues or one of several substantive issue areas. Descriptions of the critical issues and the issue areas follow below.

Identifying Critical Issues

Definition   In the American politics literature, a critical issue is an issue that is very important, dominates debate for a significant period of time, often cuts across prior coalitions, and usually has or acquires a moral dimension (see Sundquist 1973). Just as the domestic critical issues of slavery, populism, and the Great Depression shaped domestic policy for an entire generation, critical foreign policy issues dominate debate, shape overall policy, and, in fact, affect interactions on many other issues. For example, one's attitude on slavery was likely to affect one's position on the dissolution of the Union and on the South's economic future. Likewise, critical foreign policy issues shape attitudes on other minor foreign policy issues. For example, during the Cold War, anticommunism dominated debate and opinion not only toward the Soviet Union but also toward other nations and certain domestic groups.

A critical foreign policy issue is defined as the most important issue on the foreign policy agenda at a given time by virtue of the fact that it involves significant threat to the country, real or perceived, and tends to overwhelm, push aside, or subsume other issues. Leaders consider the issue the most important, and the public is aware of its importance in shaping policy. *Importance* means that the issue has great value, significance, and consequence for the country. The issue involves values that are held dear, such as liberty, prosperity, stability, democracy, or freedom. The issue is significant in that perceived threat has the potential to remove or diminish such a cherished value, and the issue is of great consequence in that if things go the wrong way, the United States will suffer a loss in value that would affect it adversely, presumably for a long time to come. The responses to this issue give a coherence to the overall foreign policy of a given era, even spanning several administrations.

The source of a critical foreign policy issue is the global political system. Critical issues arise periodically at the global level, forcing members of the system, particularly major states, to grapple with them. According to Mansbach and Vasquez (1981, 110–11), global critical issues are the most salient in the global political system, are at the top of the agenda of the major states, draw in or redefine other issues, shape the identities of global actors, and form the axes of coalitions. Global critical issues have included the French Revolution, imperialism, fascism, and communism. For states—particularly major states—actively involved in the global political system, confronting these issues is unavoidable. Global critical issues then impinge on the concerns of these states, shaping their foreign policy agendas. The reaction to the global issue produces an issue around which foreign policy is shaped, and the articulation of that issue is the critical foreign policy issue (see Vasquez 1985). Other issues or concerns are approached in terms of their implications for the critical foreign policy issue. For example, if a group of African Americans wanted to see more aid go to a particular African country during the Cold War, the first thing the foreign policy establishment would be interested in knowing would not be the country's level of need but its government's ideological orientation.

Critical issues are distinguishable from issue areas in that, although quite broad, they are issues, and as such are susceptible to resolution, unlike issue areas. They also differ from what historians might consider a driving force behind policy. For example, Gardner, LaFeber, and McCormick (1976) see the search for foreign markets as a driving force in the diplomacy of the United States as an industrial nation. They distinguish this phenomenon, however, from the issue of imperialism, the debate over which can be seen as confined to the early 1890s and the dominance of which extends only until World War I pushes it aside. Critical foreign policy issues are discrete issues that are extremely important to the direction of foreign policy.

There are two aspects to the procedure for measuring the critical foreign policy issues: identification of the most important issues in U.S. foreign policy from diplomatic history texts and the operational definition specified below. Diplomatic history texts were used as a source for identifying the most important issues in American foreign policy partly to achieve some distance from political science, partly because diplomatic history tends to take a fairly broad and sweeping approach that gets beyond minutiae, and partly because these texts are likely to define the most important issues in terms of the interests and goals of the United States as a whole and not in terms of subnational actors.

To avoid problems of idiosyncrasy of a given text, two texts with very different points of view were examined: *A Diplomatic History of the American People* by Thomas Bailey (1980), which is fairly traditional, and *Creation of the American Empire* by Gardner, LaFeber, and McCormick (1976), which is a revisionist text. The following three issues were identified as the most important foreign policy issues of the 1897–1984 period: imperialism (1897–1914), involvement in Europe (1917–45), and communism (1947–84).[18]

The operational definition of a critical issue is an issue that, summarized in one word or concept, is used as the justification for a broad range of policies over a multiyear period. It is composed of various stakes that derive their significance from the extent to which they further or threaten the values underlying the issue. For example, in the early 1900s, Nicaragua was a stake in the imperialism issue. U.S. actions vis-à-vis Nicaragua depended on its stance on the critical issue of imperialism. After 1979, however, the same country was a stake in the communism issue. If the Sandinistas had used a non-Marxist ideology for their revolution, the United States would have remained neutral toward them. However, as their rhetoric and behavior became more influenced by the Soviet Union, Nicaragua came to be seen as part of an overall threat to the American way of life and a key to its grand strategy. A behavioral way to identify a critical issue would be to identify the grand strategy in security policy and then ask "What issue does this strategy seek to resolve?" By definition, that issue would be the critical issue.

Coding for the critical issues will allow the data to reveal whether these three issues dominate the Senate's attention and whether they form an identifiable pattern in its behavior. Approximately one fourth of the roll-call votes were found to be related to one of the three critical issues of the 1897–1984 period.[19] In a coding reliability test, a random sample of 615 roll calls was coded for issue and issue area with a reliability of 87 percent.

The Issue Cycle in U.S. Foreign Policy   A critical foreign policy issue goes through several stages. First it is an issue in the global arena, then it becomes an issue for American foreign policy, then it becomes critical to American foreign policy. Next a policy is implemented, which either removes the issue from the agenda by resolving it or staves it off until a new critical issue pushes it aside or the policy ceases to work.[20] For example, communism is on the global agenda from 1848 on, and it becomes an issue in American foreign policy during the Bolshevik Revolution leading to Wilson's sending

American troops to intervene in the Russian civil war. However, communism does not become critical to American foreign policy until the Soviet Union emerges as a rival superpower after World War II. The identification of dates is an attempt to specify approximately when the issue became critical to U.S. foreign policy and when it was resolved or supplanted, even though the issue may remain on the stage in a more minor form both before and after the named period.

While patterns in the substantive issue areas are expected to differ from each other because of their different characteristics, the critical issue pattern is expected to be distinct as a result of the importance of critical issues. Critical issues are so important at least partly because they are complex and difficult to resolve. Because of the difficulty (or impossibility) of reaching a compromise and the length of time it can take to implement all of the relevant policies, such issues will tend to dominate political interaction. When an issue emerges as the most important of its time, it produces a higher than normal level of activity and contention. The debate eventually is resolved, and a solution emerges. At this point, congressional activism decreases, and policies are implemented to carry out the decision. On this basis, one can predict a rise in congressional activity, then a decline, and then relative stasis until a new critical issue arises.

The first issue, imperialism, was a driving force in global politics throughout the nineteenth century, but it did not become a critical issue in U.S. foreign policy until the 1890s. Prior to that time, overseas expansion was viewed with great caution. When a resolution was introduced in the House of Representatives to recognize Cuban insurgency against Spain in 1870, Secretary of State Fish convinced President Grant to recommend against the measure, and it was defeated 88–101 (Bailey 1980, 380). Bailey (407–20) sees a shift away from the hesitation of the 1880s to become involved overseas with Blaine's "spirited diplomacy" from 1889 to 1892. Bailey then refers to U.S. involvement in Samoa and Hawaii as "an imperialistic preview" (421).

While Gardner, LaFeber, and McCormick (1976) disagree with Bailey on the nature and extent of imperialism in American experience, these authors do identify the 1890s as the period during which the issue of imperialism captures the most attention. They describe an explicit debate with three identifiable positions: anti-imperial expansionists, who favored acquiring markets without formal colonies; imperial expansionists, who favored administrative colonialism like that of Britain in India; and pragmatic expansionists, who argued for case-by-case decisions based on cost (226–33). By 1900, the pragmatic expansionists had won, the debate subsided, and a mixture of related policies was carried out based on assessments of cost and risk. Formal colonialism in China was rejected in favor of the Open Door policy,

Pacific islands that were easily secured were used as trade stepping-stones, and in the case of Cuba, an all-out war was fought (231).

The Cuban situation brought the issue to a head and involved the most public attention, and it served as the test case for the imperial expansionists. The Cuban revolution broke out anew in 1895, and by the end of 1896, the United States was delivering a near-ultimatum to Spain. The unspoken deadline was December 31, 1897 (Gardner, LaFeber, and McCormick 1976, 245). The newly acquired significance of imperialism and the atmosphere of crisis make 1897 a logical starting point for this critical-issue period. Following the unique experience of formal colonialism in the Philippines, the United States pursued a policy of pragmatic imperialism, primarily in Latin America, well into the Wilson administration. In fact, even though Wilson earlier had opposed imperialism, "as President, he carried out more armed interventions in Latin America than any of his predecessors" (Bailey 1980, 553).

The outbreak of war in Europe in 1914 turned American attention away from imperialism and back to the old issue of what kind of relationship to have with Europe. The United States managed to stay clear of the war for quite some time, but the issues of freedom of the seas and the rights of neutrals and the German policy of unrestricted warfare finally made involvement in Europe a critical issue. The issue reached the critical stage when Germany announced on January 31, 1917, that it would resume unrestricted submarine warfare (Hawley 1979, 18). Throughout the war, the peace negotiations, neutrality in the 1930s, and entry into World War II, this issue dominated American foreign policy. Only the successful institutionalization of the peace in the United Nations finally resolved this issue for the United States.

No sooner was the issue of involvement in Europe resolved than events in eastern and southeastern Europe fueled a rivalry between the two most powerful victors of World War II. Between 1945 and 1947, there was a debate over whether the United States should try to roll back communism, hold it where it was, or cooperate with the Soviet Union. George Kennan's (1947) famous "Mr. X" letter arguing that the United States should "contain" communism and the defeat of accommodationist Henry Wallace in the 1948 election signaled the advent of a consensus on containment. The carefully developed bipartisan support Congress gave the executive on the Truman Doctrine in 1947 was the first important domestic political success for containment, although there remained resistance to this type of international involvement (J. Jones 1955; Briggs 1994, chap. 3). The outbreak of the Korean War increased the perceived importance of the communism issue, and the June 1950 decision to intervene, made unilaterally by the executive branch without any objections from Congress or the public, solidified the consensus on containment (Jervis 1980). This consensus was so secure that it gave rise to the phenomenon of bipartisanship on foreign policy and to an entire school of thought on the decline of Congress (Dahl 1950; Robinson 1962; Wildavsky 1966; Huntington 1971; Rieselbach 1973; Sundquist 1981).[21] This consensus broke down over the conduct of the Vietnam War.

 Many analysts see the 1968 Tet Offensive as a signal that U.S. strategy in the Vietnam War was failing. Although the United States was not defeated, the successes of the National Liberation Front shook public and congressional confidence in the executive's policy (Carter 1986a, 334). The secret war in Cambodia brought the crisis to a head in 1970. Manley (1971, 66) points out that by May 1971, the majority of people polled wanted troop withdrawals to continue even if the South Vietnamese government collapsed, believed sending troops had been a mistake, and believed that it was morally wrong for the United States to be fighting in Vietnam. By November 1971, the perception of the Vietnam policy as a failure had grown from a minority position to a majority position (see also Mueller 1971).[22]

The three issues of imperialism, involvement in Europe, and communism are clearly the most important of the second century of American foreign policy. No other issues come close to playing the kind of overarching role in shaping policy that these three issues did. Yet, they were not the only issues on the foreign policy agenda. During the same time period, attention was also given to the general issue of trade, to human rights, to relations with the Third World, but none of those issues caught policymakers' imaginations and shaped grand strategy the way the three critical issues did. Perhaps the clearest case of this phenomenon occurred during the Cold War. Attitudes on communism and the Soviet Union pushed aside strong arguments and even movements in favor of shifting American foreign policy toward for example, human rights or disarmament.[23] In the 1890s, the United States could well have pursued a mission to be completely self-sufficient within the North American continent, but it did not.[24] In the 1920s and 1930s, the tariff could have dominated American foreign policy, but instead it died as an issue in 1934 and was eclipsed in importance by the involvement-in-Europe issue.

The longest period of time spent on debating and settling on a basic position on a critical issue came between 1914 and 1941. When war broke out in Europe, the issue of America's role in Europe and the world was raised. The United States avoided involvement until its own ships were attacked and then joined the conflict with enthusiasm. However, once the war was over, there were many isolationists who wanted to withdraw. They defeated Wilson's League of Nations in the Senate in 1919 and 1920 and restrained Franklin Roosevelt from pursuing the internationalist policies he favored through the 1930s. Only the Japanese attack on Pearl Harbor definitively defeated the isolationists. Although which position was going to succeed was in doubt all of that time, it is still clear that the issue of what position to take on involvement in world affairs dominated foreign policy thinking.

The utility of the application of the critical-issue concept to analyses of American foreign policy can be supported by the fact that the evolution of highly important issues has influenced many works that periodize history. One example discussed earlier is the mood-cycle theory of Klingberg (1952) and Holmes (1985). It may be that the trigger to switches from extrovert to introvert moods and back again is the rise of a critical issue. Roskin (1974) relates the changes in attitudes over isolation and intervention to congressional behavior. He sees four "paradigms" since the 1870s: imperialism (1890s to 1910s), the Versailles paradigm (1920s and 1930s), the Pearl Harbor paradigm (1940s to 1960s), and the Vietnam paradigm (starting in the 1970s) (581). What is theoretically interesting about Roskin's analysis is that he explicitly hypothesizes that congressional behavior toward the executive on foreign policy will be generally obstructionist during noninterventionist periods (e.g., Versailles and Vietnam). This finding would imply a cyclical pattern of congressional behavior, with activity and disagreement high during the first period, low during the next, and so on. This also conforms to Holmes's (1985, 113–14) observation that Congress is more activist in introvert periods as it reacts to extrovert presidents.

Roskin's paradigm perspective leads him to identify different moods or different positions on an issue rather than issues themselves. When the dominant position on an issue changes, he sees a new period. By contrast, this study will use an issue perspective, identifying periods according to the rise and resolution of critical issues. Thus, a period dominated by just one issue, such as involvement in Europe (1914–45) may include shifts in the dominant mood, such as alternations between neutrality and intervention.

Critical Issues and Grand Strategy   Critical issues are also relevant to the recent literature on grand strategy. The literature defines *grand strategy* as "that collection of military, economic, and political means and ends with which a state attempts to achieve security" (Posen 1984, 7). From this perspective, three grand strategies that the United States has pursued in the twentieth century can be identified: imperialism (1897–1913), making the world safe for democracy (1917–45), and containment of communism (1947–89). From a political perspective, these three grand strategies form a coherent whole. Once the North American continent was conquered, the United States expanded its commerce overseas; protected democratic, liberal trading partners from defeat; and became the leader of the so-called Free World in a global struggle against communism. This progression in overall strategy can be seen as a response to the rise of three different issues:

imperialism, involvement in Europe, and communism. In terms of the analysis offered here, grand strategy is the foreign policy a state pursues on its critical issues.

The issue of imperialism called for a grand strategy on the part of the United States because it was emerging as a major state and all of the major states had pursued an imperial policy in the past. As much as the economic crises Gardner, LaFeber, and McCormick (1976) stress, the imperial precedent caused many domestic actors to argue that the United States should follow the same path. The crisis with Spain that erupted into the Spanish-American War set U.S. policy in the Western Hemisphere for the next century and defined U.S. foreign policy well into the Wilson administration. The overall strategy pursued was to eschew territorial, political control of overseas colonies in favor of informal commercial expansion entailing sufficient influence over domestic political forces to protect economic interests and to avoid getting very involved in European politics.

The next challenge to the United States came from the emergence of expansionist states, particularly Germany, which triggered two world wars and pushed the United States to redesign its grand strategy. The United States had to struggle with its own isolationist tendencies and overcome its aversion to getting involved in Europe. Making the world safe for democracy can be seen as a grand strategy developed by Wilson and later adapted by Roosevelt as a way of dealing with America's main external threats. Focusing on the protection of democracy was a way to make an internationalist posture palatable while pursuing traditional national interests. The Japanese attack on Pearl Harbor defeated isolationism, and the signing of the United Nations Charter definitively settled the issue of U.S. involvement in Europe.

With the end of World War II, a new challenge was perceived in the form of an ideological struggle with the Soviet Union, requiring a new grand strategy for the United States. As World War II wound down and the postwar situation took shape, the United States emerged as the most powerful country in the world and began to make commitments to lead the reaction to the Soviet Union. For the first time, the United States embraced its expanded role fairly enthusiastically, and the policy of containment became the new grand strategy. This change did not occur instantaneously, however. According to Stein (1993, 118–20), between the end of the World War II and 1950, policymakers were making commitments based on containment, but Congress acted as a constraint by being reluctant to appropriate the funds that would establish the capability needed to back up the commitment. However, by 1950, these commitments were fully supported by massive increases in defense spending and a domestic consensus on containment (Jervis 1980). Suggestions of accommodation were quickly defeated, and flirtations with the idea of rollback went down to defeat with the failure to intervene in the 1956 Hungarian revolution.

Critical-Issue Characteristics and Domestic Political Effects   It is important at this juncture to clarify the difference between a critical issue's characteristics and its effects. The two are clearly distinct (see table 2.1). Critical issues are characterized by great importance, potential threat to the perceived national interest, and a tendency to overwhelm other issues, so that minor issues are seen in terms of their implications for the critical issue. According to this analysis, critical issues are then posited to have the following effects: they create divides in the polity and produce debate, within and among the public, groups, and the branches of government, the breadth and depth of which vary depending on certain other variables; they produce assertiveness within Congress; they cause a reassessment of the "national interest" and motivate resolution of the issue so that the United States is not at a disadvantage abroad; their resolution entails choice of a policy response, which then evolves into a broad and general stance on which a bipartisan consensus emerges. Separating the characteristics of critical issues from their effects shows that critical issues are not a function of the level of conflict in Congress but rather one of several possible causes of conflict in Congress.

Another way in which the distinction between the issues themselves and conflict in Congress can be drawn is by noting that critical foreign policy issues are defined in terms of the issue that dominates relations with other nation-states (Vasquez 1985; Mansbach and Vasquez 1981). Vasquez (1985, 644) theorizes that there are significant domestic political effects of a global critical issue's passage through various stages. For example, in the crisis stage, decision makers form images of contending nations, infuse the issue with symbolic and transcendent qualities, and exaggerate the external threat. In the United States, as in most countries, the executive branch is at the center of this process. The examination of the executive's behavior toward other countries serves as the basis for identifying the critical issues of a historical period. Nothing in this definition logically implies that an issue that dominates relations with other countries must of necessity produce domestic disagreement

TABLE 2.1.   Characteristics and Effects of Critical Issues

Characteristics	Effects
come from global political system	divide the polity
high threat	domestic contention
very important	broad-based policy response
overwhelm other issues	curvilinear pattern of contention followed by consensus

or contention or any particular type of behavior within Congress. Such a relationship is historically contingent, not logically necessary.

Third, a critical issue has the characteristics of being important, overarching, and dominant in the conduct of foreign relations. Such an issue may cause internal debate, but it does not by definition require internal debate. If the executive branch dominates foreign policy (as is widely assumed, even in the current era), it is quite possible for a critical issue to enter the agenda, dominate thinking on foreign policy, and challenge fundamental values without Congress engaging in a great deal of debate. Indeed, this is what many observers of congressional behavior on foreign policy have argued (Wildavsky 1966). Thus, it is not a given that critical issues will produce domestic contention and an increase in congressional activity on foreign policy.

Fourth, the realist paradigm sees grand strategies and the critical issues to which they respond as being developed in terms of a state's national interest irrespective of contention within the state or other domestic pressures (see Posen 1984). In this view, the anarchic international system produces challenges to which individual states must respond (Waltz 1979). A state's grand strategy consists of a policy response to the critical issue shaping foreign policy concerns. Whether there is domestic contention over the issue is usually irrelevant in realist analyses.

The realist paradigm has often been criticized for encouraging a billiard-ball approach that assumes that states are unitary rational actors. Although realism assumes that the selection of grand strategies is unencumbered by domestic constraints, other analyses show that domestic pressures frequently either constrain a state from taking action when it should or push a state to be more aggressive than the international environment warrants (Rosecrance and Stein 1993, 18–19). Far from indicating that those issues that produce the most contention domestically are the critical issues of foreign policy, Rosecrance and Stein (1993, 17) note that "domestic constraints are sufficient to prevent or retard the policy response apparently dictated by international pressures." For example, Stein (1993) argues that the United States underreacted to foreign aggression in the 1930s until December 1941 and overreacted (compared to its capability) to the Soviet threat in the late 1940s. The domestic contention was not a defining condition of the critical issue but a constraint on the straightforward application of the strategy to deal with the issue. Stein argues that the realist framework is incomplete—that domestic constraints play a role, especially in democracies. However, the domestic reaction in no way defines the importance of the challenge to the United States.

It is also important to keep the characteristics of the critical issues operationally separate from their effects. The explanation was constructed before data collection, and diplomatic history texts were used to identify the critical issues. U.S. diplomatic histories rarely look at the role of Congress and generally conceive of U.S. foreign policy as the stance of a fairly unitary actor. The Gardner, LaFeber, and McCormick (1976) text does not even have an entry for Congress in its index, and the index to the Bailey (1980) work, whose contribution is describing the role of "the people" in influencing American foreign policy, has as many entries on China as on Congress. Using diplomatic histories as a source prevents the identification of the critical issues from being confounded with the observation of contention in Congress. After the explanation was constructed and the critical issues identified, the data were collected. The main indicator of disagreement, the number of close votes in a year, is a very objective measure, rendering the explanation falsifiable.

Finally, the fact that not all cases fit the explanation shows that it is clearly falsifiable. The theory predicts a rise in activity for 1947, but there is little congressional activity in that year, and there are years with a high level of activity that is not explained by the theory. Thus, while critical issues are likely to cause debate, it is not part and parcel of their definition that they are characterized by high debate in Congress. Critical issues also do not necessarily have to be the only cause of an increase in congressional activism (presidential misconduct could do so). A critical issue is a sufficient condition for contention, not a necessary or defining condition. If it were, all serious contention would be over critical issues, and all critical issues would be "characterized" by (i.e., followed by) the same level of conflict, but such is not the case.

Of course, other variables affect the level of congressional contention, and many of them have been treated in the literature and will be excluded from this analysis. However, the final chapter will assess the role of some intervening variables: party control of the branches, presidential honeymoon years, war. These variables will play only a minor role here. While it may seem obvious that there is more conflict under divided government, focusing on party control alone would give a very incomplete picture. The amount of conflict depends much more on the type of issue at stake and at what stage in the life cycle the issue is. Whether Congress becomes assertive depends on the critical issue. The intensity of the conflict is then in turn affected by party distribution and the president's position, attitude, and behavior.

Substantive Issue Areas

The Concept of Issue Area   Lowi (1964) and Rosenau (1971a) suggested decades ago the idea that political behavior varies by issue area. Lowi posits four issue areas, the last of which is foreign policy. Likewise, Rosenau views foreign policy as an issue area, distinguishing it from domestic policy. Conceiving of all of foreign policy as one issue area is limited of course by the fact that there are significant variations within foreign policy (R. Moe and Teel 1971, 38–49). For this reason, the study will look at various issue areas within foreign policy.

While an issue is contention over the disposition of stakes, an issue area, by contrast, must be sufficiently broad and abstract to encompass past, present, and future issues (Rosenau 1971a, 405). *Issue area* is defined as a cluster of related issues linked together either by the substance with which they are concerned or by a characteristic or set of characteristics that are thought to be theoretically significant. The issues that fall into a substantive issue area are linked by their content. One asks what an issue is about to assign it to a category. A substantive issue area can be as broad as economic or military issues or as narrow as tariff policy or conscription policy. By contrast, issues in an issue area based on theoretically significant characteristics are linked by a variable thought to affect the behavior on those issues or processes they produce. An example of such a characteristic is Lowi's disaggregatability of the resources involved in an issue's resolution. Issues of varying substance could clearly fall into the same category, such as tariff before 1934 and defense contracts, depending on how broadly a category is defined. Likewise, one substantive issue could change on such a characteristic and be placed in different categories at different times. This is Lowi's (1964) important contribution in demonstrating that the tariff is distributive before 1934 but regulative after.

A substantive issue area, such as tariff policy, or a theoretical issue area, such as distributive issues, remains identifiable over long periods of time, even as individual issues and policies come and go. An issue area is a component of a classification scheme: it does not get resolved. The concept of issue area is an analytical construct used by scholars and politicians to organize issues. It is useful to the extent that it summarizes information and elucidates theoretically significant differences among types of issues.

Several typologies of issue areas have been offered in the political science literature. Among the substantive typologies is that of Brecher, Steinberg, and Stein (1969), which has four categories: military-security, political-diplomatic, economic development, and cultural-status. Hoggard (1974, 380–81) offers a much more detailed typology, which includes 35 subcategories that make coding more reliable. The 10 issue-area categories are: military and political; nuclear; territorial, boundary, and colonial; trade and economic; technical and scientific; sociocultural; general relations; international organization and law; miscellaneous; no explicit issue area. Hermann and Coate (1982, 92–108) offer an even more detailed list of 66 "substantive problem areas." This list is so long, however, that it ceases to comprise areas and becomes more of a list of problems and behaviors.

There are also several typologies based on theoretically significant issue characteristics. Rosenau's (1971b) typology is based on the tangibility of the means and ends of issues. Lowi's (1964) typology is based on the disaggregatability of political goods and how equally they are distributed. He argues that different types of issues produce different policy processes. Hayes (1981) builds on this notion, introducing types of supply and demand patterns as the basis for his typology. Data-based studies have found that conflict/cooperation varies according to certain issue characteristics, especially tangibility (Henehan 1981; Vasquez 1983b).

The issue areas used for this study are based on the substance they concern for two practical and theoretical reasons. First, there have been observations of different patterns of behavior in Congress on different substantive issue areas, such as tariff, immigration, national defense, and foreign aid (Chamberlain 1946; R. Moe and Teel 1971; Hinckley 1978; Carter 1985; Rourke 1987). Recent research confirms that congressional behavior varies by issue area. For example, analyses of changes in Congress's role in foreign policy during the 1980s find little increase in the trade area but substantial increase in the defense area (Peterson 1994a, 11; Carter 1994; Destler 1994). This finding indicates that activity and disagreement within the Senate are likely to vary by issue area. Dahl (1961) predicates his study of the role of elites in different issue areas on the expectation that they will activate different interests, which will attract a different set of actors to each area. More to the point of this study's expectation that different patterns of behavior will emerge is Rosenau's (1971b, 141) argument that issue areas produce unique forms of interactions among actors.

The second reason for using substantive issue areas is that Congress organizes its work around substantive issue areas. Proposals are assigned to committees and subcommittees based on the substantive area with which they deal. Furthermore, members of Congress who serve on these committees develop specializations in these areas. The number and identity of these areas may change over time: as new issues arise, subcommittees are formed to deal with them. Since, as Keohane and Nye (1977, 65) point out, issues are fundamentally perceptual in origin, a selection of issue areas based on actual behavior in Congress should produce categories that will be empirically useful.

Five Issue Areas   Issue areas should cover a wide range of foreign policy; differ enough to show different patterns, if they exist; and be representative of U.S. foreign policy even if they are not exhaustive. Since R. Moe and Teel's

(1971, 38–49) study found different patterns of congressional behavior in four different areas of foreign policy, the first three of their areas will be chosen for this analysis: tariff questions, immigration policy, and national defense. Their fourth category is "foreign policy other than immigration, tariff, and defense," which is obviously too broad. Such a category would make the list logically exhaustive but would do so at the expense of the lack of any basis on which to expect a characteristic pattern to emerge. Instead, foreign aid, which is often selected for separate analysis (Morgenthau 1962; Franck 1981a; Lumsdaine 1993), will be the fourth issue area.

These four issue areas clearly do not cover all votes on foreign policy, and indeed, many votes do not fit into any of the areas.[25] However, it is not necessary to trace every issue area that faces Congress to show that patterns of behavior vary by issue area. Two classic studies in American politics demonstrate that political behavior varies by issue by focusing on only three issue areas. Miller and Stokes (1963) show that there is a very close correspondence between representatives' votes and their constituents' attitudes in the area of civil rights, while there was little correlation in the area of foreign policy. This finding was presented as evidence that constituency influence in Congress is stronger on issues that are more important to the constituents. Similarly, Dahl (1961) shows that different elites arise to deal with three different issue areas in New Haven. Thus, a sample of several important issue areas can suffice to show that issue areas make a difference.

To create a logically exhaustive typology, two more categories were added. "Routine diplomatic activity" was added to contrast with the other highly important issues. This issue area is somewhat broad, since the substance of the votes may vary. The category is defined as comprising decisions on routine matters of relations with foreign states, such as sending ambassadors; funding the Department of State; and declarations of policy that do not require appropriations. Something in this category will occasionally be controversial, but most activity will probably not engender much conflict. It generally can be seen as the mechanics of maintaining a foreign policy bureaucracy. Since these five categories still do not form a logically exhaustive typology, all remaining roll calls were assigned to a "miscellaneous" category.

The area of tariff questions will be interesting to observe because much of the literature has pointed out significant changes in Congress's role in this area between the 1930s and the 1960s (Lowi 1979; Hayes 1981; Haggard 1988). Immigration policy is an important area to observe because it has been an issue for the entire span of this study, it concerns U.S. relations with every country in the world, and it has traditionally been an area of foreign policy that Congress dominates (Chamberlain 1946; R. Moe and Teel 1971). Foreign aid and international assistance is not relevant for the whole period, and its nature changes dramatically after World War II. However, it is an important category to include, because some of the hypotheses on congressional behavior are derived from arguments about how U.S. foreign policy has changed since World War II as a result of to the prominent role of foreign aid (R. Moe and Teel 1971; Franck 1981a; Pastor 1994). Therefore, the key observation in this area will be to see what type of pattern emerges after the war.

National defense was chosen both because of its relevance to the possibility of war and because of the large proportion of the budget it can comprise. Also, since there are such important domestic economic implications of defense spending, if a unique pattern of behavior emerges on this issue area, it will be desirable for future research to discover whether that pattern is more similar to patterns that would emerge on domestic issues than to those on other foreign policy issues. Finally, the category of routine diplomatic activity was added as an example of an area to capture some of the everyday activity on foreign policy. For Sigelman (1979), such issues are trivial and not even worthy of study when it comes to assessing the relative influence of the president and Congress. And yet, as R. Moe and Teel (1971) point out, the sum of all of the small and routine decisions can add up to a significant role in foreign policy.[26]

One common issue area not used here is national security, although many votes on national security issues will fall into the defense category. Usually there is one overarching issue that shapes how national security is perceived. For example, during the Reagan administration, Nicaragua was presented as an important national security issue, not because of any objective assessment of its capability or even of its intentions toward the United States but because the nature of its government was contrary to the prevailing anticommunist thrust of American foreign policy. Thus, most issues that are identified as dealing with national security are linked to the critical issue of their time. If national security were used as one of the issue areas, if would probably comprise most of the activity on the various critical issues. Instead, roll calls of this type will be coded for the individual critical issues.

Coding and Reliability

The roll-call votes on foreign policy were coded for the issue variables discussed earlier. Each roll call was examined and coded as either one of the critical issues or one of the issue areas/categories. This created nine categories: imperialism, involvement in Europe, anticommunism (including votes on withdrawal from Vietnam), tariff, immigration, foreign aid, defense, routine diplomatic activity, and miscellaneous. A random sample of 615 roll calls was chosen and coded by a researcher with a doctorate in political science. The reliability score was 87 percent on the first try. (See the appendix for coding rules and discussion of reliability.)

IV. Predicting Trends in Senatorial Behavior on Foreign Policy

There are two main tasks for the data analysis in this book: to reveal patterns in activity and disagreement in the Senate's roll calls on foreign policy and to assess the critical issue theory. This section will delineate the patterns hypothesized in the literature and specify what observations would support these claims. The following section will explain how the impact of critical issues will be assessed.

Deriving Predictions from the Literature

The various claims made in the literature were reviewed in chapter 1; in this section, some specific predictions will be derived to stipulate what will be accepted as evidence of the validity of their claims. Predictions will be made about the kinds of patterns that would emerge if a given perspective were correct. The figures presented here will be very general and are not expected to be duplicated perfectly in the data. The observations will probably be much more complex. The predictions are intended only to indicate general trends, such as those produced by long-term simulation models like Meadows et al. (1972). The authors of that study explained that their findings were based on a theoretical model that would describe overall trends, not make specific predictions. Likewise, the figures that follow give general indications of trends, and the observed data do not have to match exactly to suggest confirmation of one of the perspectives.

The first perspective, as exemplified by Huntington (1971), Robinson (1962), Koh (1986), and Silverstein (1994) predicts a gradual decline in congressional activity from the beginning of the twentieth century and especially since World War II. A line graph of such a trend would be easy to recognize and would look like this:

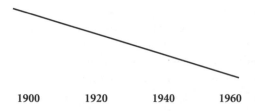

| 1900 | 1920 | 1940 | 1960 |

Sundquist's (1981) prediction is a little more complex. He sees a general decline in congressional activity with spurts of activism:

The second perspective posits increases in congressional activity. R. Moe and Teel (1971) see an increase since World War II that should look like this:

Franck and Weisband (1979) focus on an increase in activism beginning in the 1970s:

Much of the literature of the 1980s and 1990s simply documents a general increase since 1970, although these works differ in terms of how much of an increase has occurred and whether it is sustained:

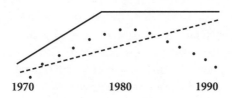

There could be either a ratchet effect (———), a steady increase (----), or an upsurge followed by relative decline (. . . .).

The third perspective indicates that congressional behavior varies in cycles. If this perspective is correct, then there should be periods of opposition of approximately equal magnitude evenly spaced across time. There may be periods of high bipartisan support in between, but the literature is not explicit on this point. The implication of a cyclical perspective is that some force, such as the Constitution for Crabb and Holt (1992, 286), allows Congress to become only so militant before the executive branch counterbalances the trend by asserting itself. These authors mention periods before 1812, after 1848, and before and after World War I as times of congressional assertiveness (286–87). The curve they predict should look like this:

          1812   1848   1914

Although Klingberg's (1952) theory does not explicitly address congressional behavior, his cycles are much more precise. Holmes (1985, 4) presents an update to 1980 of what he calls the "American Liberal Mood Curve," as shown here:

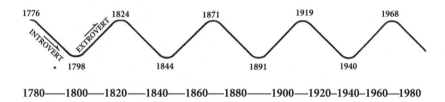

(Copyright © 1985, from *The Mood/Interest Theory of American Foreign Policy,* by Jack E. Holmes. Reprinted with permission of the University Press of Kentucky and Jack Holmes.)

The Predictions of the Critical-Issue Explanation

The critical-issue explanation differs from the first three perspectives in that changes in congressional behavior are linked to the rise and resolution of critical foreign policy issues. As a result, the critical-issue explanation lies in the fourth perspective of explanations that identify some variable that produces changes in behavior. Various explanations of this type would have to be tested individually, although it will be possible to eliminate some of them by looking at the longitudinal data. For example, it will be feasible to observe the data and see whether activity and disagreement are highest after wars. This analysis will be most concerned with observed activity and disagreement after the rise of critical issues.

Each period covered by one of the critical issues can be seen as having four stages. During the first stage, which is a debate that occurs within Congress and in the nation as a whole, activity and disagreement are predicted to be high. In the second stage, a position emerges through political victory, compromise, or consensus. This stage concludes with a decrease in activity and disagreement. The third stage is the implementation of the policies relevant to the issue, and activity will remain low. The fourth stage is the resolution of the issue. Either the issue is resolved with successful policies, in which case activity remains low until the emergence of another critical issue, or a major policy related to the current critical issue turns out to be a failure.

In the case of a policy failure, the original issue is debated again, and if the domestic costs were high, the debate can be quite bitter. Activity will increase until either a new solution is found to the old issue or it is abandoned as no longer important. The Vietnam policy can be seen as a failure of containment, which produced a great amount of congressional activism, shaking the tradition of bipartisan support for the president on foreign policy. This experience left an unstable situation, because there was still concern over the issue of communism but no consensus emerged. As Holsti and Rosenau (1984) have found, retrospective opposition to the Vietnam policy does not occur from only one direction: it is bimodal (see also Wittkopf and Maggiotto 1983). Many of those who defeated the policy and who are still in Congress feel that the United States tried to do too much in Vietnam, whereas others feel the United States did not do enough.

In sum, the critical-issue theory predicts that activity and disagreement will rise after each of the following: the emergence of imperialism as a critical issue in 1897, the crisis over involvement in Europe in 1917, the heightened importance of the response to communism in 1947, and the perceived failure of the containment policy in Vietnam between the Tet Offensive in 1968 and the bombing of Cambodia in 1970:

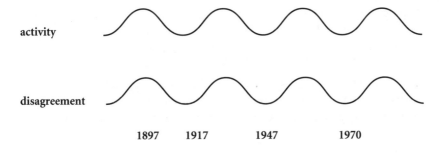

activity

disagreement

1897   1917   1947   1970

V.   Impact Assessment of Critical Issues

Observation of the series of roll-call votes will reveal whether there are increases in activity in response to the rise of a critical issue or the failure of a policy on a critical issue. However, mere visual inspection cannot produce precise inferences on the significance of the increases and the magnitude of the impact of the critical issues. For these reasons, econometricians and statisticians have developed autoregressive integrated moving averages (ARIMA) analysis for describing a series and forecasting from it (Box and Jenkins 1970) and impact analysis (or interrupted time-series analysis) for assessing the impact of an external event or variable on the level of the series (Box and Tiao 1975; McDowall et al. 1980; Enders 1995, chap. 5, pt. 1). International relations has adopted this method to analyze a variety of longitudinal questions, such as the impact of war on the growth of the state (Rasler and Thompson 1985) and the lagged effect of power and alliance polarization on the magnitude of war (Wayman 1984). For this analysis, ARIMA will be used to determine what is driving the patterns in the data. Then impact analysis will be used to assess the impact of critical issues and policy failure on the levels of senatorial roll calls.

One of the problems with any analysis that focuses on one particular variable is the question of whether other variables would also be important. This analysis does not deny that there may be other variables affecting increases in activity and disagreement but merely assesses the extent and duration of the impact of critical issues. The absence of other variables does not cause the impact of critical issues to be overestimated.

Identifying the ARIMA Model

The first step in an ARIMA analysis is to identify what type of model accurately describes the process in the data.[27] Any given series can be said to have "noise" in it, meaning that the values in the series are not completely independent of each other. If each value is partially a product of preceding values, the series is said to be autoregressive (AR), and the "order" is either AR(1), AR(2), AR(3), or AR(4), depending on how many of the previous values are shaping the current value. The letter p represents the order (1, 2, 3, or 4). If there is a trend in the data, or even if there is not a statistical trend but the series moves up and down, or "drifts," then it is said to have an integrated (I) component, the value of which is referred to as d. It used to be the case that a series with a trend would simply be "detrended," which means to regress the values with time and plot the residuals, but given that assumptions of linearity do not always hold in these cases, it is now more common to "difference" the series—that is, to subtract from each value the preceding value.[28] Once the trend is removed, the series is considered "stationary"—that is, the mean of the series is the same over time.[29] If the values of the series are shaping the values that follow them, the series is said to have a moving averages component (MA), which can also be MA(1), MA(2), MA(3), or MA(4), depending on how many subsequent values are affected by the current value. The order of the MA component is referred to as q, so that the order of an ARIMA model is represented as (p,d,q).

Whether there is a trend can be determined by statistical tests or by simply looking at the series in the case of an obvious trend. There are various criteria by which one can determine the appropriate values of p and q and thus the nature of the model that best fits the data. Two widely used criteria are formulas called the Akaike information criterion (AIC) and the Bayesian information criterion (BIC). When these statistics are run for all combinations of AR(1, 2, 3, and 4) and MA(1, 2, 3, and 4), one chooses the model with the lowest values of the AIC and BIC as being both statistically accurate and parsimonious. For this analysis, the model with the lowest BIC was chosen.[30]

Once the three components are identified, it becomes possible to remove the noise from the model. The residuals are checked for autocorrelation, and if there is no longer any dependence of the values of the series on each other or on time, the series is said to be random, or "white noise." Achieving white noise is the main goal of an ARIMA analysis, and the value of doing so is to make accurate forecasts. For this analysis, forecasting is not the goal; rather, the noise is removed so that the impact of critical issues can be assessed as distinct from other factors such as time or the values' effects on each other.

Estimating the Parameters

The second step in ARIMA analysis is estimation. In this case, the impact of the critical issues will be assessed jointly with the estimation of the ARIMA model. The technique used is maximum likelihood estimation, and the statistical package used for this analysis is Regression Analysis for Time Series (RATS). Coefficients are calculated for each component of the optimal model and for two measures of impact. The model with the most statistically significant parameter estimates is chosen.

The analysis assesses four different types of impact that an event can produce: gradual and permanent, gradual and temporary, abrupt and permanent, and abrupt and temporary. Diagrams corresponding to the four types can be observed in figure 2.1. Two statistics measure the extent and the duration of the impact: omega and delta. The omega shows how much the level of the series changes, and the delta is a rate, indicating over how much time the

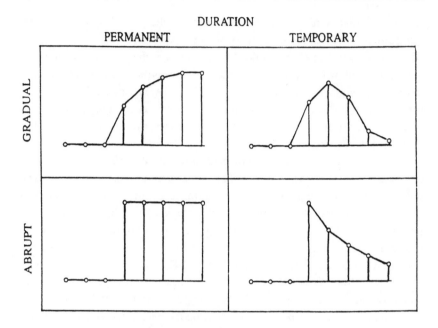

Fig. 2.1.   Four types of impact. (Reprinted by permission from
David McDowall, Richard McCleary, Errol E. Meidinger, and Richard
A. Hay Jr. 1980. *Interrupted Time Series Analysis,* p. 66. Copyright ©
1980 by Sage Publications.)

impact occurs. The larger the omega, the larger the size of the impact. If the
delta is zero, the impact is abrupt. If the delta is above zero and below 1.0, the
higher it is, the more time the gradual impact takes to reach its new level.

Diagnosis of the Model

The third step in the process is diagnosis. Because more than one model can
fit a series and because choosing a model depends a great deal on the
researcher's judgment, two more procedures are used to confirm that the
model chosen is optimal. Autocorrelation functions (ACFs) are run on the
residuals to ensure that there remain essentially no autocorrelations. If the
series is white noise, then the model chosen was the best. If there are a couple
of significant autocorrelations, a Q-statistic is calculated to see if the residuals
are white noise or significantly different from zero. If the Q is statistically
significant, the model must be rejected, because then there are significant
autocorrelations. If the Q is nonsignificant—that is, higher than $p < .05$—
then the residuals are not significantly different from white noise, and the
model can be accepted (Enders 1995, 87–88; McDowall et al. 1980, 50).

Two of the critical issues, involvement in Europe and communism, and the failure of containment will be assessed in terms of their impacts on the level of roll-call activity.[31] The conclusions drawn will depend on which impact model produces significant findings for each case. A strong finding consists of a model with statistically significant ARIMA parameter estimates, statistically significant impact parameters (omega and/or delta), and statistical evidence that the series is white noise (a statistically nonsignificant Q).

VI. Summary of Query and Hypotheses

The questions and predictions made in these two chapters can be summarized as follows:

QUERY: What is the nature of the pattern in the Senate's behavior on foreign policy issues: is it downward, upward, cyclical, or irregular/curvilinear?

PROPOSITION 1: Critical foreign policy issues dominate senatorial behavior on foreign policy.

PROPOSITION 2: This domination of the Senate's activity creates a curvilinear pattern.

PROPOSITION 3: Activity on foreign policy and disagreement within the Senate over foreign policy increase after the emergence of a critical issue. This is a significant increase, its impact measurable by Box-Tiao analysis.

PROPOSITION 4: With the choice of a policy to respond to the critical issue, activity and disagreement decrease as long as there is no dramatic failure in the policy.

PROPOSITION 5: The failure of a major policy response to a critical issue also produces increases in activity and disagreement followed by a decrease.

PROPOSITION 6: While there may be increases in activity and disagreement at times other than in conjunction with a critical issue, the critical-issue explanation holds that both activity and disagreement rise together.

PROPOSITION 7: The patterns in activity and disagreement vary by issue area.

VII. Preliminary Validity Test

The validity of this research design hinges on the validity of roll-call votes as an indicator of the Senate's behavior on foreign policy issues. Although the argument has been made that legislation is the main function of Congress,

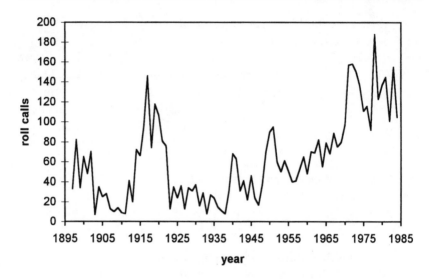

Fig. 2.2.   Foreign policy roll calls minus tariff

looking at only roll-call votes leaves out not only other aspects of behavior, such as consultation by the executive and hearings, but voice votes as well. As a preliminary validity test, the data were examined to see whether the number of roll-call votes is indeed unusually high during known periods of congressional activism. Two famous examples of congressional activism, debate, opposition, and even defeat of the president involve the Treaty of Versailles and the ending of the Vietnam War. If the number of roll calls were low during these two periods, there would be grounds for abandoning roll calls as the indicator. However, they are expected to be among the highest.

Figure 2.2 confirms this expectation. It shows all roll-call votes on foreign policy except tariff for each year from 1897 to 1984.[32] The number of votes in 1919 is higher than any other year prior to World War II, and the number of votes in 1971–74 is exceeded only in 1978. Thus, even if the number of roll-call votes does not tap all aspects of congressional behavior, measure influence, or indicate the state of congressional-executive relations, when the Senate becomes very involved in foreign policy, this activism can be seen in the number of roll-call votes.[33] This preliminary evidence suggests that important and interesting patterns will be found in the roll-call data. The analysis of roll-call activity will be presented in chapter 3, and the findings on disagreement will be reported in chapter 4.

Long-Term Trends in Foreign Policy Activity in the Senate and the Impact of Critical Issues

Now that foreign policy activity in the Senate has been defined, the questions are: How does it vary over time? Was the increased activity of the Vietnam years an unprecedented anomaly? Has activity generally increased or decreased? Has it been cyclical? Are increases in activity associated with the rise of critical issues? The empirical answers to these questions can be found by conducting various analyses on a series composed of the roll-call votes on foreign policy for each year from 1897 to 1984. First, the series will be examined to see whether there are any patterns discernible in the data that conform to any of the predictions in the literature or to the predictions of the critical-issue theory and its corollary. Second, an impact analysis will be performed to assess the extent and duration of the effects of the critical issues and major policy failure. Third, a separate analysis will be conducted on the votes on critical issues to confirm that these issues are shaping the overall pattern in the data. These observations will allow many of the claims in the literature to be evaluated and will serve as a test of the critical-issue theory elaborated in chapter 1.

I. Patterns in Overall Foreign Policy Activity

As reviewed in chapter 1, there are four strands in the literature describing congressional activity on foreign policy. The first posits overall decline, the second asserts that the role of Congress in foreign policy has increased, the third perceives a cyclical pattern, and the fourth identifies variables associated with spurts in activism at irregular intervals. This analysis presents the argument that there is an increase in activity at the rise of a critical issue and a gradual decline as it is resolved, forming a curvilinear pattern through history and resulting in an increase in activity following a major policy failure related to a critical issue. The first step is to examine the series of roll-call data for evidence of patterns that have been hypothesized here and in the literature.

A Secular Trend

Figure 3.1 presents all roll calls on foreign policy for each year from 1897 to 1984. The proposition that gets the most support from this data is that of R. Moe and Teel (1971). There is indeed a steady increase in activity after World War II. This finding does not mean, however, that activity is always higher after World War II than before. In fact, there are ten years in the prewar period that have a higher number of votes than any of the years between 1945 and 1971. The significant difference between the pre- and postwar eras is that in the former, the level of activity always drops back down to a low to moderate level after peaks. In the latter period, however, after each new peak, the level of activity never drops as low as it had been before the peak, and each new peak is higher than the last, starting in 1949 and continuing through the 1980s. The trend is quite obvious to the naked eye but can also be seen in two simple statistics. First, there is a difference in the average number of roll calls in the two halves of the series. Even though there are occasionally very large numbers of roll calls in the pre–World War II era, the mean number of roll calls is higher in the post–World War II era, 88.23, than in the prewar era, 63.51. Second, a trend can be seen as the correlation between the series and time. When the variable of number of roll-call votes in each year is correlated with the variable year (1897–1984), the Pearson's r for 1897–1945 is null at $-.153$, whereas the Pearson's r of .783 for 1946–84 indicates a strong relationship between the series and time—in other words, an upward trend. Thus, Moe and Teel's claim that congressional involvement has increased since World War II seems to be borne out at least in terms of the number of roll-call votes. This increase is also congruent with more recent studies that demonstrate an increase in activism in the Senate (Sinclair 1989) and Congress in general (Ripley and Lindsay 1993a).

Huntington (1971) and Sundquist's (1981) decline thesis seem to be quite soundly disconfirmed by the data. Huntington's diatribe on the decline of Congress is unpersuasive when one sees the number of roll calls climb steadily over the years. Sundquist's argument that there are occasional spurts of activity within an overall pattern of decline seems more theoretically plausible, but the strong, steady increases in roll calls contradict this proposition. Of course, an increase in roll calls is not synonymous with an increase in influence but certainly does not indicate abdication.

There is some support for the claims of Robinson (1962) and others in the 1960s that Congress experiences a decline after 1930. Compared to the

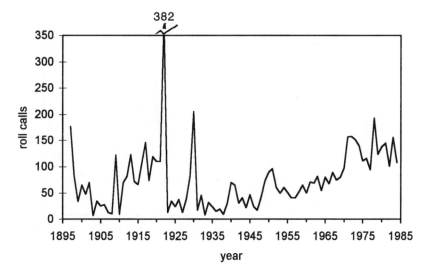

Fig. 3.1.   Roll calls on foreign policy

rest of the 88-year period, the years from 1931 to 1948 represent a decline, but the 1950s and 1960s cannot be considered the "nadir" that Sundquist calls them. Rather, the steady increase in activity starts with 1949 and continues unabated.

A slightly different perspective can be gained by looking at foreign policy's percentage of all roll call votes. Figure 3.2 shows that the foreign policy share of senators' attention has declined. Thus, although the absolute amount of activity on foreign policy has increased a great deal, the amount of activity on domestic policy has increased even more. This finding would allow an emendation of Huntington and Sundquist to the effect that the proportion of time given to foreign policy issues has declined.

As for the period after 1970, Franck and Weisband (1979) argue that there was a revolutionary increase in Congress's role and that it was permanent. The increase from 1970 to 1971 is indeed dramatic, but it cannot be characterized as revolutionary, since other increases of the same magnitude have occurred before and even since (e.g., 1897, 1909, 1913, 1917, 1922, 1930, 1950–51, and 1978). The only unusual aspect of this period is that activity is sustained at a high level for four years, but it does decline again, although not all the way to pre-1970 levels. Thus, neither the dramatic revolution of Franck and Weisband nor the back-to-business-as-usual prediction of Congress's detractors seems to be borne out by these data. In fact, the most recognizable

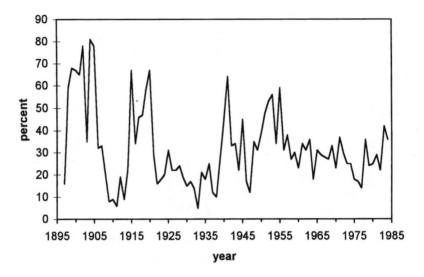

Fig. 3.2.   Foreign policy as percent of total

pattern in the 88-year span of the data is the curvilinear pattern associated with critical issues.

A Curvilinear Pattern

One of the goals of this study is to overcome the time-bound nature of many analyses by looking at 88 years. The entire 1897–1984 period will now be observed to see how well long-term generalizations apply to senatorial behavior. None of the propositions delineated from the literature purport to apply to the entire temporal domain of this study, except for Klingberg/Holmes, but that is a cycle in foreign policy, not in congressional behavior per se. Only the critical-issue theory is sufficiently generalizable to apply to the entire period, attempting to answer the question of why congressional activity rises and falls when it does.

It is hypothesized that three very salient, critical issues have played a key role in directing American foreign policy since the late nineteenth century: imperialism, the U.S. role in Europe, and communism. It is expected that senatorial activity will be high as the issue of imperialism comes to a head in 1898, decrease when the war ends, and wane as the policy of nonterritorial imperialism is institutionalized. The next spurt of activity should come with the conflict in Europe, wane after the peace of Versailles, and rise as the same issue arises again in the 1930s, to fall only with the final resolution of German expansion in the late 1940s. Almost immediately, anticommunism becomes the main driving force of foreign policy, launching the Cold War, and senatorial activity is expected to rise again by the end of the 1940s.

The rise of a critical issue is one sufficient condition for an increase in roll-call activity, but it is not the only condition. The second condition hypothesized here is the failure of a major policy response to a critical issue. Rosenau (1971b) long ago hypothesized that a rise in domestic costs would increase the role of Congress in foreign policy, and Mueller (1971) shows public support for the president's policies in Korea and Vietnam falling with the rise in casualties. Nevertheless, cost alone does not govern congressional involvement—very costly policies are frequently tolerated unless they do not achieve the goal they seek to achieve. The war in Korea was fought to a stalemate, which was not a success, but it was seen as successful containment. U.S. involvement in World War II was extremely costly but effective. With Vietnam, conversely, as the costs rose, especially in lives, and no success was in sight, debate within the society became intense and divisive. The fact that certain segments of the population saw the war as not only costly and unsuccessful but illegitimate surely contributed to the intensity, and the debate was also reflected in Congress. Thus, a corollary to the critical-issue theory is that activity increases when a major policy response to a critical issue fails. In this case, roll-call activity in the Senate is expected to increase until the Vietnam issue is resolved and then to decrease but not disappear, because the critical issue of communism is still not resolved.

At first glance, the data for 1897–1944 in figure 3.1 do not seem to encourage pursuit of this line of theorizing. There are indeed peaks in activity, but they appear to be fairly random. However, an examination of the content of the highest peaks in the pre–World War II period reveals that they are made up largely of votes on the tariff. The tariff clearly was a key issue until the 1930s (Haggard 1988), but it does not seem to be related to the critical issues. Since the original reason for a tariff was to raise revenue for the federal government, and its later purpose was to protect "infant" industries, its heavily domestic component may make it behave differently from other foreign policy issues. It has become common to distinguish between "intermestic" (Manning 1977) and foreign policy issues, and there is empirical evidence that congressional behavior and particularly congressional-executive relations differ between these two issue types (Rourke 1987). Thus it seems justified to remove the votes on tariff to see if a clearer pattern emerges.[1] Figure 3.3 presents the 5,477 roll-call votes on all foreign policy issues except the tariff. Now there appears to be another pattern besides the upward trend. To facilitate observation of this pattern without the secular trend, the

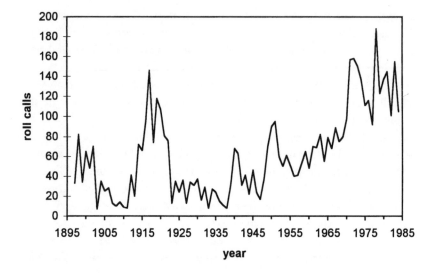

Fig. 3.3.   Foreign policy roll calls minus tariff

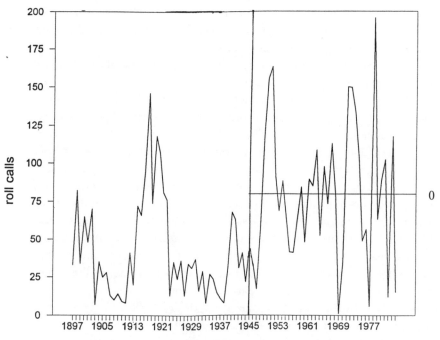

Fig. 3.4.   Foreign policy roll calls detrended from 1946

post–World War II part of the series was detrended. Figure 3.4 shows the result.

A distinct curvilinear pattern is now clearly observable. It was predicted that senatorial activity would rise subsequent to the years 1898, 1917, 1947, and 1968 in response to the critical issues of imperialism, involvement in Europe, and communism and the failure of containment. There are peaks of activity in all of the years predicted by the critical-issue theory and its corollary.

The first set of peaks comes in the alternate years of 1898, 1900, and 1902. The peaks are not very large, but they certainly overshadow the lull that follows from 1903 to 1913. The largest number of votes occurs between 1898 and 1902, the period during which decisions were being made about the type of role the United States would play abroad. The second obvious set of peaks occurs in 1917 and 1919–20 and consists of a very large number of votes, unsurpassed until the 1970s. These peaks stand out clearly as evidence that roll-call activity in the Senate increased because of the issue of involvement in Europe.

It was predicted that activity would rise in 1947 or after. Figure 3.4 shows a significant number of roll-call votes in 1949, 1950, and 1951. The amount of activity is not as great as in 1919–20, but considering the generally accepted notion of congressional acquiescence in the Cold War era, the spurt of activity in these three years is fairly impressive. A preliminary guess when observing the peak in 1950 might be that it is composed of votes on Korea. However, such is not the case. The Korea decision was dominated by the executive (Paige 1968) and did not involve any congressional voting. The Korea situation served as the catalyst for the consensus that emerged on containment (Jervis 1980). The increase in activity predicted by the critical-issue theory is composed mostly of votes on the Marshall Plan and foreign aid generally, which was the major tool of the containment policy. Contention over using foreign aid as a tool of anticommunism resulted from this critical issue. As Hartmann (1983, 394–95) puts it, "Increasingly, the program took on the attributes of a cold war weapon." Votes on foreign aid were such a significant part of this contention that, as much as the foreign aid program has grown since that time, the 34 roll calls on foreign aid in 1949 has been exceeded only once, in 1965, which saw 40 roll calls on foreign aid, and matched one other time, in 1963 (see fig. 5.5). As the theory predicts, activity decreases after 1951 as consensus forms.

The fourth increase was predicted to occur not because of a new critical issue but as a result of the failure of containment as the major policy response to the critical issue of communism. The Tet Offensive in 1968 signaled that U.S. policy was failing in Vietnam. Disillusionment with the policy is expected to reveal itself in a subsequent rise in roll-call activity. The detrended series in figure 3.4 shows that the number of roll calls is relatively low from 1951 until 1971. Unprecedented numbers of roll-call votes are recorded from 1971 until 1974, declining only in 1975 with the final evacuation from Saigon. This high level of activity can be seen as a reevaluation of the overarching policy of containment as applied in Vietnam.[2] Thus, there is a rise in activity with the outbreak of the Cold War followed by a decline with consensus over containment. Then there is a sharp increase in senatorial participation on the Vietnam War policy as a reaction to the failure of the policy of containment.

Five other peaks occurred that were not predicted by the critical-issue theory, but they are all related to one or another of the critical issues. High levels of votes are found in 1917, 1940, 1978–79, 1981, and 1983. Most of the roll calls in 1917 and 1940 are related to the draft. In both cases, the Senate is involved in the mobilization effort for war, and in each case the war is related to the question of involvement in Europe. However, the individual roll calls are not on the question of whether to get involved but rather on raising the troops and production needed to prosecute the war.

A large pair of peaks in 1978–79 is comprised mostly of votes on the Panama Canal Treaty. This last high peak of the data set represents the final disposition of a major stake in the first critical issue, imperialism. The theory cannot predict the timing of disposition of individual stakes after the decline in salience of the critical issue, which means that there may be surges of activity in a given period that do not result from the current critical issue. The fact that this peak is only one year in duration indicates that it is not a result of the rise of a new critical issue: it is merely related to the critical issue of imperialism.

The high levels in 1981 and 1983 are not specifically predicted by the theory, but they are related to the critical issue of communism. A look at the content of these two years' roll calls reveals that they concern mainly defense and aid, fairly stock items in the postwar era. The defense component may be seen as an indicator of the "new" Cold War under Reagan, but it is not really a new issue.

To confirm that the peaks associated with critical issues and the failed containment policy really shape the pattern and that the smaller peaks (such as 1932 and 1983) are unimportant, the series was smoothed. Figure 3.5 confirms that the critical-issue peaks are the most robust. There are still six clearly identifiable peaks: 1898, 1919–20, 1940–42, 1951, 1973, and 1980. In contrast to figure 3.4, the peak in 1973 emerges as higher than the one in 1980 because of the significance of the sustained level of activity from 1971 to 1974. Most notable, however, is the fact that the peaks identified with the critical issues do not disappear when the series is smoothed: instead, six robust peaks

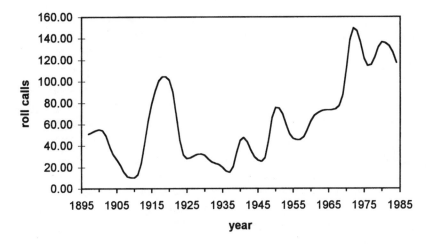

Fig. 3.5.   Foreign policy roll calls smoothed

remain. Four are quite high (1898, 1919–1920, 1973, and 1980), one is modest (1950–51), and one is small (1940–41). These results are consistent with the interpretation based on figure 3.4. The peaks in 1898, 1919–20, and 1951 result from the rise of critical issues, the one in 1973 results from the failure of containment, the one in 1940–42 is related to the involvement-in-Europe issue, and the one in the 1980 is related to imperialism.

The Impact of Critical Issues and Failure of a Policy on a Critical Issue

Observation of the series clearly indicates that roll-call activity in the Senate rises in response to the rise of a critical issue or the failure of a policy on a critical issue. However, mere visual inspection cannot produce precise inferences on the significance of the increases and the magnitude of the impact of the critical issues. As explained in chapter 2, the impact of the critical issues can be assessed by fitting a Box-Jenkins time-series model to the series and then measuring the extent and duration of the impact according to procedures developed by Box and Tiao.[3]

The first step in ARIMA modeling is to determine whether there is a trend in the series. There are various statistical tests for trend, but they are not necessary in this case, as the trend is clearly visible. When there is a trend in a series it is usually differenced and then treated as an integrated model of the order $(p,1,q)$.[4] A different procedure will be used for this analysis. Since the trend is actually very interesting to this analysis (i.e., the R. Moe and Teel

[1971] hypothesis), instead of removing the trend by differencing, the trend will be measured in two ways, by a trend dummy variable, which codes the onset of a trend, and by a break-trend function, which codes the increase in the trend. This way, the trend will not confound the results but will be explicitly measured and reported separately from the other results. Without the *d*, or integrated, component, the ARIMA (*p,d,q*) model becomes an ARMA (*p,q*) model. Once the trend variables are taken care of, the next step is to identify the appropriate ARMA model for each part of the series by estimating the values of *p* and *q*. Finally, the four types of impact are assessed for each case.

The first critical issue is imperialism, and it is hypothesized to have an impact in the 1890s. This issue defined the beginning of the temporal domain for the study. Unfortunately, impact analysis cannot be performed for this critical issue, because it would necessitate data for about 30 years before the impact. In the absence of such data, the observation of the raw data in the previous section will have to suffice. For the rest of the cases, the series is divided into three parts, and models are estimated for the time periods corresponding to the other two critical issues, involvement in Europe and communism, and the failure of containment in Vietnam. These become the three cases for the impact analysis.[5]

It is predicted that each of the critical issues and the policy failure will have an impact on roll-call activity—that is, it will increase. The questions are whether the impact is statistically significant, whether the impact is abrupt or gradual, and whether the impact is permanent or temporary. For each critical issue and the policy failure, statistics are calculated for each of the four possible types of impact. The type of impact is then identified by which set of findings has the most significant parameters.

Since the critical-issue theory predicts that activity will increase with the rise of a critical issue and then decline with its resolution, the impact pattern that one would be most likely to expect would be an abrupt, temporary impact, but all four types are run to test that expectation. In the case of the failure of containment, the impact might be of longer duration. Many analyses attribute a general increase in congressional activism to the effects of Vietnam, and the raw data in figures 3.1 and 3.3 show an increasingly steep upward trend in roll-call votes after 1970 as well as the 1971–74 peak. Thus, the impact might be abrupt and permanent.

For the first case, 1917, the model with the lowest BIC score is an ARMA(4,2) model. Statistics are run for all four types of impact on this model, and, as the theory expects, the strongest findings are for an abrupt, temporary impact, and the findings for the other three are largely nonsignificant (see table 3.1). The Q statistic is nonsignificant, well above $p < .10$, confirming that there is no autocorrelation in the residuals, so the series is white noise. The trend dummy is nonsignificant, confirming that there is no trend in this part of the data, as expected on the basis of simple visual inspection. Most of the coefficients are statistically significant at the .05 level or better ($t > 1.645$). Only the constant is not statistically significant, and the AR(1) component is borderline (1.46). Most importantly, the omega term is strong and significant (1.124; $t = 2.609$; $p < .011$), clearly indicating an abrupt, temporary impact of the involvement-in-Europe critical issue.

For the second case, 1948, the BIC suggests that the optimal model is ARMA(0,3). Again, as the theory expects, the strongest findings are for an abrupt, temporary impact (see table 3.2). Also again, the Q is nonsignificant ($p < .162$), indicating a white noise series. This time, the trend dummy is significant, indicating the beginning of the trend observed in the data. All of the coefficients are significant except the constant and the MA(2) term. The omega is strongly significant (.984; $t = 2.417$; $p < .019$), as in the previous case, indicating an abrupt, temporary impact for the communism critical issue.

The third case, 1968, presented a somewhat more complicated picture. The BIC indicated that the optimal model is ARMA(2,1). With the trend removed, there were no statistically significant findings to indicate an impact for the Tet Offensive. Thus, the case was reanalyzed without removing the trend, treating it as a stationary series.[6] Under this assumption, the findings showed a strong abrupt and permanent impact (see table 3.3). The series can

TABLE 3.1.   The Impact of the Involvement-in-Europe Critical Issue

Impact year: 1917
ARMA model (4, 2)
Abrupt and temporary impact

Variable	coefficient	std error	t-statistic	significance
constant	−.034	.085	−.399	.691
AR (1)	.209	.143	1.46	.149
AR (2)	−.351	.054	−6.519	.000*
AR (3)	−.599	.092	−6.543	.000*
AR (4)	.345	.091	3.788	.000*
MA (1)	−.741	.103	−7.181	.000*
MA (2)	1.298	.112	11.615	.000*
Trend dummy	.001	.002	.625	.534
Omega	1.124	.431	2.609	.011*

AIC = 181.313   BIC = 201.420
Q = 13.564   .258

*statistically significant at $p < .05$

TABLE 3.2. The Impact of the Communism Critical Issue

Impact year: 1948
ARMA model (0, 3)
Abrupt and temporary impact

Variable	coefficient	std error	t-statistic	significance
constant	−.025	.023	−1.109	.272
MA (1)	−.627	.127	−4.952	.000*
MA (2)	−.045	.139	−.326	.746
MA (3)	−.596	.133	−4.485	.000*
Trend dummy	.001	.000	3.037	.003*
Omega	.984	.407	2.417	.019*

AIC = 181.587   BIC = 194.992
Q = 19.069   .162

*statistically significant at $p < .05$

TABLE 3.3. The Impact of the Failure of Containment in Vietnam

Impact year: 1968
ARMA model (2, 1)
Abrupt and permanent impact

Variable	coefficient	std error	t-statistic	significance
constant	5.184	.397	13.043	.000*
AR (1)	−0.509	.124	−4.105	.000*
AR (2)	0.521	.119	4.368	.000*
MA (1)	1.156	.092	12.557	.000*
Trend dummy	0.028	.008	3.707	.000*
Omega	0.930	.340	2.740	.008*
Trend function	−0.044	0.13	−3.492	.001*

AIC = 188.749   BIC = 204.388
Q = 23.104   .059

*statistically significant at $p < .05$

be considered white noise, as indicated by the Q statistic ($p < .059$), meaning that the residuals are not correlated with each other. All of the coefficients are statistically significant. The significant constant, AR(1), AR(2), and MA(1) terms confirm the ARMA (2,1) model. The omega of .93 indicates an abrupt impact. If there were no significant difference between the trend coefficients pre- and post-1968, then there would be no grounds to infer an impact for the Tet offensive. However, a significant shift in the trend is indicated by the findings. The pre-1968 coefficient is .028, the post-1968 coefficient is −.016, and the difference between the two is −.044 (see table 3.3). The strong statistical significance of all of the coefficients indicates that the level of roll calls increased after Tet to a permanently higher level.

The fact that the findings indicate a permanent impact in contrast to the temporary impacts for the two critical issues is evidence that the failure of a major policy can produce not only an increase in activism to rectify the current situation but a permanent change in how the Senate participates in making foreign policy. Anecdotal evidence from the literature includes highlighting the legislation to end military action in Southeast Asia as situation-specific activism in combination with legislation such as the War Powers Resolution, which is designed (though with limited success) to institutionalize a larger role for Congress in decisions to go war (see Destler 1981a, 168; Katzmann 1990, Burgin 1993a, 337). Thus, critical issues produce a temporary increase in activity that wanes as the policy response to the issue is implemented, and the failure of a policy response to a critical issue produces an increase in activity but also a permanent impact as the legislature engages in new types of activity designed to prevent analogous future situations.

In summary, the postwar period exhibits two patterns simultaneously. First is the secular trend identified by R. Moe and Teel (1971), which continues through 1984 (observed in figs. 3.1 and 3.3). Second is the pattern of peaks and valleys associated with the critical issue of communism (observed in figs. 3.3 and 3.4). Furthermore, the interrupted time-series analysis confirms that the critical issue of involvement in Europe, the critical issue of communism, and the failed policy of containment in Vietnam have a statistically significant impact on the Senate's roll-call activity. These observations provide evidence that the critical-issue theory is supported, that the corollary on failed policy is valid, and that the burgeoning literature on the growing role of Congress is documenting a real increase in activity.

For the 88-year period covered by this study, the critical-issue theory fits the data very well. It is the only generalized statement of congressional activity that successfully captures nearly a century of its history. Since the critical-issue theory has gained empirical support, the next section will examine the votes on the critical issues alone to better observe the substantive content of the largest numbers of roll calls and to confirm that roll calls on critical issues comprise the peaks that have been measured and observed so far.

II. Patterns in Roll Calls on Critical Issues

This theory hypothesizes that critical issues and failure of a policy on a critical issue overwhelm smaller foreign policy issues, dominate debate, and shape the overall direction and tenor of foreign policy. Observation of the series and the impact analysis have confirmed that there are significant increases in roll-call activity at the times predicted by the theory. It is assumed that the largest peaks in the data set are indeed comprised of votes on critical issues and that roll calls on critical issues drive the curvilinear pattern but not the upward trend. To confirm this, all of the roll calls not involving critical issues were removed so that the roll calls on critical issues could be observed in isolation.

The first step in this analysis is to create a subset of just the roll-call votes on critical issues. When just the votes on critical issues are selected out of the 5,477 roll calls on foreign policy minus tariff, the result is a subset of 1,553 cases over the 88 years. Figure 3.6 shows the number of votes on critical issues each year. This graph has two striking characteristics. The first is its similarity to figure 3.4, the detrended series of all foreign policy roll calls except tariff, which means that critical issues themselves are responsible for the years with large numbers of roll-call votes.[7] The second striking characteristic is that the secular trend of the post–World War II period that is so obvious in figures 3.1 and 3.3 is totally absent from figure 3.6. Thus, critical issues account for the curvilinear pattern but do not play a significant role in the secular upward trend.

The characteristic critical-issue pattern can be seen in the form of peaks during most of the same years as in the overall data. The set of peaks produced by the first critical issue of imperialism, 1898–1902, stands out much more than in the overall data (fig. 3.3). In fact, this period has the second most activity in the pre–World War II era. In 1898, most of the votes are on resolutions regarding Cuba, as Congress demanded that the McKinley administration take a more aggressive stance toward Spain. Votes in the other years are all produced by issues closely related to the issue of imperialism: Hawaii, the Panama Canal, occupation of the Philippines. Also included are votes on sending troops to various countries in Latin America and involvement in and final annexation of Hawaii. By 1906 activity on imperialism reaches a low ebb and remains low except for some activity on the building and running of the canal in 1913, 1914, and 1921 and on legislation in 1932 providing for the independence of the Philippines, a stage in the movement away from territorial imperialism. Senatorial activity on this issue produces a classic curve of the type predicted by the theory: several years of high levels of activity followed by low to moderate levels that gradually decrease to insignificance.

The second set of peaks is formed by the large numbers of votes on involvement in Europe in 1917, 1919, and 1920. By 1917 unrestricted German submarine warfare made involvement in Europe a critical issue for the United States whether it wanted to face the problem or not. In response to

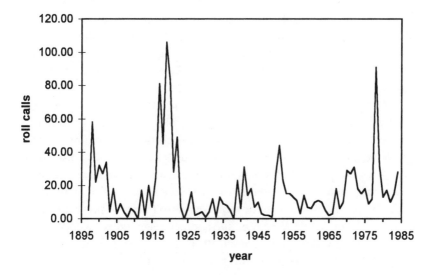

Fig. 3.6.   Roll calls on critical issues

this threat, the Wilson administration began mobilization for war, and the Senate was very active in roll-call votes on the draft and other mobilization measures. Once the war was under way, Wilson had a fair degree of freedom, but the issue of involvement in Europe was salient and divisive enough that once it came to an area in which Congress, specifically the Senate, has a constitutional role—treaty ratification—the pent-up opposition exploded. The combination of Henry Cabot Lodge's leadership of Republican isolationist sentiment and Wilson's unwillingness to compromise produced a debate that spawned so many reservations that the original supporters of the treaty ended up voting against it. The number of votes regarding the treaty is a historical record—between 1919 and 1920, it produced 186 roll calls. Not only is the level of activity high, but the Senate handed the president a major defeat by keeping the United States out of the League of Nations, which indicates that although the United States was willing to enter a European war, it was not ready to stay involved abroad in peacetime.

The issue of America's involvement in Europe is more complex than imperialism because two world wars were needed to finally resolve it. The Senate's defeat of Wilson did not produce a consensus: the debate over internationalism continued through the 1930s and up to the beginning of World War II, observable in the graph as peaks in 1937, 1940, and 1941. These votes reflect the attempt to hammer out neutrality legislation in the interwar period. The final disposition of this issue is represented by the major role played by the United States in the formation of the United Nations and its commitment to the organization, the votes on which produce the last peak on this issue, 1945. Even though the resolution of this issue occurs in three stages (World War I and aftermath, neutrality debate of the 1930s, and United Nations), it does produce a curve that conforms fairly well to the theory.

The third major peak is associated with the critical issue of communism. Activity on this issue includes votes with wording on fighting communism, votes that punish countries because they are socialist or communist, votes on involvement in the wars in Korea and Vietnam, and votes on the dismantling of the Vietnam policy. Roll-call votes on foreign aid and Senate resolutions are generally coded as anticommunist only if there was explicit mention that the reason for the amendment or measure was to thwart or prevent communism, harass the Soviet Union, or single out foreign aid recipients for cuts because they were socialist or communist. Thus, the large number of votes on foreign aid in 1949 drop out of this graph, but in 1950 and 1951 there are a growing number of votes that explicitly mention fighting communism. With the application of containment in Korea, consensus forms, and activity drops off. Indeed, between 1952 and 1964 there are few roll calls on this issue.

The fact that activity rises in 1950 and not in 1947 as predicted bears some explication. Between 1945 and 1947, the relationship between the United States and the Soviet Union evolved from war allies to rivals. A variety of policy responses were considered, from accommodation as proposed by Henry Wallace to rollback as attempted later by General MacArthur in Korea. According to the critical-issue theory, this debate, culminating in the granting of aid to Greece and Turkey as a method of containing communism, should produce a rise in activity. However, there are actually very few roll calls in 1947. Does this result mean that the theory is wrong? Not necessarily.

First, while most interpretations of executive-congressional relations in the period between World War II and Vietnam focus on the considerable extent of consensus between the two branches and the acquiescence of Congress, the Senate did not roll over and play dead with the three roll calls on the Truman Doctrine. It is easy in hindsight to perceive complete consensus on the containment policy, yet from the first feelers on the Truman Doctrine through aid to Yugoslavia, there was significant resistance to both the whole idea of sending taxpayers' money overseas and to military aid to these countries. The lull in congressional activity in 1947 was only temporary. Despite the generalizations about the quiescent 1950s, the decade started with a high level of roll-call activity on foreign policy.

Second, roll call votes are only one indicator of the Senate's activity. In this case, there was significant potential for opposition within the Senate to the Truman administration's proposed aid policy, and only the rhetorical force of Acheson's argument won over Vandenberg, who eventually brought the Senate along (J. Jones 1955:142). Thus, instead of significant roll-call activity, there was consultation involving a historically significant role for at least one senator and only two failed roll calls attempting to amend and table the bill.

The proposals of aid to Greece and Turkey, the Marshall Plan, and Kennan's articulation of the policy of containment caused considerable debate, with significant numbers of roll calls. With the Korean War, consensus formed, and the number of roll calls (excluding the secular trend) fell off as containment was implemented as the major postwar foreign policy.

It is natural in the division of tasks between the two political branches that the executive branch should dominate implementation. Thus, as case after case arose of responding to communism, especially in the Third World, Congress allowed the executive a free hand, perhaps most significantly in rubber-stamping the Gulf of Tonkin Resolution. This relative quiescence can be seen in the lower levels of votes between 1952 and 1970, in accord with the prediction of the theory that activity would decrease as the policy response to the critical issue is implemented. What changed the behavior of Congress regarding Vietnam was the combination of costliness and failure in a major policy that was not merely important but was a defining aspect of U.S. identity in the world as the defender of freedom against communism. By 1971 the Senate was beginning to use legislation as a tool to force the withdrawal of U.S. troops from Southeast Asia. The fourth major peak in figure 3.6 is comprised of a historically large number of roll calls over a sustained length of time—140 roll calls between 1970 and 1974—on the Vietnam issue.

Once it is understood that the failure of the policy accounts for the changes in activity, it is not surprising that the communism issue emerges again in the late 1970s and accounts for increases in votes in the 1980s. The issue has not been resolved; containment has failed, and detente and a renewed Cold War have been attempted in turn to replace a bankrupt policy, but communism itself remains on the agenda. Concern about communism in Central America keeps this issue on the agenda throughout the Reagan administration.

What makes the critical issue of communism different from the previous two is that, given the immense power of the two contenders and the high risk involved in settling their differences through war, the issue is less susceptible to permanent resolution until Gorbachev unilaterally opts out. Thus, the issue of how to deal with communism dominates American foreign policy for a long time—more than 40 years—and the failure to enforce containment in Vietnam produces a new upsurge in activity.

In sum, the pattern produced by votes on the critical issues is clearly similar to the overall pattern, lending considerable support to the claim that critical issues dominate overall activity and produce the dominant pattern. Generally, the critical issue of imperialism is responsible for peaks from 1898 to 1904, involvement in Europe accounts for the spurts in 1917, 1919–20, and 1940, communism produces the peaks of 1949–51, and the failure of containment in Vietnam lies behind the surge of 1971–74.

The similarity between figures 3.3 and 3.6 is the curvilinear pattern produced by the critical issues. The difference is that figure 3.6 does not show an upward trend. There is only a very slight stepwise increase, producing generally higher levels in the 1970s and 1980s than in the 1950s and 1960s, but nothing like the steep and steady climb in figure 3.3. This result confirms the assertion that critical issues account for the curvilinear pattern but not for the secular trend. Therefore, other issues besides critical issues must produce the secular trend.[8] It is interesting, given the potency of critical issues in shaping the overall pattern, that the number of votes on the critical issue does not increase during the burgeoning of senatorial involvement on foreign policy in the post-1945 period. Thus, the secular increase is not driven by the most important issues. More routine issues take up more votes over time, in a finding consonant with R. Moe and Teel's (1971) observation that the role of Congress has grown since World War II because of Congress's increased role in routine issues, especially foreign aid (see also chap. 5), and critical issues produce a curve quite similar to previous eras.

III. Conclusion

The critical-issue theory and corollary have achieved considerable support from the findings reported in this chapter. Observation of just the roll-call votes on critical issues as well as all those on foreign policy shows that the patterns produced by the critical issues is nearly the same as the pattern in the overall data. Although there are irregularities in the empirical data in its raw form, the shape of the curves that emerge when the data are smoothed is consistent with the predicted shape. This finding confirms the hypothesis that critical issues so dominate debate that they influence the shape of overall behavior.

The data on imperialism lend a great deal of credence to the critical-issue theory. Those on involvement in Europe show 1919–20 to be completely dominated by the isolationism/internationalism issue. Despite the lore on the consensus over containment, the years 1949–51 reveal significant, if modest, activity. Finally, the surge in activity over policy in Vietnam offers very clear evidence of an increase in activity over a failed policy. The impact analysis provides further evidence that the two critical issues of involvement in Europe and of communism produce abrupt but temporary impacts on the level of roll calls and that the failed policy produces an abrupt, permanent impact.

What is important about these findings is that they show, first, that the Senate's activity on foreign policy has neither steadily declined nor steadily risen over the years. Nor has the pattern been strictly cyclical. The findings support the fourth perspective's notion of an irregular curvilinear pattern. Second, and more important, the findings show that the critical-issue theory can predict when these spurts in activity will begin and explain why the activity rises and falls when it does. That the critical-issue theory explains and predicts long-term trends in senatorial behavior and is confirmed by the empirical data represents important progress in this research area by providing a more accurate description and explanation of overall congressional behavior than do the other theories in the literature.

The critical-issue theory asserts that debate over the critical issue produces increased activity. This notion raises the question of whether disagreement within the Senate also increases and decreases with the rise and resolution of critical issues. The next chapter will measure the level of disagreement in the Senate to see whether the patterns in contention are similar to those in amount of activity and whether disagreement is related to level of activity.

Disagreement over Foreign Policy in the Senate

The findings in chapter 3 showed that there is a distinct curvilinear pattern in the Senate's roll-call activity that conforms to the predictions of the critical-issue theory. The impact analyses confirmed that the Senate's roll-call activity on foreign policy increases significantly during the periods following the entry of critical foreign policy issues onto the agenda or the failure of a major policy response to a critical issue. The critical-issue theory not only predicts increases in activity but also explains these increases in terms of debate over the critical issue and disagreement over policy. It is thus hypothesized that disagreement within the Senate will also rise and fall with the rise and resolution of critical issues.

According to the critical-issue theory, the rise of a new critical issue in foreign policy is followed by a debate within the United States that manifests, among other places, in disagreement among senators over what policy to choose to deal with that issue. If the theory is correct, there should be a relationship between the increases in activity observed in chapter 3 and increased disagreement among senators. If disagreement over the issue produces the increase in activity, then there should be some observable indicator of that disagreement during the periods in which the critical issues emerge. If there is no evidence of disagreement during these periods, then the theory is wrong. If there is such evidence, it would show that disagreement lies behind the increases in activity.

This chapter will trace and explain patterns in disagreement among senators and delineate the nature of the relationship between the amount of roll-call activity and the amount of disagreement. The first section will analyze the data set consisting of all of the foreign policy roll calls except tariff, first to see whether disagreement follows the same pattern as activity and then to test their relationship to each other. The second section will examine the data set composed of roll calls on just the critical issues to see whether they are producing the curvilinear pattern. The third section compares the relationship between activity and disagreement on critical issues with the relationship between activity and disagreement on noncritical issues to highlight the fact that contention lies behind overall activity on critical issues.

I. Patterns in Disagreement

To test these propositions, the roll-call behavior of the Senate is disaggregated and identified as being characterized by more or less disagreement. Disagreement within the Senate is defined as differences in opinion among members over the matters of public policy before the Senate. These differences manifest themselves in committee debates and votes and in amendments to and passage of specific pieces of legislation on the floor. This chapter will focus on disagreement among senators as observed in roll-call voting behavior. When bills pass or fail by a narrow margin or are amended a great deal, it indicates that there is a great deal of disagreement in the Senate. Conversely, when legislation is passed by very broad margins and when bills pass easily without being changed by many amendments, it indicates more consensus.

As stated in chapter 2, two sets of indicators are used to operationalize disagreement. The first is based on the size of the margin of victory of each roll-call vote. The number of votes each year with a close margin of victory indicates disagreement, while the number of votes with a very wide to unanimous margin indicates consensus. Close votes are those for which one side receives 50–55 percent of the vote, and unanimous or near-unanimous votes are those to which 10 percent or fewer votes are opposed. The second indicator of disagreement is the number of votes each year taken on amendments or on matters of procedure. The number of votes on bills and conference reports indicates consensus. The amount of disagreement in a given year is operationalized as the number of close votes in that year and by the number of amendments and procedural votes in that year.

Close Votes versus Unanimous Votes

If the theory is correct that disagreement is the reason for the recurring increases in activity, then both close votes and the number of amendments and procedural votes should vary in a pattern similar to that of the number of foreign policy roll calls. This section uses the measure based on the size of the margin of victory to indicate the amount of disagreement, with close votes indicating the most disagreement and unanimous votes indicating the least. The database consists of 5,477 roll-call votes on foreign policy.[1] The first set of findings plots the number of close votes for each year and the number of unanimous and near-unanimous votes for each year. The expectation is that the longitudinal pattern in close votes will be very similar to the pattern in overall activity, because disagreement produces the increases. The pattern in the unanimous votes is expected to be flat by comparison, as the periodic peaks are not thought to be caused by an increase in consensual activity.

Figure 4.1 shows the raw number of close votes and unanimous and near-unanimous votes. The pattern that was identified in figure 3.3 in chapter 3 is clearly recognizable in the data on close votes. There are three small peaks of close votes at the beginning of the imperialism period, in 1898, 1899, and 1902. Each is small, but together they add up to more than 40 close votes. One reason there are few close votes is that much of the disagreement over imperialism at that time occurred between Congress and the president, not within the Senate. The issue of involvement in Europe makes 1919 the highest year on close votes and 1940 a moderately high peak. Finally, 1950, which had a great deal of activity on the use of foreign aid to contain communism, also has a large number of close votes, especially considering assumptions about the quiescence of Congress in that period. The surge in the early 1970s that can be observed here and that corresponds to the surge in overall activity indicates that the increase in activity resulted in great part to an increase in close votes. The same four-year period, 1971–74, that stands out as a very active period also has a large number of close votes. This curvilinear pattern in close votes is striking evidence that the theory was correct in hypothesizing that periodic surges in activity result from disagreement.

There are two differences between the pattern of close votes and the pattern of all foreign policy roll calls that provide additional evidence in support of the theory. First, the pattern in all roll calls reveals an upward secular trend in the post-World War II era, while the close votes do not display a steep trend. In fact, the number of close votes actually decreases between 1954 and 1958 and between 1962 and 1969. This decline is consistent with the claims in the literature that Congress was quiescent in the 1950s and 1960s, and it is also consistent with the critical-issue theory's explanation for this decline, which is that contention decreases after initial debate over a critical issue produces a policy and does not increase again until the adopted policy fails or a new issue emerges. However, there is a slight ratchet effect after 1974, which no doubt contributes to the finding of the impact analysis of a permanent impact after Vietnam. Thus, while unanimous votes drive the upward trend, close votes make the trend steeper after 1974.

The second difference between activity and close votes is in 1978, which was a very active year, mostly because of the Panama Canal Treaty. Although this treaty involved the final resolution of one of the stakes of the critical issue of imperialism, it did not entail the same level of debate as would a new critical issue or the failure of a major policy. This is reflected in the fact that, although 1978 stands out as one of the highest peaks in overall activity (see fig. 3.1), it does not have a particularly large number of close votes, as shown in figure 4.1. These two aspects of the pattern of close votes demonstrate the validity of this indicator of disagreement, but more important, they provide

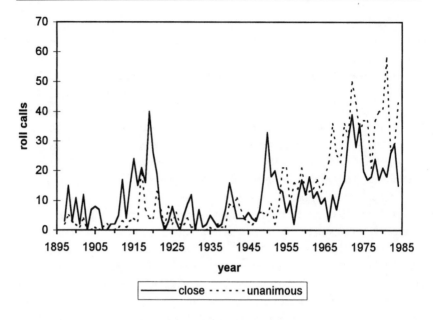

Fig. 4.1.   Close votes and unanimous votes

stronger evidence than merely the level of activity that the critical-issue theory is correct that contention drives the curvilinear pattern in Senate roll
calls.

   To conclude that disagreement co-varies with activity, it must be shown
that consensus does not. Consensus is indicated by unanimous and near-
unanimous votes, which can be expected to vary in a pattern that differs
greatly from the pattern in activity—that is, the number of unanimous and
near-unanimous votes should be significantly lower than the number of close
votes in the critical-issue years. As expected, the pattern in unanimous votes
in figure 4.1 is quite different from that in close votes and from that in figure
3.3, with much lower peaks during the critical-issue years than the close votes
have until 1971.

   There is a very small peak in 1898, which may again reflect the agreement within the Senate against the president, but it is only five votes compared to eighteen close votes. There is a peak of 21 votes in 1917, which is
associated with involvement in Europe, but these votes concern war mobilization, not debating the issue. Likewise, the prosecution of World War II
produces between seven and eleven votes in the years from 1940 to 1943. By
contrast, there are only four unanimous votes in 1919 and 1920, whereas
1919 is unsurpassed in number of close votes. In general, the number of

unanimous votes is low in very active years (1950 = 5, 1971 = 31,[2] and 1978 = 37),[3] and relatively high in the quiescent years of the late 1950s and '60s (1954, 1955, and 1959 = 21, 1967 and 1970 = 36). The pattern is not the opposite of close votes, but it differs considerably. The point is that most of the years that stand out as high in unanimous votes—1955, 1956, 1967, 1970, 1972, and 1981—are not critical-issue years (except for 1972), and the critical-issue years of 1898, 1919–20, 1950, and 1971 are not high in unanimous votes.[4]

After 1970, the graph of unanimous votes is actually somewhat similar to that of close votes. The large number of each in the early 1970s may reflect both disagreement over Vietnam and growing consensus against President Nixon. The difference between the two, however, is that the number of close votes declines after Vietnam, as predicted by the critical-issue theory, whereas the number of unanimous votes continues to climb, which is related to the upward trend associated with the R. Moe and Teel (1971) hypothesis. Thus, there is enough of a difference between close votes and unanimous votes to conclude that disagreement shapes the critical-issue pattern.

One can conclude from figure 4.1 that the peaks in close votes correspond with the critical-issue theory and that the unanimous votes are more instrumental in driving the upward trend, but it is useful to smooth the series to see how robust these patterns are. There are several peaks in close votes for which the theory does not account, such as 1912, 1930, and 1983, but they fade in significance when the series is smoothed.[5] Figure 4.2 shows that the highest peaks are 1919, 1951, and 1972–73. There is a long, sustained plateau from 1897 to 1906, although it is not high. The smoothed series of unanimous votes shows some small curves, but the upward trend is clearly the more salient characteristic of the series. It climbs steeply through the early 1970s and remains at the new level until the end of the series. By contrast, the close votes show a rise in the early 1970s followed by a decline, but the series settles at a higher level than prior to 1970.

Unanimous votes drive the secular increase in activity in the post–World War II period, meaning that consensus is driving the overall trend, while close votes shape the periodic increases associated with the critical issues or the failure of a major policy. The important conclusion to be drawn from figures 4.1 and 4.2 is that there is generally more disagreement in the years dominated by debate on critical issues than in the years in between, that the pattern characterizing close votes is very similar to that which characterizes overall activity, and that unanimous votes do not drive the critical-issue pattern. This means that increases in disagreement (as indicated by close votes) co-occur with increases in activity. In conclusion, the strong similarity between the curvilinear patterns in close votes and in overall activity coupled

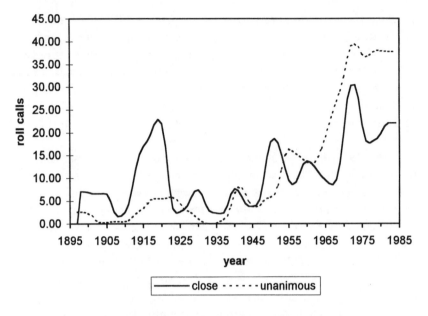

Fig. 4.2.   Close votes and unanimous votes smoothed

with the dissimilarity between the unanimous votes pattern and the overall pattern give considerable credence to the critical-issue explanation.

Amendments and Procedural Votes versus Bills and Conference Reports

The second measure of disagreement consists of amendments and procedural votes. Amendments and attempts to block amendments and bills by tabling them or recommitting them are used as an indicator of disagreement because these tactics are employed by senators to thwart each others' actions. If the theory is correct, their incidence should vary in a pattern that is similar to overall activity. Bills and conference reports, however, are more likely to be associated with consensual behavior in the Senate, and they are not expected to correlate with the critical-issue pattern in activity.

    The patterns in the number of amendments and procedural votes and the number of bills and conference reports are shown in figure 4.3. The most significant characteristic of the pattern in amendments and procedural votes is its striking similarity to the overall activity pattern in figure 3.3. Every peak and valley in activity is present in the graph of amendments and procedural votes alone. Each critical-issue period has a large number of amendments and

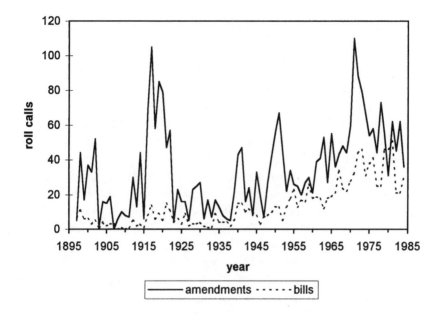

Fig. 4.3. Amendments and procedural votes and bills and conference reports

procedural votes in its first several years. There are large numbers of these votes in the 1898–1902 period, very high levels in 1917 and 1919–20, and moderately high levels in 1940–41 and 1945. There are also high levels in 1950–51 and 1971–74, all of which are years with large numbers of roll-call votes. Each of these sets of years is followed by relatively lower numbers of amendments and procedural votes, in keeping with the prediction of the critical-issue explanation that disagreement rises with the rise of a critical issue and declines as consensus over the issue emerges. In addition, the number of amendments and procedural votes shows a steady increase starting in 1949, which means that all of the increases in number of roll-call votes result mainly from increases in amendments and procedural votes, including both the critical-issue pattern and the post–World War II upward trend. That is, the amount of disagreement rises with the emergence of a critical issue and falls with its resolution, and the absolute amount of disagreement increases in the post–World War II era.

The link between amendments and procedural votes and overall activity is meaningful only if bills and conference reports do not exhibit the same patterns. If the pattern in the bill/conference report variable were the same as the amendment/procedural one, then this variable would be irrelevant, because the two variables would just be two identical subsets of the indicator of activity. If the bill/conference report pattern is similar to unanimous votes, as hypothesized, and they increase gradually in the post–World War II era but not in the critical-issue years, then amendments and procedural votes will be shown to be important in producing the critical-issue pattern.

The number of bills, resolutions, veto overrides, nominations, and conference reports for each year is also shown in figure 4.3. Naturally, the absolute number of bills and conference reports is a good deal smaller than the number of amendments and procedural votes, but there are no peaks in bills and conference reports that can compare with the dramatic peaks in amendments and procedural votes. Particularly striking is the absence of a peak in 1919–20; the large number of votes in these years is clearly produced by votes on reservations to the Treaty of Versailles. The main difference is the height of the peaks and depth of the troughs in amendments and procedural votes compared to the much smaller variation in bills and conference reports.

Again, there are peaks in 1898, 1917, and 1940, which are also peaks in amendments and procedural votes, but these peaks are much smaller and are mostly on war mobilization rather than on debating the issue. There are also peaks in the early 1970s and 1980s as well as others that are not in critical-issue periods, such as 1921 and 1967. Because there is some similarity in shape between the graph of amendments and that of bills, although not in the height of the peaks, it will be useful to contrast the two in terms of their relationship with critical-issue years in the next section.

Although not as steep as the upward trend in amendments, there is a slight upward trend in bills and conference reports from 1946 on. The fact that the bill/conference report variable and the amendment/procedural vote variable both exhibit the postwar secular increase means that neither one explains it: that increase is made up of growing numbers of both bills and amendments. It must be concluded that the utility of the bill-versus-amendment distinction is confined to accounting for the periodic increases in activity associated with the critical issues. Amendments and procedural votes are clearly responsible for the critical-issue pattern in activity, especially in 1919–20 and 1949–52, and bills and conference reports are not. To highlight this difference, the two series are smoothed and displayed in figure 4.4. The contrast is far sharper here: the peaks during critical-issue years are the distinguishing characteristic of the amendments and procedural votes, while the line graph of bills and conference reports is nearly flat except for the upward trend. The nature of the trend seems to differ a bit for the two: it appears that the number of amendments is growing continuously, while the increase in bills may be just a stepwise increase. The data set ends too soon to tell for certain, but the widening gap between the two may mean that the impact of

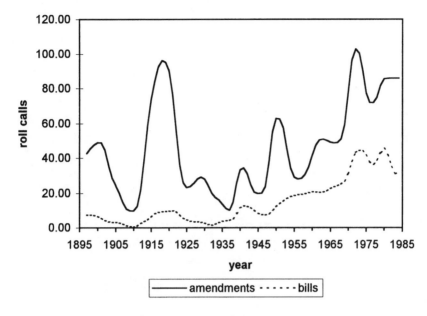

Fig. 4.4.   Amendments and bills smoothed

Vietnam is a one-time increase in activity but a continual increase in disagreement.

An interesting difference has emerged between the two indicators of disagreement. While the level of close votes returns to nearly the same level after 1949–52 and falls fairly far after the 1971–74 peak, the level of amendments and procedural votes climbs steeply in addition to revealing the two peaks. The ever-rising baseline is quite similar to that in overall activity. When amendments and procedural votes are smoothed and displayed together with the smoothed close votes, one can see that the same peaks of 1919, 1951, and 1972–73 appear in each, with a peak in 1898 of amendments and a plateau in close votes (see fig. 4.5). The difference in the period after 1952 is clear: close votes exhibit only a very slight stepwise increase, but amendments climb up in a steep trend.

This finding is important for sorting out the effects of critical issues from other influences on increased activity of Congress in the post–World War II era. For example, Sinclair (1989) traces long-term trends from the 1950s to the 1980s in the increase in senators' activism, which she explains in terms of the change in ideological composition of the Senate and in terms of the increased influence of groups. Thus, the increase in amendments and proce-

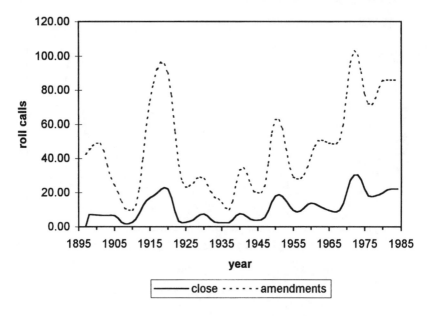

Fig. 4.5.   Close votes and amendments smoothed

dural votes can be seen as part of this secular phenomenon, while the pattern in close votes can be seen as related to critical issues.

Nevertheless, all four indicators seem to play at least a part in the post–World War II upward trend. The steepest climb is exhibited by unanimous votes. Also steep, and larger in absolute value, is the increase in amendments and procedural votes, which also includes a surge related to the failure of containment. Bills and conference reports account for a small part of the trend. Finally, close votes provide a surge followed by a decline, but they do not fall as low as the pre-1970 levels. To isolate the pattern in disagreement over critical issues from disagreement over other issues, roll calls on critical issues need to be observed alone.

Controlling for Critical Issues

Observing the 1,233-case subset of roll-call votes on just the critical issues can verify that votes on critical issues are responsible for the increases in disagreement and that critical issues produce the curves but not the upward trend. Also, activity and disagreement should be more strongly correlated in the critical-issue subset.

Figure 4.6 presents close votes and unanimous votes only on critical

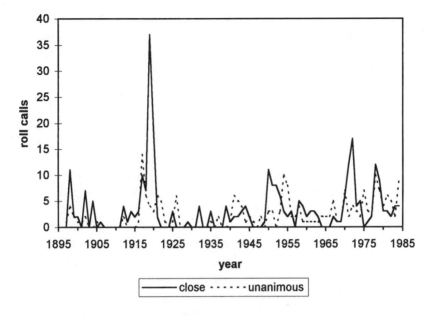

Fig. 4.6.   Close votes and unanimous votes on critical issues

issues. The figure confirms the interpretation in the first section of this chapter, as the major peaks in close votes all appear in years associated with critical issues: 1898, 1917, 1919–20, 1950, 1971–72, and 1978.[6] The shape of the pattern of close votes on critical issues is quite similar to the pattern of total close votes, except that there is even less of an increase in the post–World War II period, thus justifying the conclusion that critical issues shape senatorial disagreement over foreign policy. In fact, the pattern in figure 4.6 is even more similar to the overall activity pattern shown in figure 3.3 than is activity on critical issues (fig. 3.6). Thus, disagreement over critical issues lies at the root of the overall pattern of senatorial roll-call voting on foreign policy.

The graph of unanimous votes on critical issues is similar to unanimous votes overall in that the only significant peak in the pre–World War II period is a modest one (14 votes) in 1917. The other years have very low values, including the otherwise active years of 1898 and 1919–20. The salient difference between the two is that there is nearly no upward trend in the post–World War II period in unanimous votes on critical issues (the lowest points increase from zero to two). Thus, the upward trend is driven by consensual activity on issues other than critical issues. There is also no pattern of peaks related to critical issues. However, it is interesting that the surge in close votes in 1950 is followed by a peak in unanimous votes in 1954–55: this finding could indicate contention over containment, followed by the emerging consensus over the policy, which is predicted by the theory. Whereas the close votes exhibited three distinct peaks in 1950, 1972, and 1978, the unanimous votes are marked by numerous small peaks without any particular pattern.

Earlier findings showed that close votes differ from amendments and procedural votes in that the number of close votes does not steadily increase after 1945, whereas the number of amendments and procedural votes increases in a secular trend. Since there is no upward trend in close votes on critical issues (only a slight ratchet effect from 1980), it will be interesting to see whether there is a difference between close votes and the amendment/procedural vote variable in this subset.

The shape of the pattern in amendments and procedural votes on critical issues is basically the same as that in close votes, as figure 4.7 shows, with high peaks in all the same places. However, the numbers of amendments and procedural votes are much greater. The amendments and procedural votes on critical issues form a pattern that is also similar to that in overall amendments and procedural votes (fig. 4.3), except that there is no clear upward trend in figure 4.7. Overall, the pattern in amendments and procedural votes on critical issues is most strongly characterized by the curvilinear pattern corresponding to the critical-issue theory.

Of course, the validity of this conclusion depends on the absence of the same pattern in the bills and conference reports on critical issues, also shown in figure 4.7. As expected, they do not reveal any significant peaks. There are small peaks in 1898, 1900, and 1917–21 and a bit of activity from 1941 to 1943, but some additional consensual activity during war years can be expected. However, none of the peaks really stand out. In fact, even the years that spawn very large numbers of amendments and procedural votes have very modest levels of bills and conference reports (1898 = 6, 1919 = 6, 1920 = 5, 1951 = 7, and 1972 = 0). After 1945, there is no distinct pattern at all. This finding gives ample support to the proposition that disagreement follows a pattern similar to overall activity and that the source of the pattern is contention over critical issues.

These longitudinal patterns show that close votes vary in a pattern that is much more similar to the overall activity pattern than does the pattern in unanimous votes. The pattern in amendments and procedural votes is most similar to the overall pattern. Close votes are the most important in shaping the overall critical-issue pattern. While amendments and procedural votes on all foreign policy issues make up a great deal of the upward trend, votes solely on critical issues are much more characterized by the pattern associated with critical issues.

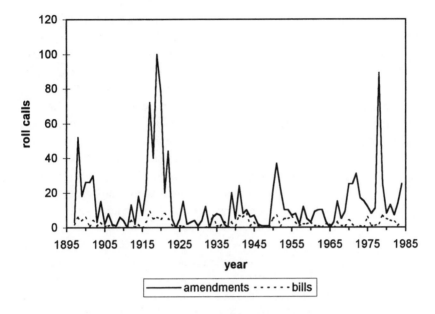

Fig. 4.7. Amendments and bills on critical issues

II. The Relationship between Activity and Disagreement

Peak Years and Disagreement

The patterns in figures 4.1 through 4.7 demonstrate fairly clearly that disagreement co-occurs with overall activity, and the more consensual votes do not. However, some unanimous votes and bills and conference reports occurred in some of the critical-issue years, so it is wise to confirm the relationship by calculating a summary statistic. To look at the relationship between overall activity and the indicators of disagreement/consensus without the confounding influence of the upward trend, a dichotomous measure was created to distinguish the active years from the less active years.

To control for the variation in activity in different time periods, the time span was divided into the four critical-issue periods, and the active years in each period were coded as peak years. In the case of the first three periods, the peak years in activity were the three highest years in that period. In the case of the fourth period, 1971–84, the peak years were the four highest except for 1978, which was not included because the activity in that year was on imperialism rather than on the failure of containment. In the imperialism period, 1897–1913, the peak years in activity are 1898, 1900, and 1902; in the involvement-in-Europe period, 1914–45, the peak years are 1917, 1919, and 1920; in the communism period, 1947–70, the peak years (correcting for the upward trend) are 1949, 1950, and 1951; and in the Vietnam era (the era of the failure of containment), there are four peak years, 1971–74. These 13 years are coded as peak years, and the other 74 years are coded as nonpeak years. To show the relationship between the now dichotomous independent variable and the interval-level dependent variables of number of close votes, unanimous votes, amendments and procedural votes, and bills and conference reports, the statistic *eta* was used. Table 4.1 shows the *etas* for peak years and the four measures of disagreement/consensus.

The use of this measure of activity distinguishes clearly between disagreement and consensus. Close votes are related to the peak years, with an *eta* of .590 ($p < .05$), whereas unanimous votes are totally unrelated, with an *eta* of .136. For amendments and procedural votes, the relationship is moderately strong (*eta* = .536 [$p < .05$]), while for bills and conference reports, the relationship disappears (*eta* = .199). These findings lend support to the critical-issue theory and separate its effects from the upward trend. This test confirms that disagreement, whether indicated by close votes or by amendments and procedural votes, is closely associated with the peaks that occur in the theoretically important critical-issue years.

Controlling for Critical Issues

For further confirmation of the significance of critical issues in the relationship between activity and disagreement, the data were divided again into votes on critical issues and on noncritical issues. The *eta* for amendments and procedural votes is not appreciably different from the *eta* for bills and conference reports (not reported). However, the *etas* for close votes and unanimous votes are very different from each other as well as statistically significant. Table 4.2 shows that the *eta* for close votes goes up in the critical-issue subset

TABLE 4.1.   The Relationship between Activity and Disagreement

Peak versus Nonpeak Years by	eta
Close votes	.590*
Unanimous votes	.136
Amendments and procedural votes	.536*
Bills and conference reports	.199

*statistically significant at $p < .05$

TABLE 4.2.   Critical Issues versus Noncritical Issues

Peak versus Nonpeak Years by	Critical Issues	Noncritical Issues
	eta	*eta*
Close votes	.616*	.341
Unanimous votes	.157*	.117

*statistically significant at $p < .05$

($eta = .616$ [$p < .05$]) and down in the noncritical-issue subset ($eta = .341$). This finding means that the relationship between activity and disagreement is much stronger when critical issues are involved. In other words, when it comes to critical issues, increased activity in the Senate is likely to be contentious, whereas with regard to other issues, there may be an increase in activity without as much disagreement.

When activity is measured in terms of peak years and correlated with the two indicators of disagreement, the role of critical issues receives more support. The key finding in terms of the adequacy of the critical-issue theory is that close votes and amendments and procedural votes are strongly related to the peaks in activity, while unanimous votes and bills and conference reports are not at all related to the peaks in activity. Furthermore, the relationship between activity and disagreement (as indicated by close votes) is a good deal stronger for critical issues than for noncritical issues.

III.   Conclusion

Considerable evidence has been provided in this chapter for the critical-issue explanation for variations in senatorial roll-call behavior on foreign policy. First, it was shown that overall disagreement, as indicated by two different measures (close votes and amendments and procedural votes), increases after the rise of a critical issue or the failure of a major policy and decreases with the issue's resolution or the policy's reversal. This interpretation was confirmed by the fact that unanimous votes and bills and conference reports do not follow the critical-issue pattern. Second, when votes on critical issues are observed alone, both close votes and the amendment/procedural vote variable follow the same pattern produced by overall close votes. Third, close votes are a purer indicator of disagreement over critical issues in that they are more closely related to critical issues than are amendments and procedural votes.

The findings on disagreement confirm the critical-issue explanation for the long-term trends observed in chapter 3 and help explain the literature's contradictory descriptions of congressional behavior. Chapter 3 showed that activity increases when a new critical issue comes onto the agenda or a major policy dealing with a critical issue fails. The explanation also holds that the debate surrounding a new critical issue or failed policy will produce an increase in disagreement, which is supported by the findings presented in this chapter.

In addition, the findings resolve the contradiction in the literature between the assertion that Congress became quiescent in the post–World War II period and the observation that activity had in fact increased a great deal. Two patterns were found in activity during this time span: the increases associated with critical issues in 1950 and 1971–74 explain the troughs in between, and the overall upward trend explains the perception of increased activity. Disagreement was found to be associated with activity in 1950 and 1971–74, but in the period between 1952 and 1970, amendments and procedural votes did not increase any more (proportionately) than did bills and conference reports, and close votes decreased, thereby providing evidence that activity increased without a proportionate increase in disagreement. The fact that disagreement is not related to the secular increase in activity only heightens the strength and significance of this chapter's major finding: that disagreement rises as a result of the entry on the agenda of a critical issue or the failure of a major policy response to a critical issue.

The effects of critical issues clearly need to be reckoned with in future studies of congressional behavior on foreign policy. One step in this direction is to elucidate how the findings of this study fit into the broader study of Congress and foreign policy. Chapter 6 will take up this task. Chapter 5 will analyze the Senate's foreign policy behavior in five substantive issue areas. The purpose of that analysis is to delineate what other patterns exist in the data besides the critical-issue pattern.

CHAPTER 5

Variations in Behavior
by Issue Area

The importance of issue areas in foreign policy has been widely recognized in the literature (Dahl 1950; Rosenau 1971a, 1971b; C. Jones 1995), but the body of empirical findings has not been commensurate with the amount of theoretical attention issue areas have received. So far, this analysis has demonstrated an important role for critical issues in the Senate's foreign policy behavior, but there are clearly other issues within foreign policy. The major reason for observing other issue areas is to discover what other patterns exist besides the critical-issue pattern. The general proposition guiding this chapter is that since issues shape behavior, different issue areas will create different patterns in behavior. Patterns in activity and disagreement will be observed in six different categories: tariff, immigration, foreign aid, defense, routine diplomatic activity, and miscellaneous foreign policy.

The previous chapters have shown that the amount of contention over time is affected by the rise and resolution of critical issues. This chapter will explore whether different issue areas in foreign policy have their own patterns of contention or are characterized by more or less disagreement and activity. If contention on different issues areas is the same as the overall pattern, then there is no need to look at issue areas individually. If, however, there are different patterns for different issue areas, then it is important to look at issue areas separately. There is already evidence suggesting that the latter is more likely: the fact that the analyses in chapters 3 and 4 revealed two basic patterns (the curvilinear critical-issue pattern and the post–World War II secular upward trend) strongly suggests that there are different patterns in behavior. It remains only to delineate the role of issue areas in producing different patterns.

There have been two major threads in the literature regarding the role of issue areas in explaining foreign policy. First is foreign policy as an issue area in itself. This is most common in studies of American politics in general, such as Miller and Stokes (1963), Clausen (1973), and Lowi (1964). The notion of foreign policy as an issue area was brought into the international relations field by Rosenau (1971a). He then developed the second thread, which is to differentiate among various types of issues within foreign policy. Rosenau's (1971b) typology is based on the tangibility of the means and ends of foreign policy. Others have constructed typologies based on the substance of the issues areas (Brecher, Steinberg, and Stein 1969; Zimmerman 1973).

There are several hypotheses on the role of issue areas in foreign policy. For example, in a challenge to the realist paradigm, Coplin (1974) and O'Leary (1976) point out that behavior in foreign policy varies by issue, with some issues, like security issues, looking like power politics behavior, but other issues, such as the environment, eliciting behavior that does not conform to the predictions of realism. More specifically, Rosenau (1971b) indicates that the amount of conflict involved in a foreign policy decision depends on characteristics of the issue at stake: tangible issues will be resolved with less conflict, and intangible ones will involve more conflict.

R. Moe and Teel (1971) proposed explicit hypotheses regarding variations in congressional behavior by issue area. Their categories are tariff, immigration, foreign aid, defense, and the catchall "foreign policy exclusive of tariff, immigration, foreign aid, and defense." The first four are conventional and widely recognized as discrete issue areas.[1] It is basic to Moe and Teel's argument that the growth in the role of Congress in foreign policy is based on the observation that as the place foreign aid takes in overall foreign policy grows, the role of Congress in foreign policy will grow because of the importance of appropriations to foreign aid policy.

Studies that have controlled for issue area have often found that different explanations are needed for different issue areas. For example, in his study of municipal politics, Dahl (1961) found that different groups of actors emerged to handle different issue areas and that some issues were characterized by more pluralist dynamics, while others were more elitist. In a test of several foreign policy typologies against each other, Henehan (1981) found that Rosenau's typology based on tangibility was most able to predict levels of conflict/cooperation.

The query for this chapter is what patterns characterize different issue areas. While Dahl found different actors and different decision-making processes depending on issue area, in this analysis, it is expected that different issue areas will produce different patterns of activity and disagreement and different absolute amounts of activity and disagreement. Each issue area will be expected to have its own distinct life cycle. Furthermore, some will be linked to the critical issues, and others will not.

In the analysis that follows, six different categories of foreign policy will be observed to see whether issue areas are characterized by different life cycles, which issue areas have the most and least contention, and whether activity and disagreement vary by the salience of an issue, by the type of issue, and by the substance of issues. Since the previous analysis revealed both a critical-issue pattern and a secular upward trend independent of the critical issues, it will be useful in this analysis to observe which issue areas are components of each pattern.

Tariff is a key issue to observe for the same reason it was excluded from the previous analyses. In the earlier analysis, votes on the tariff were removed on the grounds that the tariff is an intermestic issue with characteristics sufficiently different from "pure" foreign policy to warrant being analyzed separately. Now the votes on tariff will be observed alone to see how tariff differs from overall foreign policy.

Immigration is an example of a generally "low politics" issue. As such, it should provide a stark contrast to the very highly salient critical issues. It is expected to have its own pattern unrelated to critical issues and is likely to be characterized by low levels of contention.

Foreign aid is a key issue area because of the importance of appropriations and because it is closely linked to the critical issue of communism. In fact, this category did not really exist before that critical issue. Despite its recent advent to the U.S. foreign policy agenda, it is probably here to stay as long as the United States is a major state. For the post–World War II period, activity on foreign aid is expected to increase generally over time.

Defense is a core issue area because it is related to critical issues, which seem frequently to be resolved by war. It is predicted that the number of votes on defense will be high around the times when critical issues come onto the agenda.

One more category, "routine diplomatic activity," has been added in the effort to tap what might be expected to be the least contentious issues. This category includes nominations and routine appropriations for the State Department. When arguing that there are certain issues that create patterns of contention on foreign policy, the unspoken assumption is that there must also be aspects of foreign policy that simply reflect a kind of overhead necessary to keep the bureaucracy functioning. This issue area is generally expected to be relatively free of disagreement, although the Clinton administration has faced some difficulties with nominations and funding the State Department. In any case, the pattern of votes on routine matters of funding and nominations is expected to differ from that on critical issues.

A significant number of roll-call votes will not fit into any of the five categories, such as votes on law of the sea, human rights, international tax agreements, and so forth. These votes are gathered into a sixth, "miscellaneous," category.

The two issue areas that are related to the critical issues are expected to vary in a pattern similar to the critical-issue pattern. Tariff will have a pattern completely unique to itself. Immigration should differ from any other issue area. The final two categories, routine diplomatic activity and miscellaneous, may either be low and constant or may increase over time after World War II as part of the upward trend.

I. Tariff

The first issue area to be observed is truly unique among foreign policy issue areas. As an issue that is highly contentious yet not central to foreign policy, its characteristics as an intermestic issue make it a key case to observe for similarities to and differences from the dynamics of critical issues.

Figure 5.1 contains two line graphs: one of all the roll-call votes on the tariff and one of all the close votes on the tariff. It is immediately apparent that the Senate's voting behavior does indeed vary by issue area. There are several years of very high levels of activity in the pre–World War II era: 1897, 1909, 1913, 1922, and 1930. After 1934, however, the tariff virtually disappears from the Senate's agenda.

The significance of the tariff issue for the earlier findings is that it accounts for most of the activity in the years with the most roll-call votes in the pre–World War II period. Of the seven most active years before the war, five are these peak years in tariff activity. In fact, there are more votes on tariff alone in each of these five years than there are all together in any of the years between 1945 and 1970. Also, because of the tariff issue, three years in the prewar period (1897, 1922, and 1930) have vote totals higher even than the totals for the 1970s and 1980s, except that 1978 has ten more votes than 1897. It is also almost exclusively because of the large number of roll calls on the tariff that 1931–60 appears to be a period of decline compared to 1897–1930. Thus, in the 1897–1930 period, the Senate's activity on foreign policy was dominated by the issue of the tariff. Considering that the tariff was such a major source of revenue, it makes sense that the legislature was heavily involved. Based on the analyses in the previous two chapters, it was concluded that the issue of imperialism dominated foreign policy, but up until 1930, the issue of the tariff dominated roll-call voting overall, producing more roll calls than the rest of foreign policy and domestic policy together in the years 1897, 1909, 1922, and 1930.[2]

As was observed in chapter 3, when the votes on the tariff are included, the pattern in overall activity on foreign policy is characterized by wide swings from very high to very low levels of activity, whereas without the tariff issue, the dominant patterns are the curves produced by critical issues and the upward trend. As for the post–World War II period, since tariff activity drops to practically nothing, it plays no role in the increase in overall activity in that period. In other words, while the tariff issue often produced most of the for-

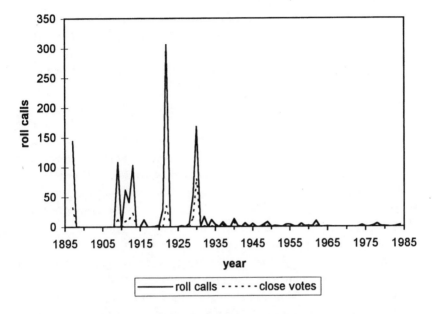

Fig. 5.1.   Roll calls and close votes on the tariff

eign policy roll-call voting in the pre–World War II era, foreign policy activity burgeoned after 1945 without any activity at all on the tariff.

The pattern on the tariff shows that roll-call behavior does vary by issue area. In addition, behavior also varies by issue type. As Lowi (1964) argues, the nature of the tariff issue changes in the 1930s. He points out that the tariff is still distributive in 1930, so that all of the contenders can gain some of the disaggregatable political goods. Starting with Reciprocal Trade Act of 1934, however, the president is given power to negotiate reciprocal trade treaties with America's trading partners, which means that the domestic contenders now stand to lose out. Lowi (1964) calls this type of issue regulative and states that this shift in the nature of the issue accounts for congressional delegation of most tariff decision making to the executive branch. This delegation can be seen in the dramatic drop in congressional roll-call voting on the tariff after 1930.

As with activity, disagreement over the tariff has its own pattern, and it too is completely unrelated to the critical-issue pattern. The tariff pattern has a sequence of peaks starting at a moderate rate in 1897 and going from a small peak in 1909 to the highest peak in 1930. While the peaks occur in the same years as the peaks in activity, the four peaks in 1909, 1913, 1922, and 1930 in disagreement form an upward trend. In contrast, the highest peak in activity is in 1922, and the actual number of roll calls decreased in 1930. Thus, although 1922 had the most activity on the tariff, the amount of disagreement increased over time to reach a high in 1930. Of course, the Smoot-Hawley Tariff is famous for the contention it spawned. It is noteworthy that the 91 close votes on the tariff in 1930 represents the largest number of close votes in one year on any issue area or critical issue examined in this study.[3]

This finding is also consistent with Lowi's (1964) analysis of the increasingly regulative nature of the tariff. As legislators have more to lose, there is more conflict over the issue, until it is finally less costly to hand it over to the executive. In sum, while the pattern of activity is periodic peaks of varying height, the pattern of disagreement is one of steady increase over time until the issue virtually disappears (in terms of the number of roll-call votes it generates) from the Senate's agenda. In this regard, tariff is unique.

Not only is the pattern of disagreement on the tariff completely unrelated to and unaffected by the critical-issue pattern, but disagreement and activity are not as strongly related to each other on the tariff as they are when looking at just the critical issues. The significance of this phenomenon is that the critical-issue theory predicts that both activity and disagreement will increase when a critical issue comes onto the agenda, meaning that these two phenomena will co-occur. Activity and disagreement on other issues are not necessarily related to each other: both simply vary by issue area. In contrast to disagreement over critical issues, which waxes and wanes with the rise and resolution of critical issues, disagreement over the tariff increases over a long period of time until the issue is removed and disagreement within the Senate over the tariff disappears. The difference between the tariff and critical foreign policy issues is that the domestic aspect of tariff means that there are real losers within Congress, making it difficult to reach a satisfactory resolution of the issue. The result is delegation of responsibility to the president. In critical foreign policy issues, however, consensus can be reached on the basis of some conception of the national interest. Senators are less likely to be permanent losers and more likely to change their minds as a consensus emerges.

This discussion reveals at least three levels of issue effects: the salience of issues, the substance of issues, and the characteristics of issues. Very salient issues such as critical issues form patterns that are distinct and different from the patterns on tariff. The pattern of votes on the tariff, however, also differs markedly from any of the other substantive issue areas. Finally, following the insights of Lowi and others (e.g., Haggard 1988), categorizing issues according to substance alone does not tell the whole story. When the tariff has the characteristics of a distributive issue, it produces dramatic levels of activity by the Senate, but when it becomes a more regulative issue, Senate activity on the tariff falls to insignificance.

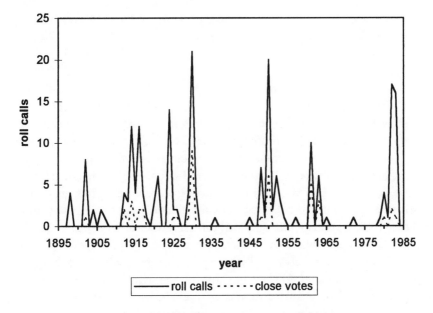

Fig. 5.2.   Roll calls and close votes on immigration

II. Immigration

Figure 5.2 plots the number of roll calls and close votes on immigration. R. Moe and Teel (1971) state that congressional activity in this area has been significant and constant throughout U.S. history. Indeed, over the 88-year period of this data set, there are no significant changes in the amount of attention the Senate devotes to immigration. There are variations, however. There is a moderate level of activity during the Spanish-American War, in response to the large numbers of immigrants of the late 1800s. A larger peak occurs during World War I, and the largest is in 1930. Activity suddenly falls and does not rise again until 1950. There are just two more spurts, 1960–63, and 1980–83, the latter produced by the attempt to cope with illegal aliens entering and working in the United States.

The lack of great variation in the level of activity on immigration adds to the evidence that behavior varies by issue area. Roll-call voting on immigration differs from that on foreign policy overall, the critical issues, or any of the other issue areas examined. Immigration is a different type of issue from critical issues, because it is not as highly salient and threatening—it does not involve the possibility of war—and it is not susceptible to permanent resolution. Rather, immigration is more of a chronic situation that will remain on the agenda as long as the demand exists for entry into the United States. As such, immigration produces small spurts of activity every few years in a pattern that is unrelated to the critical issues and at levels that do not exceed 25 roll calls in a year.

The number of close votes on immigration is generally quite small, with only three years having more than four: 1930, 1950, and 1961. These three years were also peaks in activity, but, in addition, five other years had comparable levels of activity (10 or more roll calls). Thus, five years are fairly active without being contentious, demonstrating once again that, while disagreement is a major factor in high levels of roll-call voting in the critical issue years, high levels of activity on issue areas that are unrelated to the critical issues can be produced either by increased disagreement or simply by more activity.[4] Close votes on immigration peak in one critical-issue year, 1950, but that result is apparently coincidental, as there is no other indication of a systematic relationship between disagreement on immigration and disagreement on critical issues. In general, voting on immigration follows a pattern unrelated to any other issue area or issue type. The issue areas that follow patterns similar to the critical-issue pattern are foreign aid and defense.

III. Foreign Aid

The graph in figure 5.3 dramatically corroborates the assertion that much of the growth in congressional activity in foreign policy since World War II results from its ever-expanding role in the foreign aid program (see Crabb 1965; R. Moe and Teel 1971). There is almost nothing that can be characterized as foreign aid activity in the early years of the data. Starting in 1925, with collection of debts incurred by the belligerents in World War I, there is a small to moderate amount of activity. The unprecedented commitment of the Marshall Plan triggers the high level of senatorial involvement in this issue area during the postwar period. The level of activity is always moderate or high (10 to 39 roll-call votes), except for 1945–47, 1954, 1970, 1975, 1976, and 1982, which have only four to nine votes.

The most significant characteristic of this post–World War II pattern is its similarity to the pattern of votes on the critical issue of communism. For this reason, the graph of roll calls on the issue of communism is printed with the postwar foreign aid data in figure 5.3 for comparison. The key similarity is that there are high numbers of votes on both foreign aid and communism in 1950 and in 1971 and 1972. The implementation of the foreign aid program as an instrument to contain communism produced roll calls on the issue of communism as well as on the program itself. Nineteen forty-nine is

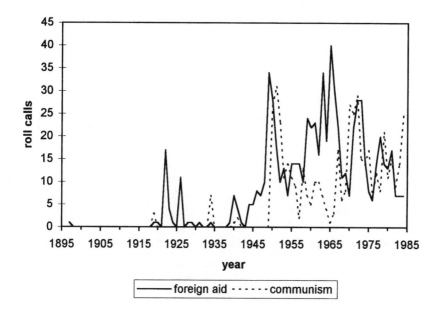

Fig. 5.3.   Roll calls on foreign aid and communism

one of the three highest years in votes on foreign aid, and 1951 is the second-highest year in votes on communism. Likewise, when activity on the critical issue rises in 1970, an increase in foreign aid votes follows in 1971, 1972, and 1973. Thus, both the critical issue itself and the program instituted to respond to it receive high levels of attention when the issue first comes onto the agenda and when the policy of containment fails.

These are not the only peaks in activity on foreign aid, however. There are large numbers of votes in 1963 and 1965, when the number of votes on the critical issue is quite low. During this period, the foreign aid program itself was under scrutiny. As the amount of money appropriated and the number of recipients increased, there were more amendments to reduce the amount appropriated or to attach conditions to the aid, without raising the issue of communism. In sum, the foreign aid issue produced large numbers of roll-call votes (1) at its inception as a major program in response to the rise of a new critical issue, communism, (2) when it grew substantially in size during the Kennedy administration, and (3) after the Vietnam policy became perceived as a failure. As an issue area, foreign aid produces its own pattern, but it is heavily influenced by the critical issue of communism.

The growth in importance of appropriations for foreign aid since 1945 was a key component of R. Moe and Teel's (1971) argument that Congress

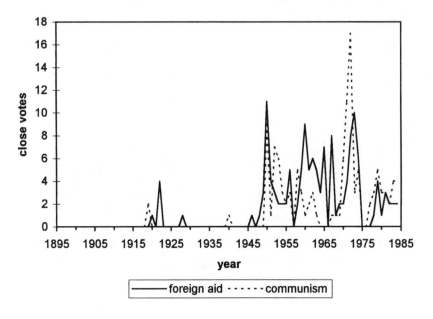

Fig. 5.4. Close votes on foreign aid and communism

has become more involved in foreign policy. Figure 3.3 confirmed their assertion, showing overall foreign policy activity climbing steadily from 1949 to
1984. Observation of the graph on foreign aid will reveal that, although activity in this issue area has grown dramatically, votes on foreign aid alone do not
account for the upward trend in the overall data. The difference in foreign aid
before and after World War II is indeed dramatic: while most years before
1944 have no votes on foreign aid, from 1944 on, there are always some votes.
The number of roll calls ranges from four to thirty-nine, rising and falling
over time. There are high peaks in the late 1940s, 1950s, and 1960s and low
valleys in the 1970s and 1980s. The high levels of activity in the 1960s are a
major contributor to the upward surge in the data in that period. However,
activity does not continue to rise but falls and rises four times over the
post–World War II period. In fact, the level of foreign aid voting during the
purported revolution of the 1970s is lower overall than it is in the 1960s.

    Close votes on foreign aid and close votes on communism are plotted in
figure 5.4. Close votes on foreign aid follow a pattern that is fairly similar to
close votes on communism except between 1959 and 1965. The highest levels
of disagreement over both foreign aid and communism occur in 1950 and
1972, but in between those two years, there is more disagreement over the
foreign aid program itself than over the issue of communism. When commu-

nism becomes the critical issue, the pattern of disagreement over foreign aid parallels disagreement over communism fairly closely, but when consensus over the critical issue is at its height, disagreement over foreign aid is at a higher level than that over communism. Thus, while disagreement in other issue areas, such as tariff and immigration, forms patterns that are unrelated to the critical-issue pattern, disagreement on foreign aid varies with disagreement over communism, sometimes at the same level, sometimes at a lower level.

IV. Defense

There remains a linear upward trend in overall activity for which none of the issue areas observed so far can account. Figure 5.5 reveals that roll calls on defense (which includes the draft and military sales) grow in number steadily through the 1960s and exhibit a stepwise increase after 1966, with a trough in the late 1970s and a downturn in 1984. The growth in activity on defense from 1960 to 1983 combines with the high levels of activity on foreign aid between 1949 and 1967 to account for much, but not all, of the overall pattern of linear growth in foreign policy behavior.

As for the question of whether activity on defense is the same as or different from the critical-issue pattern, there does seem to be a relationship, but it is not as close as that between communism and foreign aid in the post–World War II period. Nevertheless, defense is unique in that it is the only issue area that is related to critical issues throughout the temporal domain of the study, as can be observed by comparing the two line graphs of roll calls on defense and roll calls on critical issues in figure 5.5. The pattern of roll-call votes on defense is fairly closely associated with that of critical issues: the years with the most roll calls on defense are 1900, 1901, 1916, 1940, and 1971, and there are high levels of roll calls on critical issues in 1900, 1901, 1917, 1939, 1941, and 1972. In general, the patterns are similar, with active years on defense occurring at around the same time as each of the active years on critical issues.

There are two major differences between defense and critical issues. The first is the stepwise increase in votes on defense resulting from the steep climb from 1966 to 1969, while no such increase is observable in votes on critical issues. The second is the absence of many votes on defense in 1898, 1919–20, and 1978. What makes the pattern look so similar is the peaks just after those years: in 1900–1901, 1921, and 1980 and 1983. The reason for the relationship between defense voting and votes on critical issues is undoubtedly the link between critical issues and the possibility of war, but the differences between

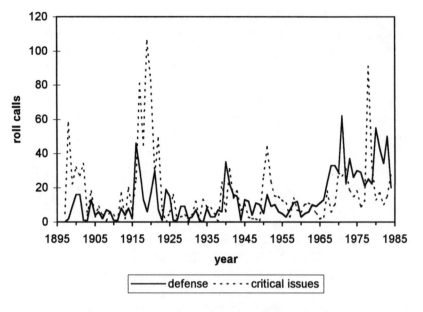

Fig. 5.5.   Roll calls on defense and critical issues

the two result from the limits to that relationship and to the variety of ways
that defense legislation has been used to shape policy. It can be concluded
from figure 5.5 that when a critical issue is resolved by war or when a failed
policy involves a war, there is a great deal of activity on defense. There are
peaks in defense in 1916–17, 1940, and 1971 and a very modest peak in 1951.
There are also repercussions after wars, as seen in the peaks in defense in
1900–1901, which also appear in the critical issues, and in 1921, which does
not appear in the critical issues. When the issue is not resolved by war, the
Senate resolves the issue by other means more suited to its constitutional
powers, such as reservations to treaties, which accounts for 1919–20 and 1978
being so high in the critical-issue graph and being virtually absent from the
defense graph.

The number of votes on defense is also low in 1898, 1950, and 1951.[5]
This phenomenon results from consensus in the Senate on U.S. involvement
in these conflicts. In the case of the 1898 Cuban crisis, consensus existed
within the Senate: the disagreement was with the president. The 1950 Korea
decision, which was dominated by the executive, was supported by the Senate
because the consensus on containment had been forged between 1947 and
1949. During the introduction of troops into Vietnam, there is also very little
activity on defense, again because of the Cold War consensus. Conversely, the
two world wars involve presidential leadership of a reluctant Senate (at least

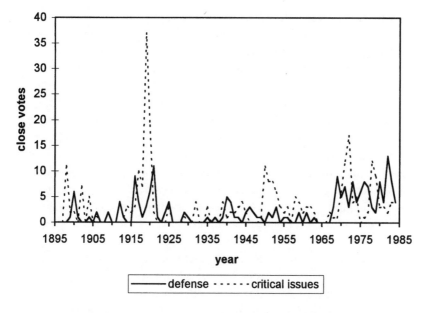

Fig. 5.6.   Close votes on defense and critical issues

before Pearl Harbor), and the withdrawal from Vietnam involves a struggle against the president, producing more numerous votes.

The graphs of close votes on defense and on critical issues, displayed in figure 5.6, confirm that disagreement on defense is related to disagreement over certain critical issues. On the involvement-in-Europe issue, there is no significant disagreement on defense in 1919–20, as this debate centers on a treaty, but there is in 1916 and 1940: U.S. entry into both world wars centered on the question of how involved the United States was willing to become in Europe. With the debate over the withdrawal from Vietnam, of course, it was defense legislation that Congress used as the major tool to achieve control of policy.

The other two critical issues do not produce close votes on defense. By the time Congress had pressured McKinley into going to war with Spain in 1898, there was such consensus that there was no contention in the form of close votes on defense in the Senate. With regard to the communism issue, the pattern in close votes on defense is consonant with the conventional wisdom that says that Congress was acquiescent in the early Cold War years. From Pearl Harbor until the Tet Offensive, the number of close votes on defense was negligible.[6] Thus, while four cases is a small number from which to generalize, it seems that critical issues are likely to be associated with contention over defense unless there is consensus in Congress, which can be a function of a united Congress in opposition to the president (1898) or a united Congress in support of the president (1942–68).

In addition to spurts in close votes on defense before and after most wars, there is a stepwise increase in disagreement over defense after 1968. The failure of the policy in Vietnam lent legitimacy to the use of defense bills as a means for modifying foreign policy. The stepwise increase observed in figure 5.5 can be seen here again as close votes on defense, after proliferating in the Vietnam era, decrease only slightly and remain at a level that is consistently higher than in the pre-1971 period, never falling below two per year. Two votes is not a large number, but the 1969–84 period is the only long stretch of time in this study during which there are always close votes on defense, usually more than six. Previously, the number of votes had frequently fallen to zero.

In sum, disagreement on defense does not follow the critical-issue pattern in the post–World War II period but is affected by it. There are increases in the number of close votes on defense after each war (1900, 1921, 1945–46, 1953, and 1975). In addition, many of the votes on critical issues are closely related to defense. In both 1898 and 1950, there are no close votes on defense, but half of the close votes on the critical issue concern mobilizing the economy for war. Thus, while little disagreement existed over mobilizing the military, there remained disagreement over the depth of the economic commitment. In the Vietnam era, the number of close votes on defense declines. However, the high peaks of votes on the failing policy in Vietnam in 1971 and 1972 include many amendments to defense bills. After the Vietnam issue is resolved, defense legislation is the object of more contention than previously, as evinced by the consistently elevated levels of close votes on defense through 1984.

The pattern in these data is very straightforward: both activity and disagreement on defense increase with the advent, fighting, and failure of wars and with the Reagan administration's defense buildup. Two wars provide exceptions because of consensus within the Senate. Defense is the only issue area that produces a pattern similar to both the overall secular increase and the critical-issue pattern. Critical issues, being so salient, tend to result in arms races and wars, thus shaping activity on defense. In addition, the defense budget during the Cold War became a vehicle for congressional influence on foreign policy, shaping the upward trend of the post–World War II era. In conclusion, the significance of the pattern of senatorial activity on defense is that defense as an issue area is a major source of the growth in foreign policy activity overall since 1945 as well as a major factor in the 88-year critical-issue pattern.

V. Routine Diplomatic Activity

A significant part of congressional activity on foreign policy does not deal
with any particular issue but simply comprises legislation that keeps the
United States in the foreign policy business. Senator Jesse Helms's obstruc-
tionism on the State Department budget during the Clinton administration
notwithstanding, most congressional action on keeping the State Department
funded and sending ambassadors overseas is noncontroversial. Such a category offers a control of sorts for the various observations of contention. If
contention generally varies in a curvilinear pattern over critical issues and
forms unique patterns on other issue areas, then it should be expected to be
low and constant on routine kinds of questions.

Figure 5.7 shows senatorial activity and disagreement on routine diplomatic questions. There is no particular pattern related to war as in the overall
data, nor is there a great deal of activity until 1973. The routine diplomatic
activity area is the only category of those observed here to increase only after
the "revolution" of the 1970s. Up until 1972, activity in this area is low to moderate. In 1972, it begins to climb for the first time, and, while it falls to under
five votes in 1974, it remains above three votes per year through 1984, exhibiting a stepwise increase similar to though much smaller than that found on
defense. Thus, while there is no growth from 1945 to 1972, the small stepwise
increase after 1972 combines with that on defense issues to contribute to the
linear growth in foreign policy overall in the 1970s and 1980s. It is interesting
that the year with the most roll calls on routine diplomatic activity is 1973, the
year marked by a most nonroutine piece of legislation—the War Powers Resolution. Most significant is the absence of any other pattern besides the
increase. The fact that activity in this routine issue area does not vary in a pattern similar to critical issues offers additional evidence of the significance of
the variations observed in the more controversial issues.

Routine diplomatic activity produces a nearly negligible number of close
votes—never more than three in a year (see fig. 5.7). What disagreement
exists is clustered in the early 1970s and from 1978 on. However, most of the
increase in activity in the post-1972 period does not occur in the form of disagreement. In fact, the slight stepwise increase observable in the number of
roll calls does not result from amendments and procedural votes but from
bills and conference reports, meaning that there are simply more bills or that
bills in this area are getting closer scrutiny by being subjected to roll-call
votes, but there is not a great deal of contention over those votes. The lack of
any systematic pattern in or even a significant number of close votes on routine diplomatic activity confirms that most contention is centered on issues
other than this one.

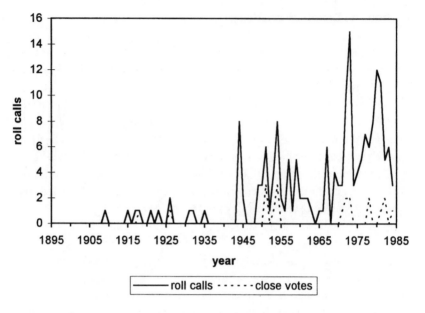

Fig. 5.7.   Roll calls and close votes on routine diplomatic activity

VI.   Miscellaneous Foreign Policy Issues

Even with routine diplomatic activity accounted for, there remains senatorial
behavior that does not fit into the categories of critical issue or issue area. The
remaining votes were gathered into a miscellaneous category and plotted
across time in figure 5.8. For comparison, the graph of all votes on critical
issues and issue areas together is also plotted in figure 5.8. The sum of these
two subsets is the total of all foreign policy roll calls, which was reported in
figure 3.1 and is reprinted here. Three patterns can be seen in the miscellaneous votes. First, they are basically a post–World War II phenomenon. Second, in the late 1940s and early 1950s, the large surge in activity is composed
nearly entirely of votes on critical issues and the issue areas (mainly foreign
aid and defense), while the number of miscellaneous votes remains low. Even
as the overall number of roll calls gradually increases in the 1960s, miscellaneous votes remain low, which means that the examination of the critical
issues and the issue areas reported previously gave a fairly complete picture of
foreign policy roll-call voting up to 1970. The third pattern can be perceived
in the Vietnam and post-Vietnam era. While votes on Vietnam produce the
major portion of the 1971–73 peak, a surge in miscellaneous votes in 1974
sustains the high levels and contributes to the stepwise increase of the 1970s.

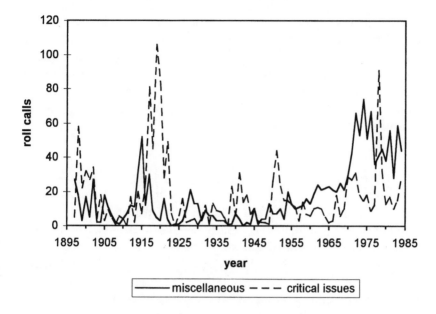

Fig. 5.8.   Roll calls on miscellaneous foreign policy issues

In 1974 and 1976 there are more miscellaneous votes than votes on the critical and substantive issues analyzed here. Except for 1982, each new low point is higher than the previous one (1980 is higher than 1977, and 1984 is higher than 1980). It is consistent with the findings of the impact analysis, which showed a permanent impact for the failure of containment, to observe that the failure of containment produced an immediate increase in votes on the Vietnam issue followed by a decrease on that issue once it was resolved and an increase in the level of miscellaneous votes that is stepwise and permanent.

The increase in miscellaneous issues may result both from the transition away from the critical issue of communism and from the reaction to containment in Vietnam. In the 1970s and 1980s, the critical issue of communism was on the wane, and other issues were emerging, such as human rights, North-South issues, supporting democracy abroad, and interventionism. However, miscellaneous roll calls did not increase at the demise of earlier critical issues and so cannot be the only explanation. The dynamics of the reaction to a failed policy are different from contending over a new issue. The fact that the Senate took on roles over Vietnam that it had eschewed in the past opened doors in issues other than Vietnam. The number of foreign policy issues on which the Senate sees a legitimate role for itself has increased as a result of the activism and reforms of the 1970s. Thus, while the critical-issue dynamic produces a decrease in activity on the critical issue with the withdrawal from Vietnam, activity on miscellaneous issues surges in the 1970s and remains higher in the 1980s (except for 1982) than at any time prior to the 1970s. Looking at this category suggests that senatorial behavior on foreign policy follows a curvilinear pattern based on critical issues until a major policy fails, at which point it exhibits a sharp and apparently permanent increase in activity.

VII. Conclusion

The findings presented here clearly demonstrate that the Senate's roll-call behavior varies by substantive issue area as well as by issue type (critical versus noncritical and distributive versus regulative). The reason it is so important to treat issue areas separately is that, because they produce different kinds of behavior, they will require different explanations. Also not only is activity on tariff different from activity on other issues, but tariff has its own life cycle.

Another reason to look at issue areas is that some issues are related to and affected by critical issues. Activity on defense increased in the 1970s because Congress perceived a major military policy of the executive as a failure and moved in to take more control. Not only did Congress become active on specifics of the Vietnam debacle, but it also passed general legislation, such as the War Powers Act, to institutionalize its increased involvement. The fact that levels of activity do not return to the lower levels of the 1960s either in foreign policy overall or on defense is evidence that Congress has not returned totally to business as usual, as some analysts asserted in the 1980s (Cronin 1983; Sundquist 1981).

The finding that behavior varies by issue is important also because it demonstrates the limited utility of a general statement that congressional activity has increased or decreased. Issue area must be specified. While Congress has delegated away much of its role in tariff policy, it has become much more involved in defense policy. Yet although overall activity in the post–World War II period has increased in a steady linear fashion, as observed in figure 3.2, much of the increase after 1976 is accounted for by the miscellaneous category.

The findings also have implications for those seeking to predict when Congress is likely to become more involved in foreign policy. One can expect Congress to be moderately involved in immigration, not very involved in tariff, somewhat less involved in foreign aid than in the 1960s, more involved in defense than before 1970, and increasingly involved in routine diplomatic activity. Given the link between foreign aid and the critical issue of communism, congressional activity on foreign aid should be different now that communism is no longer the dominant issue, reflecting more isolationist or budgetary concerns. Given the link between defense and all critical issues, one could expect congressional activism in this issue area to surge anew once a new critical issue emerges. The recent debates over the role of the United Nations, peacekeeping, and human rights in China indicate that in this era of transition between the critical issue of communism and a new critical issue, concerns with national security will again come to the fore.

CHAPTER 6

Conclusion: Theories and Research on Congressional Behavior on Foreign Policy

The findings presented in this book confirm an explanation that accounts for fluctuations in congressional behavior that had previously been only poorly understood. The first part of this chapter will relate the findings reported in chapters 3–5 to the claims and findings in the existing literature to determine which claims are correct and under what conditions they apply. In addition, several competing independent variables will be examined. The result of this integration of findings will be an elaboration of the critical-issue explanation developed herein. The second part of the chapter will summarize this book's contributions and point the way toward future research that would test other questions this study raises.

I. Constructing a Theory of Congressional Behavior on Foreign Policy

Resolving the Contradictions

Myriad claims have been made in the literature regarding Congress's behavior on foreign policy. Although many such claims are plausible, they cannot all be correct because they contradict each other. Without scientific evidence, no progress can be made in resolving the contradictions. There is a need to be more precise in specifying the conditions under which certain claims hold and to test them empirically. The findings from this study can be compared to the findings and conclusions of other studies in an attempt to refine and extend the explanations offered in earlier chapters.

The major contradiction in the literature is that various studies, even some done at the same time, draw opposite conclusions about whether Congress's role in the post–World War II era has declined or grown. One school of thought is characterized by studies in the 1960s and early 1970s that stress the decline of Congress (Huntington 1971; Robinson 1962) and subsequent analyses that dismiss the assertiveness of the 1970s as an aberration in an overall pattern of decline (Sundquist 1981; Cronin 1983; Koh 1986; Silverstein 1994). The other school stresses the growth of Congress's role in foreign policy, including early arguments that the increased reliance on foreign policy programs that require appropriation augments the role of Congress (R. Moe and Teel 1971) and later studies that see the increase in congressional assertiveness in the 1970s as a permanent or continuing phenomenon (Franck and Weisband 1979; Mann 1990a; Ripley and Lindsay 1993b; Peterson 1994b). Both sets of arguments suffer from an assumption that trends in congressional behavior are linear. The tendency to see linear trends often results from looking at too short a period of time and proceeding without a theory of long-term behavior. This study's findings help to resolve some of the contradictions.

It is obvious that the works of the 1960s that characterized Congress as being in decline failed to anticipate the resurgence of the 1970s, just as the heralding of the congressional revolution failed to recognize the extent to which the pendulum would swing back. Yet it is far too simplistic to explain away variations with the pendulum analogy. It may seem unfair to fault these analysts for not being able to read the future, but they clearly lacked a theory of long-term behavior. The weakest analyses were those that attempted to definitively state the nature of congressional behavior without recognizing that it varied over time. Those who looked at longer periods were likely, as did Crabb and Holt (1992), to mention a cyclical pattern, but rarely was such a cycle explained.[1]

This study shows that senatorial behavior on foreign policy issues does indeed vary and, more important, explains why. The critical-issue explanation shifts the focus away from making universal descriptions of congressional behavior to specifying why different behaviors occur when they do. Different types of behavior correspond to different phases within the life cycle of critical issues. A period of relative assertiveness is thus seen in the context of the rise of a new critical issue or the failure of a major policy, and a period of relative quiescence is seen as the implementation period for a policy response to a resolved critical issue. Thus, this study improves on earlier time-bound studies by specifying the time period during which various descriptions are correct.

In addition to being contradictory, descriptions of growth and decline are sometimes unclear on the meaning of these terms. Descriptions of the growth of Congress may refer to an increase in activity, conflict, control, initiative, or influence.[2] R. Moe and Teel (1971) distinguish between amount of activity and the significance of certain policies. They concede that Congress may not be very active on great foreign policy matters but argue that Congress's role in foreign policy has increased. Moe and Teel argue that there has been such an increase in the amount of congressional activity on foreign policy matters and in the time spent on aspects of foreign policy in which Congress plays a major role, such as foreign aid, that the sum of congressional activity is significantly greater than in the past. Hinckley (1994) purports to find little in terms of substantive policy, but the fact that there was twice as much in the 1970s than in the 1960s or 1980s is a significant finding. Furthermore, Lindsay (1994a, 282–83) cautions students of Congress and foreign policy to look beyond substantive legislation to procedural innovations that allow Congress indirectly to exert its influence. The findings in chapter 3 showing the upward trend in senatorial roll-call voting after 1945 are consistent with these works observing an increase in Congress's role.

The arguments that Congress has declined are more complex. They depend on an assessment of the relative influence of Congress and the president, which this study does not attempt to measure, but they also make assumptions about the nature of congressional behavior that the findings from this study can address indirectly. The literature refers to three ways in which Congress has declined. First is Congress's alleged unwillingness and/or incompetence to engage in the formulation of national-level policy, leaving this area to the president's discretion. Second is that Congress has less influence on policy than does the president, a hypothesis that is very hard to measure, as discussed in chapter 2. Third is Robinson's (1962) win-lose criterion, by which he finds that Congress usually loses to the president. The relevance of this study's findings to these three points will be dealt with in turn.

The first claim is soundly falsified by the data. The characterizations of a Congress ready to abdicate all authority may have had merit for the short term of the 1950s and 1960s, but a longer view shows that it is a mistake to dismiss Congress as an important actor in high politics. Rather, Congress can be counted on to become vitally active in the most crucial of foreign policies every 20 years or so. The most active years in the data set are not filled with roll calls on routine matters: they are the years of debate over the Versailles treaty and the Vietnam War. The Senate has been more than willing not only to vote on matters of policy but also to engage in internal debate in the form of amendments and other modifications to shape policy. There was such a long period during which Congress was branded as impotent because this kind of intense activity takes place only every 20 years or so with the emergence of a critical issue. The critical-issue explanation suggests that debate within Congress and congressional activity on foreign policy increase with the introduction of a new critical issue or the failure of a major policy response to a critical issue and that they remain high until a policy is chosen in response. As a result, Congress is not only willing to engage itself in high politics but is a key player in shaping the fundamental tenets of a generation's foreign policy. This finding provides the necessary perspective that the periods of abdication are better characterized as relative passivity while Congress acts as a watchdog and the executive carries out the policy that Congress either helped to formulate or at least approved.[3]

There is one caveat to the conclusion that congressional activity on foreign policy increases in the post–World War II era. Although the number of roll-call votes increases, the number of votes on domestic policy increases even more. Chapter 3 showed that the percentage of roll calls devoted to foreign policy is generally lower in the post–World War II period than earlier. Thus, the increased attention given to foreign policy is a function of an overall increase in congressional activity in policy-making, and, in fact, activity on foreign policy has not increased as much as has activity on domestic policy. A combined interpretation of both the roll-call data and the percentage data makes sense of Sundquist's (1981) characterization of congressional activity as exhibiting occasional spurts in an overall pattern of decline. The peaks in roll calls are the spurts, and foreign policy's decreasing share of overall activity can be seen as relative decline.

Of course, Sundquist is not talking solely about the amount or percentage of foreign policy activity: he is referring to a decline in the Congress's influence relative to the president over foreign policy, which is the second claim mentioned earlier. Although there are many arguments that stress the president's advantages in foreign policy and see the congressional assertiveness of the 1970s as ephemeral, the perspective offered by the critical-issue explanation—that Congress plays a key role in formulating the policy that shapes a generation's foreign policy—suggests that Congress has more influence over foreign policy than is generally acknowledged. It is not that there is no difference between the congressional-executive relationship of Woodrow Wilson's "congressional government" and that of the post–World War II era—the differences are marked and well documented. The critical-issue explanation suggests that Congress is heavily involved in the process that gives rise to a policy in response to a critical issue.

The critical-issue explanation, however, emphasizes effects that occur prior to the influence of either the president or Congress and that constrain and shape their choices. An issue arises in the global arena and causes debate within both the legislative and executive branches. The issue is so salient that it dominates debate, reducing the amount of time and attention available to consider other issues. The outcome has less to do with the institutional strengths or interests of the two branches than with the global situation and prior decisions or nondecisions. For example, even though Congress had declared war in World War I, the Senate was not willing to follow Wilson's internationalist lead after the war and fought instead to keep the United States out of the League of Nations. In the case of the establishment of the United Nations after World War II, the Senate was much more supportive (producing only nine roll-call votes on the ratification of the Charter). It is not that Congress had no influence; rather, over the experience of World War II, most members of the elite had changed their minds and supported an internationalist policy, and a consensus emerged. Likewise, this incident was not a loss for Congress as an institution but instead showed the effect of changes of issue position and of personnel.

As a result, the third claim, that the president usually wins and Congress usually loses, requires some rethinking. Robinson's (1962) findings seem so clear-cut, yet they produce a picture of congressional-executive relations that is at best incomplete and at worst a distortion. First, it is a conceptual error to see the two sides in a zero-sum game, since Congress is not a unitary actor. The president has allies in Congress as well as adversaries; a win for the president is not necessarily a loss for Congress. Even when Congress pushes a policy on a president, it is not necessarily a loss for the president. The only two events that are really losses are vetoes and veto overrides. Second, looking at only the most important decisions ignores the larger number of smaller decisions on which Congress might have prevailed. Third, Robinson's sample does not account for the fact that some of those decisions were logical extensions of the basic policy already approved by Congress. When the administration submits a proposal and Congress passes it, this is not a loss for Congress. It is important to remember Chamberlain's (1946) point that many policies proposed by the administration have congressional roots as well as the fact that the administration often, though not always, shapes its requests so that they will be met.

While Robinson's (1962) study is limited by the fact that he looks at only the most important cases, there is an interesting perspective to be gained by looking in a different way at a very small number of important cases. According to the critical-issue perspective, there have been four major foreign policy decisions to which the Senate devoted a great deal of attention during the 88 years covered here: to fight Spain over Cuba, to defeat the Versailles treaty and keep the United States out of the League of Nations, to institute a set of programs to contain communism, and to end U.S. involvement in the Vietnam War. Of these four major policy decisions associated with critical issues, Congress—in particular, the Senate—prevailed on three. It forced McKinley to reverse his position against war and deliver an ultimatum to Spain; it denied Wilson his dream of joining the League of Nations; it made the Nixon and Ford administrations withdraw all U.S. troops from Vietnam.

The only exception in this winning record is the post–World War II Marshall Plan and other aid programs to rebuild Europe, which the administration proposed to Congress. Although these programs were arguably in the long-term national economic interest, members of Congress were inclined to oppose spending their constituents' money abroad. Depending on how one looks at it, Senator Vandenberg was responsible either for securing an important role for the Senate or for paving the way for an easy win for the administration. Without Vandenberg, the administration probably still would have prevailed, but it would have taken much more of a fight. In sum, then, Congress won on three of the four cases, and in the fourth case, the administration had to present the issue in a particular way to gain congressional support (an eventual victory for the administration, though not necessarily a loss for Congress).

Looking at whether the president wins or loses also misses a very important factor. It seems logical and appropriate to talk about congressional assertiveness even when it is not successful. Although the period 1946–70 is dominated by presidential victories, those years were not all alike. The 1949–51 period has a significant, although moderate, amount of activity and disagreement, and it is a distortion to equate it with the rest of the post–World War II period merely because Congress did not defeat the executive on a major policy.[4] To get a complete, precise, and theoretically relevant historical picture, it is just as important to identify periods of failed assertiveness as it is to identify congressional successes. Even if 1949–51 is seen as a period of failed congressional assertiveness, the era is a crucial part of the critical-issue pattern that has proven a powerful explanation for congressional behavior.

In sum, the roll-call findings show that R. Moe and Teel (1971) are correct in their assessment of the quantity of congressional activity in the post–World War II period. Huntington (1971) and Sundquist (1981) are incorrect in characterizing Congress in decline, but they do have a point if one looks at the proportion of attention devoted to foreign policy compared to domestic policy. The findings on bills and conference reports are consistent with Hinckley's (1994) data showing a very small number of bills passed each year. The data on amendments and procedural votes, however, goes beyond the passage of substantive legislation to show how the level of disagreement within the Senate varies over time. Franck and Weisband (1979) are shown to be too shortsighted: what they offer in timely description of a contemporary phenomenon is flawed by the lack of a long-term theory and overstatement of the magnitude and duration of the increase in activity. Crabb and Holt (1992), Klingberg (1952), and Holmes (1985) are closer to the mark with a cyclical notion, although Crabb and Holt are far too vague and atheoretical and Klingberg and Holmes do not explicitly address congressional behavior. Furthermore, the empirical pattern is not truly cyclical but is irregular and curvilinear. Only the critical-issue explanation captures and explains the nature of the pattern in the roll-call data.

In addition to the overall critical-issue pattern, this study also predicted that congressional behavior would vary by issue area. The claims in the literature are generally correct in this area, although the types of issue areas specified vary widely. For example, Clausen (1973) specifies only one foreign policy issue area, international involvement, while R. Moe and Teel (1971) and Rosati (1984) divide foreign policy into various categories. Carter (1988) goes even further by dividing the category of national security policy into four types. For most of these studies, the point is that the role of Congress or the influence of the president varies depending on which type of issue is at stake. The findings on issue area in this study go much further. Once it is observed that voting on critical issues dominates the overall pattern, it is useful to know the extent to which critical issues dominate activity on various issue areas. The issue areas of the tariff, immigration, and routine diplomatic activity are independent of the critical issues, defense is heavily influenced by critical issues, and, starting in 1947, foreign aid is intimately linked with the critical issue of communism. More important is the finding that the relationship between activity and disagreement on which the critical-issue explanation depends holds only for the critical issues and to some extent for the issue areas that are related to the critical issues, foreign aid and defense. There is no statistical relationship between activity and disagreement for votes on foreign policy other than critical issues, and the graphs on tariff, immigration, and routine diplomatic activity in chapter 5 show that activity and disagreement patterns can differ greatly from each other in certain issue areas. The fact that activity and disagreement are related to each other only for the critical issues supports the critical-issue explanation by confirming that overall activity rises as a result of debate over the critical issue.

In conclusion, there is a great deal of conceptual confusion in this literature. This study's findings take a small step toward clarifying some of the more confounding issues. More important, perhaps, these findings have broken ground in what should be a continuing effort to subject theories and implicit propositions to empirical tests. This book suggests a fairly extensive research agenda. The next section compares the findings with other data-based findings in the literature and suggests directions for future research.

Counterexplanations

This section will explore several additional variables that can be raised as possible ad hoc explanations for variations in congressional behavior. The first three are competing variables suggested by explanations of American domestic politics: presidential honeymoons, presidential election years, and party control. The last variable is an international systemic variable, war, that has been offered as an alternate explanation but that can also be integrated into the critical-issue explanation. These variables will be compared to the critical-issue variable by computing simple measures of association between each and the most active years in terms of number of roll calls and number of close votes.

The critical-issue years are 1897–98, 1917–20, 1947–50, and 1968–73. Since the effects of critical issues are expected to be delayed, a one-year time lag is used in the cross-tabulation with activity and disagreement. The finding for peaks in activity is $phi = .634$ ($p < .05$); for peaks in close votes, $phi = .397$ ($p < .05$) (see table 6.1). These outcomes might be even higher with a longer lag. However, these findings do indicate that critical issues are moderately related to roll-call activity at a statistically significant level.

Two hypotheses based on domestic politics are that the honeymoon stage of the presidency accounts for lower levels of activity or that higher levels of activity occur in presidential election years. Honeymoon and presidential election year can be operationalized as dichotomous variables and cross-tabulated with activity and disagreement. All of the findings are null and nonsignificant.[5] For honeymoon years, $phi = -.018$ for peak years in activity and $-.175$ for peak years in close votes (see table 6.1). While honeymoon years are generally fairly low in both activity and disagreement, there is not

TABLE 6.1. Competing Independent Variables

	Peaks in activity (phi)	Peaks in close votes (phi)
Critical issue years with one-year lag	.634*	.397*
Honeymoon years	−.018	−.175
Presidential election years	−.018	.080
Party control	.177	.175
War endings		
one year after	.056	.077
two years after	.082	.113
last year of war plus two years	.236*	.212*
War years	.222*	.213*

*statistically significant at $p < .05$

always high activity and disagreement in the nonhoneymoon years, leaving a great deal unexplained. The findings for presidential election years are *phi* = –0.18 for peak years in activity, which is neither in the right direction nor statistically significant, and .080 for peak years in close votes (see table 6.1). These findings should put to rest any questions about whether election years or honeymoon years are more important than critical issues.

A common question after critical issues are offered as the explanation for surges in congressional activity is whether increases in activity and disagreement are not more likely occurring because different parties control the two branches, with consensus and less activity reigning when one party controls both branches. Carter (1986a, 336) found that party control makes no significant difference in the incidence of his indicators of compliant and independent behavior. It is a simple matter to measure the variable of party control to see whether it co-occurs with activity and disagreement. A cross-tabulation was run between the two dichotomous variables of party control (same party controlling the Senate and the presidency versus different party) and peak years in activity (peak versus nonpeak), producing a *phi* of .177, which confirms that there is no statistical relationship between party control and high levels of activity (see table 6.1). The association between party control and peaks in disagreement is also null (*phi* = .175).

Of course, only disagreement within the Senate is measured here, not congressional-presidential disagreement. Nevertheless, the critical-issue perspective would not have expected congressional-executive relations to be highly consensual in 1993–94 just because the same party controlled both branches or for relations to have subsequently become highly contentious merely because of split party control. McCormick, Wittkopf, and Danna (1997) show that although there is somewhat more contention when party control is divided, the more important variable in changing the level of disagreement between Congress and the president is the end of the Cold War. Even if the trauma of Vietnam makes any future era of congressional deference or abdication highly unlikely, a consensus could emerge on a new conception of the U.S. role in the world that could see relatively little difference between the parties, thereby leading to a return, after the major policies are hammered out, to relative acquiescence. As Rohde (1994b, 127) states, because most debates over foreign policy involve assessing the international situation and identifying the national interest, once a consensus on these issues emerges, divided government does not matter very much.

Although there is no statistical relationship between party control and high activity or disagreement, a look at the frequencies shows that two sets of years are characterized by divided party control and very high activity. These years, 1919–20 and 1971–74, are also the two cases elaborated in the section on Holmes as being instances of an extrovert president being overruled by Congress at the very end of an extrovert phase. Thus, divided control does not cause conflict—it is not even correlated with it. However, when a conflict does arise over a critical issue or major policy failure, if party control is divided, the level of conflict is more intense.

High activity can occur even when the same party is in control because when there is a critical issue at stake, the issue overrides party divisions and loyalties. Indirect evidence that critical issues are more important can be seen in the pattern of peak years in roll-call voting and close votes as reported in chapters 3 and 4. Critical issues can be said to have produced every peak year in activity except 1981 and 1983, indicating that critical issues have a strong relationship to high levels of senatorial activity in foreign policy. Of the 27 peak years in close votes, critical issues are related to 15, and all of the 11 highest peaks in close votes are related to critical issues except 1983.

The assumption that the most important sources of foreign policy are external suggests quite a different perspective. Such a systemic view would suggest that war affects the behavior of domestic institutions. It is striking indeed that all four periods of high activity identified in the roll-call data are related somehow to war. Gregorian (1984) contends that congressional assertiveness generally follows war as a reaction to executive dominance during the war, with the exception of the post–World War II period, during which the emergence of superpower rivalry created a consensus based on a wartime mentality. However, there is no strong statistical relationship between war and peaks in activity or close votes.

There is no relationship at all with a variable based on the year following each war or the two years following each war, contrary to Gregorian's prediction (see table 6.1). There are statistically significant but very small relationships with years during which the country is at war ($phi = .222$; $phi = .213$) and with a variable coded as the last year of a war plus the two years following it ($phi = .236$; $phi = .212$; see table 6.1). However, these relationships are not as strong as the moderate phis for critical-issue years. While there is some relationship to war, the timing differs for each war. The roll-call data show spurts of activity and disagreement before the Spanish-American War and during the Vietnam War, so the only case in this study that really conforms to Gregorian's argument is the post–World War I period. Given these inconsistencies, the critical-issue explanation provides a much more accurate picture by arguing that activity rises with the rise of a critical issue or the failure of a major policy and falls with the resolution of the issue or the reversal of the policy.

The role of war can be integrated into the critical-issue explanation by looking at its relationship with critical issues. Global critical issues are so salient that they are often resolved by war. However, increases in congressional activity are linked not to the war but to the debate on the critical issue, which may come before, during, or after the war or even when war is avoided, as in the Cold War. This distinction is important, not only because the link between critical issues and congressional behavior is more consistent than that between war and congressional behavior but also because the critical-issue explanation can better explain both the relative congressional quiescence and the moderate surge in activity in the early post–World War II period.

This period is somewhat exceptional in its lack of congressional insurgence, but not for the reason Gregorian (1984) gives. He argues that Congress is not assertive after World War II because war breaks out again in the form of the Cold War. However, the Cold War did not begin immediately with the end of World War II, so if there is normally a congressional reaction to executive dominance in wartime, Congress should be very assertive between 1945 and 1947 at least. There is indeed some activity on the United Nations Charter, but it comprises only nine roll calls, hardly comparable to the insurrection of 1919–20. The reason the United Nations does not produce the disagreement that the Treaty of Versailles did is that a consensus has finally emerged on the U.S. role in Europe. World War II produces little disagreement because a consensus is being forged on the critical issue and because U.S. involvement is successful. What shapes contention is the issue, not the timing (i.e., a postwar period). On the other side of the question, contrary to what Gregorian says and to much of the conventional wisdom, there is a surge of senatorial activity and disagreement in this early Cold War period (1949–52), although it is not very great and does not defeat the president, as in 1919–20 or 1973–74. These behaviors are not in reaction to the war, however; they are produced by debate on the policy response to the newly emerging critical issue of communism.

Empirical Findings in the Literature

Having examined several alternative hypotheses, it is now useful to look at some of the findings in the literature for ideas of how the critical-issue findings fit in and where future research should head. Although not concerned directly with congressional behavior, the Klingberg-Holmes theory of long-term cyclical trends in foreign policy moods (Klingberg 1952; Holmes 1985; Holmes and Elder 1983, 1987; Elder and Holmes 1988; Holmes et al. 1992), argues that foreign policy moods alternate between extrovert phases of approximately 27 years in length and introvert periods of approximately 21 years. The relevance of these authors' work to this study is that each of the four critical-issue periods comes at or near the beginning of a new mood phase. The resolution of the imperialism issue in 1898 follows the beginning of an extrovert period that begins in 1891. The Versailles treaty decision on the involvement-in-Europe question is at the onset of an introvert period (starting in 1919). The activity in 1950 over foreign aid and communism occurs in the second third of an extrovert phase, and the decision to withdraw from Vietnam comes after a new introvert phase begins in 1968. The two studies are obviously concerned with very different phenomena, but it is interesting that the findings from this study are compatible with the mood-cycle theory. When a new mood phase is entered, it makes sense that there would occur a debate over policy responses in the new atmosphere. Holmes has said that it is quite consistent with his theory that Congress would be in an active state at the outset of each new mood phase.[6] The fact that the data for this study follow a pattern consistent with a totally different theory for which there is also empirical evidence lends considerable support to the validity of the roll-call data and the accuracy of the critical-issue explanation. Since the theories are not contradictory, both sets of data are likely tapping aspects of the same reality.

The periods Klingberg and Holmes have identified help make sense of historical trends in American foreign policy behavior. Interestingly, the identification of introvert and extrovert periods may help explain why two of the periods of high congressional activity identified in this study are much higher than the other two. The levels of activity in 1919–20 and 1971–74 are much higher and are sustained longer than the peaks of 1898 and 1950. If it is accurate to say that the general trend in American foreign policy in the 88 years of this data set has been the pursuit of a role as a world power, then in extrovert periods this goal is pursued with gusto and in introvert periods it is approached with ambivalence.

The implication of the mood-cycle theory is that the public's mood changes, and policy changes follow. A look at the roll-call findings suggests a different interpretation. In 1919 an introvert period is said to have begun. Rather than being seen as inevitable or the result of a pendulum-type swing, it can be seen as a reaction to World War I. Congress and the public supported U.S. involvement in the war mostly because of the unrestricted submarine warfare that triggered American participation and to propaganda. Once the war ended, there was a reaction against international involvement or internationalism, characterized by Klingberg and Holmes as introversion and indicated in this study by a surge in activity and disagreement. It is not an accident that Klingberg and Holmes identify the next introvert period as beginning in 1968, when the Tet Offensive dampened U.S. optimism regarding the Vietnam War. From this time on, opinion turned against the war and, for some people, against overseas use of force in general.

What is also significant about 1919–20 and 1971–74 is that Congress (especially the Senate) handed an extrovert president a resounding defeat by pushing through an introvert policy. Given the nature of extrovert policies, especially when they involve the use of force abroad, the executive would tend to dominate. Congress would then become more involved in reacting to the costs or the failure of the policy. By contrast, 1891 and 1940 had ushered in extrovert periods, so the debate on policies of external involvement were not nearly as intense. McKinley's reluctance to become engaged with Spain was overcome in a relatively short time, and a Senate that was less than enthusiastic about spending constituents' money on foreign aid was won over on the Truman Doctrine and the Marshall Plan.

The relationship between the mood cycles and surges in congressional activity may be summed up as follows. The two cases in which Congress defeated the president, the Treaty of Versailles and the withdrawal from Vietnam, both took place at the end of an extrovert period. In 1898, an introvert phase had ended, and Congress both initiated and prevailed over the president with an extrovert policy. According to the mood theory, then, in these three cases, the president's policies were out of step with the impending or newly begun phase, and Congress prevailed with a policy more in keeping with the new mood. The way in which the fourth case, the policy of containment, differs is that it occurred in the middle (1947–51) of an extrovert phase (1940–68). In this case, the executive dominates and Congress is quite malleable. These four cases suggest two generalizations. When the executive's response to a critical issue is out of step with the current mood or comes in the third (last) stage of a mood phase, Congress can change or initiate a policy. When the executive's policy is in step with the current mood and it is initiated in the first or second stage, the executive will dominate.

The mood-cycle theory is useful for identifying long-term trends in the making of foreign policy. However, its theoretical foundation is probably too idealistic (in the philosophical sense) in assuming that public opinion is the primary force behind foreign policy. The critical-issue explanation brings into the picture the variables of global issues and war. While there is little evidence that public opinion directs foreign policy, there is considerable evidence that wars and other significant global events such as depressions and revolutions shape states' foreign policies and public opinion (Gourevitch 1978; Hintze 1975; Rasler and Thompson 1989).

In fact, the role of war could be integrated with both the mood-cycle theory and the critical-issue theory to give a potentially more complete explanation for public opinion as well as congressional behavior. Instead of assuming that the source of mood shifts is the public, in the same way that an individual has mood shifts from time to time, we can see critical issues giving rise to wars and wars producing mood changes. The experience of war changes what people in general and the elites who represent them are willing to do at any given time. War as a variable seems to hold the key to providing a more complete description of the long-term effects of critical issues, to integrating the critical-issue explanation with the mood/interest theory, and to generalizing to other cases. A research agenda informed by empirical findings on war and incorporating other cases would be a fruitful extension of this study.

Carter's ongoing data-based project is relevant to this study, although his work covers a shorter period (1945–82), because it measures various aspects of congressional behavior on foreign policy. Carter (1986a) alleges that the literature exaggerates the extent to which Congress is acquiescent in the early post–World War II period and assertive in the post-1968 period. He finds that the difference between the two periods is not as great as the literature would imply and that even though there is a significant difference in congressional activity on the war-powers issue, that is only one among many foreign policy issues, some of which have been characterized by relatively constant congressional activism or passivity. In a later study (Carter 1988), he finds that although there is a greater amount of "independent" congressional activity after 1968 in the area of national security policy—by which he means that Congress creates its own policy agenda independent of the president— there are actually more instances of "compliant" behavior, which is indicated by the *Congressional Quarterly* measure of presidential victory on a vote on which the president takes a position. Carter concludes from these findings that

> Presidents occasionally benefit from the discomfiture some members feel when confronted with the allegation that they have "undercut" the president's effectiveness in such high-risk cases. (1988, 16)

This is a reasonable interpretation of some members' reactions to the assertiveness of the Vietnam era, but Carter's findings provide only partial information because they are divided into only two discrete categories.[7] As it stands, it is hard to tell whether this study's findings are consistent with Carter's. He says that there is more assertiveness before and less assertiveness after Tet than is widely thought. This conclusion is consistent with and can be explained by the critical-issue theory. It is not that there is assertiveness throughout the 1946–68 period, and it goes unnoticed, but that it is concentrated in 1949–51. Between 1952 and 1968, Congress was relatively aquiescent because of the consensus reached on the critical issue. Likewise, it is not that there is a great deal of congressional acquiescence throughout the 1969–82 period, but it is not noticed. Acquiescence was less prevalent in the Vietnam period, because it was replaced by activism in at least some issue areas. However, after the last Americans leave Saigon in 1975, it makes sense for some degree of acquiescence to return. With all of the years from 1969 to 1982 aggregated, it is impossible to tell whether the increase in compliant behavior Carter observes is concurrent with the increase in independent behavior or subsequent to it. If the two developments are concurrent, then he has a valid criticism of the conventional wisdom. If they occur in sequence, then the critique applies only to the early incorrect assessments like those of Franck and Weisband (1979). Also if the developments are sequential, the critical-issue explanation accounts for them in terms of disagreement rising with the debate over the failed policy in Vietnam and falling after the dismantling of the policy.

It would be possible to test the critical-issue interpretation by dividing Carter's data into five time periods instead of two:

1. 1946–48
2. 1949–51
3. 1952–70
4. 1971–74
5. 1975–82

This breakdown isolates the two periods of disagreement over the critical issue and the failed policy identified in the present study, 1949–51 and 1971–74. If the assertiveness ("resistant," "rejection," and "independent" behavior) scores for periods 2 and 4 were high and the others low (and/or the others had relatively higher "compliant" behavior scores), it would offer strong evidence that the close-votes data in this study reflect congressional assertiveness as well as disagreement—or at least correlate with assertiveness. Even a correlation would lend support to the critical-issue explanation. There is no evidence in Carter's findings as they stand to indicate that the critical-issue explanation is incorrect. Support from Carter's findings for the critical-issue explanation would not only contribute to his original goal of making descriptions of congressional behavior more precise but would also help to explain the contradictions between his findings and many of the claims in the literature.

In conclusion, this study's findings cannot answer all of the questions raised in the literature on Congress and foreign policy or resolve all of the contradictions. However, several clarifications are suggested by the roll-call findings that will enable future studies to be more precise and theoretical when addressing the nature and import of congressional behavior. Furthermore, it is heartening to see indications that these findings can be integrated with the findings of other projects in the field. It bodes well for the future of the quantitative study of Congress and foreign policy.

II. Future Directions

This project has produced a new and previously overlooked dependent variable for the study of congressional behavior on foreign policy, which varies in interesting and important ways over long periods of time. A new dependent variable in and of itself is important, but the contribution is much enhanced by the fact that the patterns in the data are consistent with a theory that plausibly explains congressional behavior over time. This section will list this study's contributions and limitations and suggest avenues for future research.

The Dependent Variable: Congressional Behavior on Foreign Policy

This study has made three main contributions to the study of congressional behavior in the area of foreign policy. First and foremost is the development of a data set using the roll-call vote itself as the unit of analysis. The resultant 6,556 cases form a body of behavior that constitutes a new dependent variable not previously studied. Roll-call analysis has traditionally been the study of how members of Congress vote. It is generally the study of individual decision making (e.g., Kingdon 1989) or, more broadly, the study of how groups of people vote (Clausen 1973; Schneider 1979). This study differs fundamentally in that it focuses on the behavior of the institution as a whole, using the roll calls themselves as the unit of analysis. It has been a conscious attempt to get away from the more behavioral approaches and back to a focus on the institution but has also involved an equally conscious effort to avoid the pitfalls of a legalistic approach in favor of empirical observation. Many studies of Congress and particularly of congressional-executive relations focus a great deal of attention on the constitutional rights and powers of the branches and on the possibilities for change or reform. The theoretical perspective developed here underemphasizes constitutional powers as well as individual behavior and looks instead at the long-term output of the institution of the Senate.

The reason for the focus on the product of the institution as a dependent variable is the assumption that external constraints in the form of global critical issues are more important for shaping the broad contours of American foreign policy than are constitutional rules and individual behavior. The Constitution certainly limits the actions of government, and individuals do have an effect, but this study focuses on previously neglected aspects of the import of the global environment for long-term institutional behavior.

This study has also contributed by offering a theoretical perspective that involves a reconceptualization of congressional behavior and congressional-executive relations. Instead of seeing policy debates in terms of Congress versus the president, the critical-issue explanation posits the rise of a critical issue in the global arena, thereby producing debate not only between the branches but also within both branches and throughout the society. In fact, both sides of the debate may even be represented in one person—in a president who changes position from one time to another. This conceptualization is helpful in reducing the tendency to see Congress and the president in a zero-sum game in which one branch is bound to lose, focusing instead on the process of debate and consensus building.[8]

Third, this study responds to the need for diachronic studies of congressional behavior as called for by Cooper and Brady (1981). Chapter 1 showed that many studies were time bound and that only a longer time period would resolve the contradictions in the literature. For the most part, the flurry of journalistic and impressionistic analyses of Congress in the 1970s lacked sufficient rigor and historical perspective. Some quantitative studies cover the entire post–World War II era, but even that period is not long enough to uncover the type of pattern that has emerged in this study. While there are certain ways in which the United States in the post–World War II period differs from the pre–World War II period, this study has uncovered some interesting patterns that extend further back. The long term of the 88-year data set combined with the plausibility of the critical-issue explanation make a strong argument in favor of pursuing this line of inquiry. A major benefit of the long time span was then the possibility of performing Box-Tiao analysis on the series to both confirm the impact of the critical issues and measure the type and magnitude of the impact.

The Critical-Issue Explanation

Two extensions of this study would be quite useful. The first is to extend the study back to the First Congress of 1789. An 88-year time span is a fairly long period, but given the relatively short history of the American bicameral legislature, it is arguable that its entire history should be covered. There are limitations to the data one can collect, but the roll-call votes are on record. Given Holmes's success in testing the mood-cycle theory for a 211-year period

(1776–1987) and the apparent relationship between critical issues and mood cycles, it would undoubtedly be fruitful to extend the roll-call study back in time.[9] One difference that might be expected between the pre- and post-1898 periods would be the nature of the critical issues. According to Gardner, LaFeber, and McCormick (1976, xviii–xx), while U.S. foreign policy has been driven since 1893 or so by informal overseas commercial expansion, the first half of the history of U.S. foreign policy was concerned with the territorial expansion within the North American continent. This driving force would make for different types of issues and for less influence for the global environment.

The other major useful extension would be a replication on the House of Representatives. Given the Senate's key role in foreign policy, especially on the Treaty of Versailles and Vietnam, the findings might differ, although they would be expected to be consistent. Given the increase in the House's role and of recorded teller votes since the early 1970s, the post-1972 period would be more comparable to the Senate, and the pre-1972 era would be interesting for contrast.

These two studies would go far in solidifying both the empirical and the theoretical contributions of the critical-issue explanation. However, the use of roll-call votes still relies on aspects of only one indicator. The close-votes indicator sought to measure disagreement only within the Senate, but it would be useful to compare the measures from this study to measures of presidential-congressional relations such as the measures used by Edwards (1980, 1989), Sullivan (1991), Fleisher and Bond (1988), Carter (1986a), McCormick, Wittkopf, and Danna (1997), and Shull (1997). Also interesting from a longitudinal perspective would be to build on the work of Cohen (1991), who examined State of the Union addresses and legislation dating from 1861. Extending data collection back to 1789, though a formidable task, would be extremely valuable. It would be useful to know the relationship between activity and disagreement within Congress on the one hand and at least some measure of disagreement between Congress and the president on the other. Assuming that when there is a high level of disagreement within Congress, the president takes a position with one of the sides, he is disagreeing with the other side. On this basis, it can reasonably be predicted that periods of high levels of disagreement between Congress and the president will coincide with the periods already identified of high disagreement within the Senate.

A theory that purports to be a general explanation of foreign policy behavior must have the potential to be applied to other nation-states. One of the problems with Holmes's mood theory is that it applies only to the United

States, and this study explicitly seeks to ensure that the critical-issue explanation be generalizable. The critical-issue explanation needs to be used to
uncover deeper causal relationships that would make it possible to couch the
theory in more general terms and apply it to other cases. Even if the theory
only applied to hegemons, it would at least increase the number of cases from
one to two or three and offer possibilities for testing it across cases. One way
to make the theory more general is to look at how critical issues affect domestic institutions in general, thereby making it applicable to states that do not
have legislatures with decision-making powers.

III. Conclusion

This study has provided a new way of looking at and explaining congressional
behavior on foreign policy. The data analysis in chapters 3 and 4 and the null
findings for competing independent variables reported in this chapter suggest
that critical issues are the key to explaining increases in senatorial activity and
disagreement on foreign policy. The collection and coding of the roll-call data
for this study have laid the groundwork for future studies based on institutional behavior rather than on how members vote.

A longitudinal study that uncovers a pattern naturally raises the question of what is predicted for the future on the basis of what has been observed
in the past. The prediction that grows out of this analysis is that levels of congressional activity and disagreement will increase when a new critical foreign
policy issue arises. It may be the case that congressional involvement in foreign policy will never again decrease to the level of the late 1950s and 1960s—
the impact analysis showed that the failure of containment in Vietnam had a
ratchet effect that may never be completely reversed. However, critical issues
will still hold the key to explaining the relative rise and fall of congressional
activity.

With the Cold War over, the new critical issue is not yet clear. That it is
not known is highlighted by the fact that the new era does not yet have a name
of its own, only the "post–Cold War era." A potential candidate is the collection of issues around the "New World Order": Should the United States
actively support international norms against aggression and in favor of
democracy, and human rights abroad, or retreat to a narrow definition of
national interest? Should it be involved in peacekeeping operations? How
interventionist should it be? Should it be willing to go to war over these new
issues, as in 1991 in the Persian Gulf and in 1999 over Kosovo? What if the
next war is long, costly, or unsuccessful? If these questions come together to

form a single coherent issue unified by an underlying theme, such as the New World Order, a new critical issue will have arisen. The critical issue in turn will produce an increase in contention, regardless of whether or not the same party controls the two political branches of government.

The critical-issue explanation predicts that in the presence of a new critical issue, a major overarching policy will emerge with at least some level of bipartisanship because of the pressures of the international environment. Partisanship will decrease, and disagreement will be pushed to the margins unless or until the policy fails or a new issue emerges. A future pattern of (1) increased contention over a critical issue, (2) decreased contention as policy responses to the issue emerge, and (3) a resurgence in contention if the policy fails will serve as a real-world test of the explanation developed in this volume.

This analysis has shown that as the post–Cold War era unfolds, it will be necessary to look to the international system as a source of issues and to look at how the life cycle of critical issues shapes the level of congressional activity and disagreement on foreign policy.

Collection and Coding of Data

I. Data Collection

The data for this study consist of roll-call votes taken by the U.S. Senate from 1897 to 1984. The source from which these data were collected is the codebooks for the ICPSR congressional roll-call data. In the ICPSR data, the case is the member of Congress, and each case is coded for how that member voted on each of the roll-call votes that was taken. Since each roll-call vote is a variable, the text of each roll call is recorded in the codebook. From the information in these codebooks, each roll call was coded for date, number of yeas and nays, and margin of victory. On the basis of the descriptive text, each roll call was coded as either domestic or foreign policy and, in the case of foreign policy roll calls, for issue. The codebooks were made available to the author by the Rutgers University Center for Computer and Information Services. The Senate recorded 19,234 roll-call votes from 1897 to 1984.

The data were coded in two steps. First, each roll call was read and coded as to whether it concerned domestic policy or foreign policy, according to the coding rules in the following section. Of the 19,234 roll calls, 6,556 were coded as foreign policy. In the second step, the foreign policy roll calls were coded by issue and type (bill, amendment, or procedural) according to the coding rules given later in the appendix. Only 5 of the 6,556 cases had to be counted as missing because they lacked sufficient information for an issue code, and four cases lacked sufficient information to code the type of vote.

II. Coding Rules

Coding Foreign Policy and Domestic Policy

The coder will read each vote and decide whether it is an instance of domestic policy or foreign policy. For the purposes of this study, foreign policy is conceptualized as comprising three groups of policy types.

1. Any policy that makes reference to the world beyond U.S. boundaries is considered foreign policy. This category includes policy toward another country, for example, but not limited to, giving aid to it, trading with it, establishing diplomatic relations with it, threatening it, applying force to it, conducting covert operations in it, and entering into agreements with it. Statements, criticisms, and commendations of the behavior of another country and dealings with international organizations and foreign nonstate actors all qualify as foreign policy.

2. Policies to deal with people and things that come into the United States from abroad are foreign policy. Immigration policy, regulations for foreign workers, and import regulations are all considered foreign policy. Since the reason for tariffs is the existence of imports and since tariffs have an immediate effect on foreign trade, tariff policy is considered part of foreign policy. Although tariff policy may be heavily influenced by, even characterized by, domestic policy processes, the reason the issue exists is foreign trading partners.

3. Foreign policy includes policies that are made internally but the reason for which is the existence or perception of an external threat. Defense policy and the policy of identifying and investigating American members of the Communist Party fall into this category.

Each roll-call vote is considered individually to determine whether it is foreign or domestic. There are often domestic amendments to foreign bills and foreign amendments to domestic bills. In this situation, domestic amendments are coded as domestic, and the bill itself is coded as foreign policy. If there are amendments relating to foreign policy attached to a domestic bill, each amendment that refers to the foreign issue is coded as foreign, but the bill is coded as domestic. It is granted that the passage or failure to pass the final bill affects foreign policy, but the number of domestic bills with foreign policy amendments is probably not significant compared to the number of the foreign amendments, which will be recorded. Therefore, the decision is made to code domestic bills as domestic no matter how many foreign amendments they may have to preserve consistency and reliability.

Several issue areas straddle the foreign-domestic line. In the area of defense and military policy, all spending for defense—weapons, research, and pay, including votes on pay raises for active forces—is considered foreign policy. Legislation on benefits for veterans and for the dependents of members of the military is considered domestic policy, since these people are not currently involved in defense. Likewise, funding for secondary-school-level military academies is coded as domestic, although funding for ROTC at the college level is coded as defense under foreign policy.

Another issue that straddles the foreign-domestic line is mobilization of the economy to fight a war. This issue involves spending for defense in what otherwise would be considered domestic areas. For example, the imposition of wage and price controls, federal control of essential industries, and federal intervention in labor disputes are all coded as foreign policy when they are done as part of a legislation package the purpose of which is to mobilize the society's resources to fight a war. When the measures are repealed and there are amendments on the details of reestablishing the peacetime economy, they are coded as domestic, because they are no longer part of a war effort.

Examples:

Helms amendment to H.R. 5359, Defense Appropriations, to make abortion illegal unless the mother's life is endangered. 11/6/1979 — Domestic

Amendment to H.R. 13161, Second Supplemental Appropriations Act for fiscal 1961, to provide $190 million for Mutual Security Program. 8/29/1960 — Foreign (vote on H.R. 13161 itself is domestic)

Coding Issues within Foreign Policy

Once the foreign policy roll calls are distinguished from those on domestic policy, each roll call is coded according to an issue or issue area within foreign policy. The five main foreign policy issue areas are tariff, immigration, foreign aid, defense, and routine diplomatic activity. The three critical issues are imperialism, involvement in Europe, and communism. Roll calls not coded into one of these eight categories are coded into a ninth category: miscellaneous. Each foreign policy roll-call vote will thus receive an issue code.

As pointed out in chapter 3, what distinguishes issue areas from critical issues is that critical issues are susceptible to resolution, whereas issue areas are categories into which questions on related issues fall. What links the two together is that one can ask in either case what stake is under contention (see Mansbach and Vasquez 1981, 57–58). In the issue areas, the stake is usually quite obvious. In the case of the tariff, particular bills, such as the tariff of 1922, are typical stakes. With the critical issues, the idea of stakes becomes more important to the process of coding.

The coder must first identify the stake in each vote. Then the stake is assigned to the appropriate issue. Each critical issue and issue area is an umbrella concept under which to gather a set of related stakes. The stakes within a given critical issue together represent senatorial behavior on the most salient issue of each time period. Within each critical issue, there are numerous stakes around which contention centers. For example, Cuba, the Philippines, and Puerto Rico are all stakes in the overarching critical issue of imperialism. Also, the same entity can be a stake in more than one issue. For example, in the early twentieth century, Nicaragua was a stake in the imperialism issue, but after 1979, it became a stake in the communism issue. The coder should first identify the stake (some of them relevant only in certain time periods) and then assign the roll call to the issue of which the stake is a part. Table A1 lists all of the stakes that figure in this data set in the first column, with the issue area, critical issue, and miscellaneous issue codes in the second column.

TABLE A1. Stakes and Issues

	Stake Codes	Issue Codes
Tariff	01	1
Reciprocal trade agreements	91	1
Immigration	02	2
Foreign aid	03	3
Arms sales	93	9
Defense	04	4
Draft	94	4
Routine diplomatic activity	05	5
Trade, mail	06	9
Indian affairs	07	9
Territory	08	9
Fisheries, environment, law of the sea	09	9
International law	10	9
International organization	11	9
Arms control and nuclear proliferation	12	9
Tax	13	9
Atomic energy	14	9
Alliances (other than NATO)	15	9
Intelligence activities	16	9
International finance	17	9
Human rights	18	9
Censorship	19	9
Espionage and sedition	20	9
Gold standard	21	9
Merchant marine	22	9
Culture	23	9
Aviation	24	9
Illegal drugs	25	9
Health	26	9
Radio and telecommunications	27	9
Sanctions	28	9
Oil	29	9
Racism	30	9
Terrorism	31	9
Nontariff barriers	32	9
War mobilization		
Spanish-American War	33	6
World Wars I and II	34	7
Korea and Vietnam	35	8
War revenue		
Spanish-American War	36	6
World Wars I and II	37	7
Korea and Vietnam	38	8
Imperialism	39	6

	Stake Codes	Issue Codes
Cuba	40	6
Philippines	41	6
Panama Canal	42	6
Spanish-American War	43	6
Hawaii	44	6
Puerto Rico	45	6
Dominican Republic	46	6
Samoa	47	6
Intervention in Mexico	48	6
South Africa	49	9
Involvement in Europe	50	7
Neutrality	51	7
World War I	52	7
World War I peace terms	53	7
Treaty of Versailles	54	7
Other peace treaties	55	7
Haiti	56	9
World Court	57	7
World War II	58	7
Lend-lease	59	7
United Nations	60	7
North Atlantic Treaty Organization (NATO)	61	7
Anticommunism	62	8
Internal security	63	8
Korea	64	8
Formosa	65	8
Berlin	66	8
Vietnam	67	8
Turkey	68	9
Middle East (including peace talks)	69	9
Angola and Mozambique	70	8
Iran (American hostages)	71	9
Falklands	72	9
Afghanistan	74	8
El Salvador	75	8
Nicaragua (anticommunism)	76	8
French claims (prior to 1801)	77	9
Arbitration	78	9
War powers	79	9
Monroe Doctrine	80	9
World War II peace terms	81	7
Anglo-American rapprochement	82	9
Relations with Russia	83	9
Secrecy	84	9
Propaganda	85	9
Export-Import Bank	86	9
SEATO (unless there is explicit mention of fighting communism)	87	9
Regulations of warfare	88	9
Congo	89	9
Détente	96	9
Lebanon	97	9
Internal procedures of the Senate	98	9

The issue codes are:

1. Tariff
2. Immigration
3. Foreign Aid
4. Defense
5. Routine Diplomatic Activity
6. Imperialism
7. Involvement in Europe
8. Communism
9. Miscellaneous

1. The first area is tariff, the votes on which are almost always obvious and easy to code. Included are votes on the tariff commission and reciprocal trade agreements in addition to the bills establishing tariff rates and amendments raising and lowering the rates on specific products. Other foreign economic policy questions do not fall into this category, among them nontariff barriers such as quotas and other import restrictions; trade agreements other than reciprocal trade agreements, usually in the form of executive agreements or treaties; and legislation on American export policy and foreign trade. These questions are general trade questions and are coded as miscellaneous (9).
Examples:

To amend H.R. 18642, by adding to the free list, farm tools, machinery and parts. 5/29/1912

To amend an amendment to H.R. 22195, by discharging the present board and creating a new tariff board of five members to investigate tariff. 7/25/1912

To amend H.R. 8687, a bill providing for reciprocal tariff agreements, by making hearings public. 5/30/1934

When the United States took control over foreign possessions (e.g., the Philippines, Puerto Rico), legislation was passed to allow products from these possessions to enter the United States duty-free. The issue at hand in such a measure is not the tariff but how to administer colonial possessions. Thus, the code would be imperialism (6), not tariff.
Counterexample:

To amend H.R. 8245, by exempting from duty all articles imported into the U.S. from Puerto Rico, and into Puerto Rico from the U.S., by making articles from Puerto Rico subject to U.S. internal revenue taxes equal to those paid in the U.S. 4/3/1900 — Imperialism

2. The second area is immigration policy. This category includes all legislation on foreigners entering and remaining in the United States, including laws on citizenship procedures and legislation regarding foreign workers.
Examples:

To amend S.51, by setting up quotas on immigration for countries of the western hemisphere. 4/22/30

To amend S.2222, a bill to revise and reform U.S. immigration laws, by according a secondary preference in allocation of family reunification visas to qualified immigrants who are adult unmarried sons and daughters of permanent resident aliens. 8/12/82

3. The third area is foreign aid. It comprises all appropriations for aid, including those votes that attach strings, such as requirements to purchase American products, to spend the money in the United States, or to be paid up to the United Nations.
Examples:

To amend S. 938, a bill to provide assistance to Greece and Turkey, by providing nonmilitary assistance only. 4/22/1947

To Amend S. 1209 by requiring that commodities procured under authority of this act shall be labeled by the supplier to clearly indicate that they have been supplied by the U.S. for European recovery. 4/8/1949

Many votes bar aid to a country because it is communist or Marxist; these votes are not coded as foreign aid but as communism (8).
Counterexamples:

To amend H.R. 13175, the Foreign Assistance Appropriations Act, by requiring publication in the federal register of a report giving the President's reasons for determining that it was in the U.S. interest to aid a communist nation. 10/1/62 — Communism

Adopt committee amendments barring aid to nations which aided Cuba or permitted their ships to deliver strategic items to Cuba, and barring shipping of foreign aid cargoes in ships of nations which supplied goods to Cuba, unless the President determined that withholding aid or cargoes would be detrimental to U.S. national interests. 10/1/62 — Communism

Amend H.R. 14260 (foreign aid bill) to delete funds for Mozambique and add funds for others. 9/10/76 — Communism

4.   The fourth issue area, defense, comprises all appropriations for defense, including research, weapons procurement, testing, and pay and promotion of members of the armed forces, all votes on the draft, ROTC, and military sales. Legislation on veterans' benefits, dependents' benefits, and high school military education are not defense but domestic policy.
Examples:

Proxmire amendment to HR 5359, Defense Appropriations, to delete funds for CVN Nimitz Class Aircraft Program. 11/6/79

Trammell (Fla) To amend S.3383 by increasing the pay of the officers 23% and the enlisted men 20%. 1/27/20

5.   The fifth issue area is routine diplomatic activity, which refers to the running of the foreign policy establishment. Included in this category are all general appropriations for the State Department, confirmation of nomination of ambassadors and other officials, and declarations of policy that do not commit resources.
Examples:

Consideration of nomination of Nelson A. Rockefeller, of New York, to be Assistant Secretary of State. 12/19/1944

H.R. 7289—Appropriations for State, Justice, Commerce, and Judiciary. Case amendments en bloc reducing by $4,455,399 funds for salaries and expenses for the State Department. 6/26/1952

6.   The first critical issue is imperialism. For this issue, the stakes are the places that the United States took over politically: Cuba, the Philippines, Puerto Rico, the interoceanic canal (whether envisioned in Nicaragua, Columbia, or Panama), and any place into which the United

States sent or considered sending troops for the purpose of influencing internal politics, such as the Dominican Republic, Haiti, and Mexico. Because Nicaragua and Cuba figure again in the third critical issue, they are generally coded into the imperialism category when the vote occurs prior to World War I and into the communism category when the vote occurs after World War II. The difference is that prior to World War I, the U.S. interest in Nicaragua and Cuba was neocolonial in the sense that the United States wanted sufficient control over those countries' politics to protect U.S. economic interests. During the Cold War, the interests remained economic but were overridden by ideological concerns. The imperialism issue includes the resolutions regarding Cuba that led to the Spanish-American War as well as roll calls involving raising revenue for the war and mobilizing the economy and the society.

Examples:

Lodge (Mass) To ratify the treaty between the U.S. and Spain providing for cession to the U.S. all islands of the Philippine Archipelago lying outside lines described in article of treaty of peace of December 10, 1898, signed at Washington on November 7, 1900. 12/4/1900

Butler (NC) To amend the treaty between the U.S. and Great Britain regarding the construction of a ship canal by eliminating Section 7 of Article II. 12/20/1900

7.   For the involvement-in-Europe issue, the first stake is World War I. This issue area includes all votes on the war in Europe, reacting to it, becoming involved in it, mobilizing the society and economy, and prosecuting it. The next stake is the Versailles treaty and involvement in the League of Nations and the World Court, followed by the reaction to the war that produces the neutrality debate of the 1930s. This issue area sees World War II as a continuation of World War I, so that votes related to the war, declaring war, prosecuting the war, and creating the peace are all coded as World War II and included in this issue area. As the creation of the United Nations is the institutionalization of the peace, votes on the United Nations Charter and U.S. entry into the United Nations are coded as United Nations and are included in this issue area.

Examples:

Borah (Idaho) To permit a printing of a copy of the Versailles Treaty, which the President of the U.S. thought best to be withheld from the public. 6/9/1919

To consider Executive F 79–1: ratification of the Charter of the United Nations. 7/28/1945

Votes on the formation of the United Nations, NATO, and other post-war institutions are coded as involvement in Europe, but once they are created and their role institutionalized, their existence is no longer at issue. Further legislation providing for financing the United Nations or NATO is coded as miscellaneous (9).
Counterexamples:

Amendment to H.R. 14989 that U.S. payment to U.N. is not to exceed 25% of the total annual assessment. 6/15/1972 — Miscellaneous

Moynihan amendment to S. 1193—State Department authorizations—that it is the sense of Congress that no funds be made available for the UNESCO budget to exceed its assessed contribution less 25% of the amount made available by UNESCO to restrict free flow of information within or between nations or impose codes of journalistic practice or ethics. 6/17/1981 — Miscellaneous

Roth amendment to S. 2248 that it is the sense of Congress that members of NATO must pool resources for their own common defense. 5/13/1982 — Miscellaneous

8. The third critical issue is the American response to communism. This issue includes votes on sending troops to Russia to fight the Bolsheviks; efforts within the United States to identify American communists in the 1920s and 1950s; denial of aid to countries that are socialist, Marxist, or communist or that aid such countries; harassment of socialist and communist countries by criticizing or punishing them because of their political systems; the wars against communist regimes in Korea and Vietnam; covert operations against Marxist regimes in Chile, Angola and Mozambique, and Nicaragua; efforts to extricate the United States from military involvement in Southeast Asia; and votes on the war-powers issue, which resulted directly from executive prosecution of the Vietnam War.
Examples:

S.J.Res. 230 — To express U.S. determination to prevent the spread of communism from Cuba to the rest of the western hemisphere, by any means necessary, including the use of arms. 9/20/1962

Regarding S654, a bill to permit states to enact laws barring subversive activities: motion to table amendment providing that no act of Congress should be construed as nullifying any state law on the same subject unless Congress so specifies. 8/20/1958

To amend S3420 to bar sales of farm surpluses to countries not promising to deny support to Soviet Union in war against U.S. 3/20/1958

Several points need to be clarified about distinctions between the stakes making up the critical issues and the other issue areas. When the United States first became involved in giving aid to other countries with the aid to Greece and Turkey, a major motivation—and, in fact, a key factor in getting congressional support for the aid—was the expectation that giving aid would help prevent communism from spreading beyond the Soviet Union and Eastern Europe. However, containing communism is not the sole purpose of foreign aid. The foreign aid program has grown into an issue area in its own right, and most of the votes on foreign aid will be coded as foreign aid. A vote (usually an amendment) is coded as anticommunism only when it specifically states that aid be barred to a country because of communist or Marxist ties. Thus, the anticommunist purpose of foreign aid is assumed to be a part of the foreign aid program, but this aspect is not coded unless there is a vote explicitly and exclusively referring to it.

All of the critical issues have involved war, so that voting on defense matters will often co-occur with votes on the critical issue. If it seems that the purpose of the votes on defense is to pursue goals associated with the critical issue, there must be explicit mention of one of the stakes of the critical issue for the code to be one of the critical issues, or the vote has to involve mobilization of the society for the war. Simple defense votes, such as weapons procurement and the draft, although they are responses to the critical issue, are coded as defense.

One of the issues that arises in the 1970s is human rights. There are numerous votes on issues of human rights before the 1970s, but the issue of ideology usually intrudes. Criticism of an East bloc country for abridging an individual's rights occurs to make political capital in the East-West rivalry. That this is the reason can be determined because no mention is made before the 1970s of the many abuses of human rights by governments friendly to the United States. What distinguishes the human-rights movement in the 1970s is the attempt to be politically neutral in the identification of human-rights abuses. This goal is not always reached, as arguments existed that, for example, Eastern European countries critical of the Soviet Union were treated more leniently in the area of human rights. However, the distinction remains clear between criticisms of governments because they are communist and criticisms of governments because they are inhumane. Instances of the former are coded as anticommunist; instances of the latter are coded as human rights.

　9.　Examples of miscellaneous foreign policy issues are Indian affairs, the gold standard, votes on acquiring North American territory, international law (which includes treaties and agreements on settlement of disputes, expropriation, extradition, law of the sea, and so forth), international organization (involvement in international organizations other than the earliest considerations of the League of Nations, the World Court, and the United Nations), fisheries, questions on the international environment, foreign trade (aside from tariffs), international finance, nontariff barriers, export regulations, human rights, censorship, espionage, sedition, arms control and disarmament, mail, and so on.

Example:

Ashurst (Ariz) To agree to the conference report on H.R. 12579 on Indian Affairs. 7/24/14

Coding Type of Vote

Each roll call is coded as to whether it is a bill, a conference report, an amendment, or a procedural vote. When a vote is taken on the passage of a bill, it is coded as a bill. When the vote is on passage of a conference report, it is coded as a conference report. Both bills and conference reports are put in the same category and coded as 0, "bills and conference reports."

When the vote is whether to amend a bill or to attach reservations to a treaty, it is coded as an amendment. When there is a vote to table an amendment, recommit or refer to committee a bill or conference report, or consider or reconsider a bill, conference report, or amendment, the vote is coded as a procedural vote. The amendments and procedural votes are put in the same category and coded as 1, "amendments and procedural votes."

III.　Reliability Studies

A master's-level graduate student and a Ph.D. in political science participated in reliability studies. The first study was to determine reliability of coding foreign versus domestic policy. Although a sampling formula would call for a sample size of about 500 votes to be representative of the 19,234 roll-call universe, since this code is a fairly straightforward dichotomous distinction, it was decided that quite a small sample would be adequate for testing the reliability of coding foreign versus domestic policy.

A random sample of 100 roll calls was chosen from the 19,234 total roll calls, and the graduate student coded each as either foreign or domestic. The reliability score was 92 percent. Of the eight cases that were incorrectly coded, three were foreign policy mistaken for domestic and five were domestic policy mistaken for foreign. The three foreign policy cases mistaken for domestic policy were all borderline cases. One referred to U.S. territories, the second to the identification of American members of the Communist Party, and the third to mobilizing the domestic economy for the Korean War. With additional training, the coder could have correctly identified these cases. The incorrect coding of domestic cases as foreign policy is less easily understood. Two cases were mistaken for tariff, one for communism, one for miscellaneous, and one for routine diplomatic activity. Among these five cases, there may have been simple errors of reading and coding the wrong case.

The second study was for reliability of the issue codes. A random sample of 615 roll calls was chosen from the data set for the study. The political science Ph.D. coded each as tariff, immigration, foreign aid, defense, routine diplomatic activity, involvement in Europe, communism, or miscellaneous. On the first try, 536 out of the 615 cases were coded correctly, for a reliability score of 87 percent.

Of the 79 incorrectly coded cases, the most common source of error was the distinction between war mobilization and war revenue on the one hand (code 6, 7, or 8, depending on the time period) and defense (code 4) on the other. A secondary problem was the distinction between tariff (1) and nontariff barriers (9). Most of these problems were soluble, and the coder made the distinctions on a second try, thus indicating that a higher reliability score would be possible.

Notes

Introduction

1. The major exception is Sundquist 1981. Some others who look at the long or medium term include Dodd 1991; Rourke 1983; Carter 1986a, 1994; Hinckley 1994 (30 years); Rohde 1994a, 1994b (20, 35 years).

2. Again, Sundquist 1981 theorizes about the decline of Congress but does not really explain the resurgences.

3. Recent data projects are remedying that situation (Carter 1986a, 1990; Hinckley 1994; Rohde 1994a, 1994b; Shull 1997; Shull and Shaw 1999).

Chapter 1

1. He could not know at the time that the House would indeed develop ways to use the power of the purse to shape foreign policy to such an extent that the Senate is now seen as relatively less important in foreign affairs (McCormick 1993; Blechman 1990). The House (and Senate) has also learned to use legislation to create procedures for increasing its role in foreign policy (Lindsay 1994a; Emery and Deering 1995).

2. Additional arguments regarding congressional delegation to the executive can be found in Lowi 1979, 94–106, and Hayes 1981, 27–33, as well as in the other works cited in this section.

3. The gap between bipartisanship on foreign policy and partisanship on domestic issues is particularly striking in the case of the bombings of Sudan and Afghanistan. Newt Gingrich (R-GA) ignored claims that Clinton had ordered the strikes to distract attention from the Monica Lewinsky scandal and led bipartisan support for the policy, but Gingrich also presided over the process that resulted in the House Judiciary Committee's (totally partisan) passage of four articles of impeachment stemming from the domestic affair.

4. See Burgin 1993a for a thorough defense of Congress against its detractors. Burgin finds that constituents are a major factor in members' involvement in foreign policy issues but not in level of activism. She argues that parochialism and concern with reelection are neither very strong nor detrimental in affecting legislators' ability to participate in formulating foreign policy.

5. There is a school of "congressional dominance," referring to congressional control of the bureaucracy (McCubbins and Schwartz 1984; Fiorina 1981; Calvert, McCubbins, and Weingast 1989), but it refers mostly to domestic politics. As Lindsay (1994a, 300) points out, several of the assumptions of this approach, such as agency decisions being a matter of public record, do not always apply in foreign policy (for example, where secrecy is allegedly essential).

6. Ely (1993, 115) indicates that the War Powers Resolution has developed such a "bad aura" that there is little hope of its being effective in its current form. Hinckley (1994, 90) highlights its poor record: in 25 cases of the use of force between 1973 and

1988, the president reported to Congress in 15 (or 19 [Katzmann 1990, 55–56]), the president started the 60-day clock on only one, Congress set an 18-month clock once, and Congress started the 60-day clock in none. Ely's proposed reform is more in keeping with the resolution's original goals. The reform reduces the amount of time the president can deploy troops without authorization to only 20 days and stresses that doing so is allowed only in an emergency, eliminates the concurrent resolution provision on grounds of possible unconstitutionality and unlikelihood that Congress would ever cut off troops cold, and provides for automatic withdrawal of troops if Congress does not authorize their use (Ely 1993, appendix A). Ely (1993, 65, 189) rejects the Use of Force Act currently being proposed by Biden, Ritch, and Glennon, who argue that their revision would give Congress and the president more flexibility, because extending the "free period" to 120 days only exacerbates what Ely finds most objectionable about the War Powers Resolution: that it is unconstitutional to give the president permission to prosecute a war for any period of time without congressional authorization.

7. The Constitution grants seven powers to Congress in foreign affairs: the power to declare war; the authority to raise and support armies, regulate foreign commerce, consent to treaty ratification, and confirm ambassadors; the right to issue letters of marque and reprisal; and the authority to define and punish piracies and other offenses against the laws of nations (Warburg 1989, 9).

8. Although the urgency of the legislated foreign policy of the 1970s has abated, Congress is unlikely to abandon its new role altogether. Smyrl (1988, 141) also criticizes broad purse-string legislation, but he holds that members of Congress will not leave themselves out of the policy-making process and that the increased risk from the international environment will not allow it.

9. Although Wildavsky is found to have overstated the president's advantages, LeLoup and Shull (1979, 717) caution against erring in the other direction. Although presidential success in Congress has diminished, the president can make initiatives in foreign policy without going to Congress, particularly in high-level diplomacy and crisis and national-security decisions. Thus, the president may not have monolithic dominance, but he still has more power in foreign policy than in domestic policy.

10. Thus, the president was not so much dominating Congress as Congress and the administrations of Truman and Eisenhower were together coming to an internationalist policy centered on the containment of the Soviet Union. It is still the case, however, that Acheson changed Vandenberg's mind (J. Jones 1955). Of interest in this regard is the following example of overselling a belief: "Dean Acheson admitted . . . that the domino imagery in NSC-68 'made our points clearer than the truth [to] bludgeon the mass mind of top government'" (Snyder 1991, 279). To understand the president's influence on Congress in the halcyon days of bipartisanship, it is necessary to look behind roll-call data and understand how isolationists either changed their minds or were replaced and how a foreign policy consensus was formed that was relatively free of division along party lines. See Briggs (1994, chap. 3) for a case study of bipartisanship in the formation of NATO.

11. Although Carter does further divide his data into a variety of time periods, the additional information they supply is incomplete because there is no theoretical rationale for the divisions. Neither decades nor presidential administrations should necessarily reveal patterns in congressional assertiveness. My analysis suggests that time periods based on the life cycle of critical issues will reveal the patterns of change in congressional behavior.

12. S. Smith's (1994, 130–31) characterization of the resurgent-Congress thesis is that the expansion of television coverage of politics, increased partisanship in public attitudes on foreign policy, shrinking of the gap between domestic and foreign policy, more active interest groups and more independent legislators, democratization of Congress through reform, greater centralization of foreign policy decision making within the executive branch, and prolonged divided government and increased partisanship have increased Congress's ability and motivation to increase its influence in foreign policy. Smith asserts that this perspective challenges the two-presidencies thesis, which stresses the institutional weaknesses of Congress and its tendency to deference. The institutional weaknesses remain, and the constitutional framework is the same, but deference has been replaced with a tendency to pursue policy preferences and interests in foreign policy just as in the domestic sphere.

13. Fisher (1987, 101–3) shows that there is a gap between the Court's decision in *Chadha* and the operational reality of government behavior. Through understandings between agencies and committees of Congress, the functions of legislative vetoes will continue to be carried out because the executive branch will still want the discretionary authority, and Congress wants to control it without passing new legislation. All *Chadha* changes is that now there will be noncompliance, evasion, and a more cumbersome lawmaking process.

14. Casting "the people" in the role of prime movers in foreign policy makes assumptions about American democracy that are probably too idealistic. The basic argument can still be made, though, by contrasting the dominant mood in Congress with the actions of the president or by collapsing the mood of Congress with that of the public in a belief-sharing model. Blechman (1990), for example, argues that public pressure on Congress moved Congress to be more assertive on arms control.

15. The other two cycles are "centralization or diffusion of presidential management and 'yearning for and disillusionment with leadership' among the public" (Rockman cited in C. Jones 1995).

16. None of the issue areas is found to be characterized by congressional dominance.

17. Whether the president's party controls Congress is not related to the amount of congressional assertiveness (Carter 1986a, 336). Rourke's finding has more to do with a president's lack of success with the opposite party on domestic issues than with any increase in influence over foreign policy.

18. This finding may offer evidence that the two-presidencies thesis is at least partially applicable to the Reagan administration, but it must be remembered that Rourke's analysis was not carried out on any earlier years.

19. Waltz's second image refers to explanations of war that look at the role of national-level variables. In the area of foreign policy, an early volume on the domestic sources of foreign policy is Rosenau 1967. Examples of current research in this area include Hall and Wayman 1990 and Wayman 1995.

20. Citing Sundquist 1981, Peterson (1994a, 20) notes that "the American presidency grew in power and authority as the United States acquired international responsibilities." This statement implies that Congress has lost influence as those responsibilities accrued. Yet congressional assertiveness reached historic highs during the early 1970s, a time during which international constraints on the United States increased, spawning much commentary on increased interdependence (see Deese 1994).

Chapter 2

1. Interview with *Congressional Quarterly* editors, Washington, D.C., March 1, 1984.

2. Lindsay 1994b and Hinckley 1994 make similar points. Lindsay (1994b, 2) bemoans the fact that most commentary on Congress and foreign policy is normative, whereas instead the concern should be with the crucial questions of what members of Congress do and why they do it. While Lindsay eschews normative questions for studying influence, I call for holding off on assessing influence until there is more systematic data on behavior. Hinckley expresses dismay at the lack of information readily available on the topic of Congress and foreign policy. Her data collection on bills and hearings is an innovation in terms of looking at congressional activity rather than the voting behavior of members.

3. Collie 1987 does look at coalitions over time, but Clausen 1973 takes a short-term view and Schneider 1979 looks at only the ninety-second and ninety-fourth Congresses and subsequently calls for more research comparing the pre- and post-1971 periods (14). For a critique of cross-sectional analyses and an argument for longitudinal studies, see Van Doren 1986.

4. Baker (1989, 122–23) quotes in this regard no less a personage than George McGovern (D-SD), who described his days in the House as consumed mostly with farmers' concerns, whereas when he arrived in the Senate, he had the opportunity to speak to the issue of America's attitude toward Castro, for example. The Senate provides not only the opportunity but also the responsibility to address these issues. McGovern asserts that if members of the Senate do not examine national-level policy, then the system is not working.

5. Furthermore, a longitudinal study of the House of Representatives would be limited because of the reforms of the 1970s. Because of the dearth of recorded teller votes before 1971 and their subsequent proliferation and the advent of electronic voting in 1973, the pre- and post-1971 eras would not be comparable (see Rohde 1994b, 113; S. Smith 1989, 16–35).

6. Preference is given the term *major states* over *great powers* following Vasquez's (1993, 12–13) argument that the term *power* is a realist construct conceptualizing nation-states only in terms of their capability and that the term *great* is normatively biased in favor of the elites that run these nation-states.

7. Now that the United States has again become a debtor nation, it may be entering a new era.

8. This time period includes neither Sundquist's "golden age" nor Wilson's era of congressional government. The period before the 1890s was characterized by continental expansion of an agrarian nation concerned mostly with domestic matters and governed by Congress. It is widely agreed that the U.S. emergence as a major state has been accompanied by some increase in the influence of the president and decrease in the influence of Congress. That said, this study seeks to identify variations in the Senate's behavior during this second century of more modest influence.

9. For complete coding rules, see the appendix.

10. See Coplin 1974 for the argument that "influence attempts" are more objective and empirically observable than "influence."

11. See Roberts 1954; Burke and Greenstein 1989.

12. Nevertheless, several scholars have found it useful to use roll-call votes to observe

trends in bipartisanship in spite of its consensual nature (see, e.g., Rieselbach 1964; Kesselman 1965; Tidmarch and Sabatt 1972; McCormick and Wittkopf 1990; McCormick, Wittkopf, and Danna 1997).

13. Foreign policy roll calls as a percentage of all roll calls were plotted across time, but they produced a graph that had randomness as its only characteristic. In a very slow year with nine votes on foreign policy and one on domestic, 90 percent of the votes would be on foreign policy, but how significant are nine votes likely to be? Conversely, in the Vietnam era (1971–74), the percentage of the roll calls on foreign policy was generally around 40 percent, but there were also a large number of votes on domestic issues. So although the percentage was low, the absolute amount of activity was high and significant.

14. It may appear at first that a measure of disagreement should be based on the percentage of close votes in a year. However, a close look reveals a validity problem with such an approach. For example, if one year had eight roll-call votes and six of them were close, its score would be 75 percent. If another year had 100 votes and 50 were close, its score would be only 50 percent. It is surely not the case that the former year is characterized by more disagreement than the latter. Since 50 close votes indicates more disagreement than 6 close votes (regardless of how many of the other types of votes there are in that year), the raw number of close votes was used as the indicator.

15. In the raw data, each roll call is coded as to whether it is a bill, conference report, amendment, or procedural motion. Resolutions, nominations, ratification of treaties, veto override attempts, and votes to pass bills are all coded together in a category called "bill." Reservations to treaties are coded as amendments. Motions to table amendments, to refer bills to committee, to adjourn during debate on a bill or amendment, to consider a piece of legislation, to reconsider a vote, to close debate, or to change the rules are all coded as procedural votes. The total number of each type of vote for each year is tallied and entered as a variable for each year in the data set. The number of votes on amendments is added to the number of votes on procedural motions to form a variable called "amendments and procedural votes," and the number of votes in the "bill" category is added to the number of votes on conference reports to form a variable called "bills and conference reports."

16. For a review of definitions of *issue,* see Randle 1987, 1–7.

17. The coding rules describe in detail how stakes are identified and assigned to issue categories (see the appendix).

18. Some analysts (e.g., Roskin 1974) see the Vietnam era as a new period starting in the mid-1970s. However, the Vietnam War was more a failure of containment than the emergence of a new issue. In fact, the Cold War reemerged shortly after Vietnam. Of course, the Cold War goes beyond the 1984 endpoint of the data set; the actual span of the communism issue is 1947–89.

19. There were 452 votes on imperialism, 583 on involvement in Europe, and 518 on communism. Five votes were assigned missing, and 1,555 were assigned to a miscellaneous category. See note 25 and the coding rules in the appendix for more detail.

20. See Vasquez and Mansbach 1983 for their conceptualization of an issue cycle for global issues and Vasquez 1985 for a more detailed treatment of domestic effects of critical issues.

21. Manley (1971, 65), however, holds that the role of consensus in congressional involvement in foreign policy was "less a question of a loss of power than a change in role: from critic to supporter." For an even stronger argument against seeing decline as

the result of consensus, see Crabb 1957, which argues that bipartisanship increased Congress's role.

22. Of course there is still no solid consensus, although the publication of McNamara's 1995 memoir brings it closer.

23. The Carter administration's attempt to bring human-rights concerns into foreign policy is only the exception that proves the rule when one considers the extent to which communist countries were treated differently and the speed with which the policy was abandoned after the invasion of Afghanistan.

24. Alexander Hamilton was quite adamant that the United States should be self-reliant. See Tickner's (1987) parallels between the United States and India as newly independent nations.

25. There are 1,109 votes on the tariff, 213 on immigration, 716 on foreign aid, 1,225 on defense, and 180 on routine diplomatic activity, leaving 1,553 votes on critical issues and 1,560 votes in other categories. See the coding rules in the appendix for more detail on how roll calls were assigned to categories and for the results of reliability tests.

26. The six issue area\categories that have been chosen are not as broad as categories such as "military," "economic," or "distributive" but are broader than mere issues. The issues of the draft, arms sales, and the Strategic Defense Initiative all fall into the area of national defense, but it may be that national defense should be seen as part of a broader category, such as "military" or some other theoretical category. If similar patterns are found on more than one of the issue areas in this study, it may be because they have similar characteristics that would warrant their being grouped together. For example, tariff and immigration may resemble each other and/or other economic issues in the behavioral patterns they trigger. Also the possibility should not be overlooked that some domestic and foreign policy issues should be grouped together. While Lowi (1964) identifies only the domestic issues of social security and public assistance as redistributive, Zimmerman (1973) sees limited war as redistributive. If Lowi's underlying dimensions should prove to be empirically useful, such a conception might lead to the unorthodox procedure of putting welfare and limited war in the same category.

27. The presentation of the steps involved in ARIMA and impact analysis is based on Enders 1995, chap. 5, pt. 1, and McDowall et al. 1980, 48.

28. The integrated component is usually either 0 if there is no trend or 1 if it is "first differenced." It is rare for a series to have to be differenced more than once.

29. See Enders 1995, 179–80, for the distinction between a difference stationary model and a trend stationary model and warnings about applying the inappropriate method to remove the trend.

30. A common conventional approach for determining whether a series is white noise is to run autocorrelation functions (ACFs) and partial autocorrelation functions (PACFs). The spikes in the correlograms, which indicate autocorrelation, tell the analyst which model is most appropriate. The use of AIC and BIC supersedes the ACFs and PACFs. When the AIC and BIC are at their lowest, there are generally no spikes in the ACFs and PACFs. ACFs are then used only for determining whether there are autocorrelations in the residuals, which gives rise to the Q statistic.

31. There are insufficient data to assess the impact of imperialism.

32. The tariff produces so many votes without suggesting a theoretically interesting pattern that it was removed to see whether an interesting pattern would emerge. Chapter 3 presents the justification for this procedure.

33. The argument in favor of using roll-call votes does not depend on proving that

other indicators (e.g., voice votes) are not valid; rather, this argument rests on showing that roll-call votes have at least some validity.

Chapter 3

1. If one is discomfited by this manipulation of the data, it might help to look at it in this light: this analysis may not explain the full pattern and may not explain the tariff, but others have explained the pattern in the tariff. This analysis explains the pattern in the rest of foreign policy. The fact that the tariff is removed does not mean that the results are not valid. Explaining the pattern in all foreign policy except tariffs is a contribution, carefully and explicitly delimited, that stands on its own.

2. It is interesting and significant that the number of votes that explicitly mention fighting communism decreases greatly after 1970, as activity on Vietnam takes over. It seems that attention is turned away from general ideological statements as the Senate gets down to the specific task of extricating the United States from the current fight against communism. Also, of course, détente is defusing some of the anticommunist rhetoric. During the six years when voting on Vietnam was at its height, 1970–75, the number of votes with explicit anticommunist wording was at its lowest in the entire 1950–84 period.

3. I am indebted to Junsoo Lee, a colleague in economics at Vanderbilt University, for helping me to navigate the RATS program.

4. A trend can be removed from a series by detrending through regression analysis, but such a procedure makes assumptions about linearity that often do not hold in a time series. Instead, series are usually "differenced," which consists of subtracting each value from the next value.

5. Each impact is run separately in this analysis rather than in a multiple impact analysis because each impact is independent of the others and their effects are not cumulative.

6. I thank Junsoo Lee for suggesting this tack.

7. When this series is smoothed, the highest peaks are 1898, 1919, 1952, 1972, and 1980, plus a small hump from 1941 to 1943. This finding confirms that the pattern observed in the total data is also present in the data on just the critical issues: smoothing the data does not remove it.

8. The trends in five other issue areas will be examined in chapter 5.

Chapter 4

1. Chapter 3 showed that the critical-issue pattern is more easily observed with votes on the tariff removed. This analysis also proceeds with the 1,071 roll calls on the tariff removed, as are eight other cases that lack the yeas and nays required for the margin-of-victory measure.

2. This finding does not mean that there is no disagreement except in critical-issue years. Even in figure 4.2, there are small surges of close votes around 1930, 1940, 1960, and 1982. The critical-issue theory names two sufficient conditions for disagreement— the rise of a critical issue and the failure of a policy on a critical issue—but other factors can produce disagreement, and future research can pursue the search for these factors.

3. This number is relatively low for the 1970s: although 1971 is the third-highest year in overall activity, it ranks thirteenth in unanimous votes.

4. This number is low only when compared to its level of overall activity: 1978 has the most roll calls overall, but eight other years match or outstrip it in unanimous votes.

5. There are three exceptions to the generalization that unanimous votes are low in critical-issue years: 1917, 1940, and 1972. While the critical issues are clearly somehow related to war, there is a difference between years dominated by debate over a critical issue, such as 1919 and 1920, and years dominated by the preparation for war, such as 1917 and 1940. Preparation for war seems to be marked by a high level of activity, a high level of unanimous votes, and only a moderate level of close votes. The peak in 1972 is more problematic; however, some of the unanimous votes may result from a consensus emerging over opposition to the Vietnam War.

6. High disagreement was not predicted for 1978, but the debate over the Panama Canal Treaty is associated with the critical issue of imperialism.

Chapter 5

1. Many studies focus on Congress's role in a particular foreign policy issue area, and most edited volumes on Congress and foreign policy have individual chapters devoted to issue areas. Examples include: on tariff, Schattschneider 1935 and Haggard 1988; on foreign aid, Franck 1981; on defense, Wayman 1985, Lindsay 1987, and Stockton 1993. In addition, there are chapters and books on diplomacy (Jentleson 1990); intelligence (Ransom 1970; Johnson 1989; Treverton 1990; Smist 1990; Crabb and Holt 1992, chap. 6); war powers (Eagleton 1974; Rourke 1983; Crabb and Holt 1992, chap. 5; Katzmann 1990; Spitzer 1993; Ely 1993; Glennon 1990); trade (Pastor 1980; Crabb and Holt 1992, chap. 7; Destler 1994; O'Halloran 1993); arms control (Blechman 1990; Frye 1994).

2. For example, in 1897, there are a total of 201 roll calls, of which 33 are on foreign policy besides tariff, 24 are on domestic policy, and 144 are on the tariff. Thus, 72 percent of all 1897 Senate roll calls were on the tariff. The numbers for 1909, 1922, and 1930 are 65 percent, 64 percent, and 66 percent, respectively.

3. While 1922 is the highest year in activity on the tariff (see fig. 5.1), only 41 of the 306 roll calls (13.4 percent) are close votes, attesting to the pork-barrel nature of the tariff at this point. By 1930, however, well over half of the roll calls (91 out of 168 [54.1 percent]) are close votes.

4. The increased activity, however, occurs mostly in the form of amendments and procedural votes. Only one year, 1924, has three bills/conference reports, and all of the rest have two or fewer. Although 1950 has eight close votes, only one bill is voted on, and the nine close votes in 1930 take place on amendments or procedural votes.

5. There is a group of votes that produces approximately half of the roll-call activity shown in these years in the critical-issue graph. These are roll-call votes on mobilizing the economy for war and raising revenue for war. These two types of roll-call votes were coded as votes on the critical issue. For instance, a vote on raising revenue for the Spanish-American War was coded as imperialism, while a vote to raise revenue for the Korean War was coded as anticommunism. This coding decision could raise validity questions because there is an argument to be made that these votes could be coded as defense. The coding rules adopted, however, state that only votes referring explicitly to

defense appropriations are to be coded as defense, while decisions to mobilize the economy beyond simply defense were seen as societal decisions on the critical issue (see the appendix). The fine line between these indicators of the critical issues and indicators of defense highlights the close relationship between defense and the critical issues, a theoretical issue that will merit continued attention in future research.

6. It is notable that in the years the Spanish-American War and the Korean War broke out, 1898 and 1950, respectively, there are in fact no close votes on defense. In the first case, the debate became focused on a reluctant president, thus galvanizing opinion in Congress. In the second, the Korean War was not fought over a critical issue but rather was entered as part of a policy response to a critical issue (i.e., containment). The consensus that sustained congressional support for Truman's Korea decision was previously forged over the Truman Doctrine in 1947.

Chapter 6

1. Sundquist's (1981) study is an exception in that it covers 200 years and offers an explanation for the decline of Congress's role in national-level policy based on the effects of increased attention to constituents' local concerns. However, Sundquist's work does not explain the periodic resurgences of congressional assertiveness.

2. Peterson and Greene (1994b) distinguish between activity and acrimony. T. Moe (1987) indicates that assumptions of congressional control over the bureaucracy are probably exaggerated. Baldwin (1966) warns about confusing initiative with influence. Lindsay (1994a, 285), rejects claims about control in favor of attempting to identify influence. O'Halloran (1993, 303) concludes that Congress certainly does not dominate trade policy but does influence it.

3. This type of perspective is consistent with Mezey's (1991) representation model, which he prefers to the activist model.

4. Although the executive succeeded in pursuing the containment policy as a security policy, Keohane (1984, 140–41) points out that Congress mounted a great deal of often successful opposition to certain aspects of the international economic regime, for example, by defeating the International Trade Organization and preventing a multilateral accord on oil. Briggs (1994) and others characterize the debate over NATO as a "great debate," a label that would not be used in the case of a totally deferential Congress.

5. The measures of association for honeymoon years are expected to be negative, given the hypothesis that honeymoon years should be lower in activity and disagreement than other years. However, they are not statistically significant.

6. Remarks made at the annual meeting of the International Studies Association, Washington, D.C., April 15, 1987.

7. Although Carter 1986a divides the data by postwar decade, calendar decade, and presidential administrations, there is no theoretical rationale for these divisions (see chap. 1). He returns to the pre-Tet/post-Tet division in a later piece (Carter 1994).

8. For an analysis of long-term trends in consensus in American foreign policy, see Holmes et al. 1992.

9. Holmes (1987, 35) notes that his data are richest for the period 1800–1950 but are fairly complete from 1790 to 1970.

References

Abshire, David M., and Ralph D. Nurnberger, eds. 1981. *The Growing Power of Congress.* Beverly Hills, CA: Sage.

Adler, David Gray. 1988. The Constitution and presidential warmaking: The enduring debate. *Political Science Quarterly* 103 (spring): 1–36.

Adler, David Gray, and Larry N. George, eds. 1996. *The Constitution and the Conduct of American Foreign Policy.* Lawrence: University of Kansas Press.

Allison, Graham T. 1971. *Essence of Decision: Explaining the Cuban Missile Crisis.* Boston: Little, Brown.

Bailey, Thomas A. 1980. *A Diplomatic History of the American People.* 10th ed. New York: Appleton-Century-Crofts.

Baker, Ross K. 1989. *House and Senate.* New York: Norton.

Baldwin, David A. 1966. Congressional initiative in foreign policy. *Journal of Politics* 28, no. 4 (November): 754–73.

Bax, Frans R. 1977. The legislative-executive relationship in foreign policy: New partnership or new competition? *Orbis* 20:881–904.

Binkley, Wilfred E. 1962. *President and Congress.* 3d rev. ed. New York: Random House.

Blechman, Barry M. 1990. The new congressional role in arms control. In *A Question of Balance: The President, the Congress, and Foreign Policy,* ed. Thomas E. Mann, 109–45. Washington, DC: Brookings Institution.

Bond, Jon R., Gary W. Copeland, Lance T. LeLoup, Russell D. Renka, and Steven A. Shull. 1991. Implications for research in studying presidential-congressional relations: Conclusion. In *The Two Presidencies: A Quarter Century Assessment,* ed. Steven A. Shull, 191–204. Chicago: Nelson-Hall.

Box, George E. P., and Gwilym M. Jenkins. 1970. *Time Series Analysis, Forecasting, and Control.* San Francisco: Holden-Day.

Box, George E. P., and G. C. Tiao. 1975. Intervention analysis with applications to economic and environmental problems. *Journal of the American Statistical Association* 70, no. 349 (March): 70–79.

Brady, David W. 1985. A reevaluation of realignments in American politics: Evidence from the House of Representatives. *American Political Science Review* 79:28–49.

———. 1988. *Critical Elections and Congressional Policy Making.* Stanford, CA: Stanford University Press.

Brecher, Michael, Blema Steinberg, and Janice Stein. 1969. A framework for research on foreign policy behavior. *Journal of Conflict Resolution* 13:75–101.

Bremer, Stuart A. 1980. National capabilities and war proneness. In *The Correlates of War,* vol. 2, ed. J. David Singer, 57–82. New York: Free Press.

Briggs, Philip J. 1994. *Making American Foreign Policy: President-Congress Relations from the Second World War to the Post–Cold War Era.* Lanham, MD: Rowman and Littlefield.

Bull, Hedley. 1977. *The Anarchical Society.* New York: Columbia University Press.

Burgin, Eileen. 1993a. Congress and foreign policy: The misperceptions. In *Congress*

Reconsidered, 5th ed., ed. Lawrence C. Dodd and Bruce I. Oppenheimer, 333–63. Washington, DC: Congressional Quarterly Press.

——. 1993b. The influence of constituents: Congressional decision making on issues of foreign and defense policy. In *Congress Resurgent: Foreign and Defense Policy on Capitol Hill*, ed. Randall B. Ripley and James M. Lindsay, 67–88. Ann Arbor: University of Michigan Press.

——. 1997. Assessing Congress's role in the making of foreign policy. In *Congress Reconsidered*, 6th ed., ed. Lawrence C. Dodd and Bruce I. Oppenheimer, 293–324. Washington, DC: Congressional Quarterly Press.

Burke, John P., and Fred I. Greenstein. 1989. *How Presidents Test Reality: Decisions on Vietnam, 1954 and 1965*. New York: Russell Sage Foundation.

Burnham, Walter Dean. 1970. *Critical Elections and the Mainsprings of American Politics*. New York: Norton.

Burton, John W. 1984. *Global Conflict: The Domestic Sources of International Crisis*. Brighton: Wheatsheaf.

Calvert, Randall L., Mathew D. McCubbins, and Barry R. Weingast. 1989. A theory of political control and agency discretion. *American Journal of Political Science* 33 (August): 588–611.

Campbell, Angus, Philip E. Converse, Warren E. Miller, and Donald E. Stokes. 1960. *The American Voter*. New York: Wiley.

Carroll, Holbert N. 1966. *The House of Representatives and Foreign Policy*. Boston: Little, Brown.

Carter, Ralph G. 1985. Issue areas in the study of American foreign policy: The case of congressional behavior. Paper presented at the annual meeting of the American Political Science Association, New Orleans, August–September.

——. 1986a. Congressional foreign policy behavior: Persistent patterns of the postwar period. *Presidential Studies Quarterly* 16 (spring): 329–59.

——. 1986b. Congressional foreign policymaking in the national security versus non–national security arenas: An examination of the postwar record. Paper presented at the annual meeting of the International Studies Association, Atlanta, November.

——. 1988. Congress and national security policy. Paper presented at the annual meeting of the International Studies Association, St. Louis, March–April.

——. 1994. Budgeting for defense. In *The President, the Congress, and the Making of Foreign Policy*, ed. Paul E. Peterson, 161–78. Norman: University of Oklahoma Press.

Chamberlain, Lawrence H. 1946. *The President, Congress, and Legislation*. New York: Columbia University Press.

Clausen, Aage R. 1967. Measurement identity in the longitudinal analysis of legislative voting. *American Political Science Review* 61 (December): 1020–35.

——. 1973. *How Congressmen Decide: A Policy Focus*. New York: St. Martin's.

Clausen, Aage R., and Carl E. Van Horn. 1977. Congressional response to a decade of change: 1963–1972. *Journal of Politics* 39:624–66.

Cohen, Jeffrey E. 1991. A historical reassessment of Wildavsky's "two presidencies" thesis. In *The Two Presidencies: A Quarter Century Assessment*, ed. Steven A. Shull, 53–60. Chicago: Nelson-Hall.

Collie, Melissa P. 1987. The rise of coalition politics: Voting in the U.S. House of Representatives during the post–New Deal era. Paper presented at the annual meeting of the American Political Science Association, Chicago, September.

Congressional Quarterly Weekly Report. 1982. January 2. Washington, DC: Congressional Quarterly.

Cooper, Joseph, and David W. Brady. 1981. Toward a diachronic analysis of Congress. *American Political Science Review* 75 (December): 988–1006.

Coplin, William D. 1974. *Introduction to International Politics.* 2d ed. Chicago: Rand McNally.

Coplin, William D., Stephen Mills, and Michael K. O'Leary. 1973. The PRINCE concepts and the study of foreign policy. In *Sage International Yearbook of Foreign Policy Studies,* ed. Patrick J. McGowan, 1:73–103. Beverly Hills, CA: Sage.

Corwin, Edward S. 1948. *The President: Office and Powers.* Rev. 3d ed. New York: New York University Press.

Covington, Cary R. 1986. Congressional support for the president: The view from the Kennedy/Johnson White House. *Journal of Politics* 48:717–28.

Crabb, Cecil V., Jr. 1957. *Bipartisan Foreign Policy: Myth or Reality?* Evanston, IL: Row, Peterson.

———. 1965. *American Foreign Policy in the Nuclear Age.* 2d ed. New York: Harper and Row.

Crabb, Cecil V., Jr., and Pat M. Holt. 1992. *Invitation to Struggle: Congress, the President and Foreign Policy.* 4th ed. Washington, DC: Congressional Quarterly Press.

Cronin, Thomas E. 1983. A resurgent Congress and the imperial presidency. In *Perspectives on American Foreign Policy,* ed. Charles W. Kegley, Jr., and Eugene R. Wittkopf, 320–46. New York: St. Martin's.

Crovitz, L. Gordon, and Jeremy A. Rabkin, eds. 1989. *The Fettered Presidency: Legal Constraints on the Executive Branch.* Washington, DC: American Enterprise Institute for Public Policy Research.

Dahl, Robert A. 1950. *Congress and Foreign Policy.* New York: Harcourt, Brace.

———. 1961. *Who Governs? Democracy and Power in an American City.* New Haven: Yale University Press.

Dean, P. Dale, and John A. Vasquez. 1976. From power politics to issue politics: Bipolarity and multipolarity in light of a new paradigm. *Western Political Quarterly* 29 (March): 7–28.

Deese, David A. 1994. The hazards of interdependence: World politics in the American foreign policy process. In *The New Politics of American Foreign Policy,* ed. David A. Deese, 2–35. New York: St. Martin's.

Destler, I. M. 1981a. Dateline Washington: Congress as boss? *Foreign Policy* 42 (spring): 167–80.

———. 1981b. Executive-congressional conflict in foreign policy: Explaining it; coping with it. In *Congress Reconsidered,* 2d ed., ed. Lawrence C. Dodd and Bruce I. Oppenheimer, 296–316. New York: Congressional Quarterly Press.

———. 1986. *American Trade Politics: System under Stress.* Washington, DC: Institute for International Economics.

———. 1994. Delegating trade policy. In *The President, the Congress, and the Making of Foreign Policy,* ed. Paul E. Peterson, 228–45. Norman: University of Oklahoma Press.

Destler, I. M., Leslie H. Gelb, and Anthony Lake. 1984. *Our Own Worst Enemy: The Unmaking of American Foreign Policy.* New York: Simon and Schuster.

Dodd, Lawrence C. 1977. Congress and the quest for power. In *Congress Reconsidered,* ed. Lawrence C. Dodd and Bruce I. Oppenheimer, 269–307. New York: Praeger.

———. 1981. Congress, the Constitution, and the crisis of legitimation. In *Congress Reconsidered,* 2d ed., ed. Lawrence C. Dodd and Bruce I. Oppenheimer, 390–420. Washington, DC: Congressional Quarterly Press.

———. 1991. Congress, the presidency, and the American experience: A transformational perspective. In *Divided Democracy: Cooperation and Conflict between the President and Congress,* ed. James A. Thurber, 275–302. Washington, DC: Congressional Quarterly Press.

Dodd, Lawrence C., and Bruce I. Oppenheimer, eds. 1981. *Congress Reconsidered.* 2d ed. Washington, DC: Congressional Quarterly Press.

———. 1985. *Congress Reconsidered.* 3d ed. Washington, DC: Congressional Quarterly Press.

———. 1989. *Congress Reconsidered.* 4th ed. Washington, DC: Congressional Quarterly Press.

———. 1993. *Congress Reconsidered.* 5th ed. Washington, DC: Congressional Quarterly Press.

Doyle, Michael W. 1995. Liberalism and world politics revisited. In *Controversies in International Relations Theory: Realism and the Neoliberal Challenge,* ed. Charles W. Kegley Jr., 83–106. New York: St. Martin's.

Eagleton, Thomas F. 1974. *War and Presidential Power.* New York: Liveright.

East, Maurice A. 1973. Size and foreign policy behavior: A test of two models. *World Politics* 25:556–76.

Edwards, George C., III. 1980. *Presidential Influence in Congress.* San Francisco: Freeman.

———. 1989. *At the Margins.* New Haven: Yale University Press.

Elder, Robert E., and Jack E. Holmes. 1988. Prosperity, consensus, and assertive foreign policy: A long-term analysis of historical relationships in American foreign policy. Paper presented at the annual meeting of the International Studies Association, St. Louis, March.

Ely, John Hart. 1993. *War and Responsibility: Constitutional Lessons of Vietnam and Its Aftermath.* Princeton: Princeton University Press.

Emery, Christine V., and Christopher J. Deering. 1995. Congress and foreign policy: Substantive and procedural legislation in the post-war era. Paper presented at the annual meeting of the International Studies Association, Chicago, February.

Enders, Walter. 1995. *Applied Econometric Time Series.* New York: Wiley.

Evangelista, Matthew. 1993. Internal and external constraints on grand strategy: The Soviet case. In *The Domestic Bases of Grand Strategy,* ed. Richard Rosecrance and Arthur A. Stein, 154–78. Ithaca: Cornell University Press.

Fiorina, Morris P. 1981. *Retrospective Voting in American National Elections.* New Haven: Yale University Press.

Fisher, Louis. 1987. *The Politics of Shared Power: Congress and the Executive.* Washington, DC: Congressional Quarterly Press.

———. 1991. War powers: The need for collective judgment. In *Divided Democracy: Cooperation and Conflict between the President and Congress,* ed. James A. Thurber, 199–217. Washington, DC: Congressional Quarterly Press.

———. 1995. *Presidential War Power.* Lawrence: University Press of Kansas.

————. 1997. Sidestepping Congress: Presidents acting under the U.N. and NATO. *Case Western Reserve Law Review* 47, no. 4: 1237–79.

Fleisher, Richard, and Jon R. Bond. 1988. Are there two presidencies? Yes, but only for Republicans. *Journal of Politics* 50 (August): 747–67.

Franck, Thomas M. 1981a. Congress and human rights: A case study on the origins of congressional imperialism. In *The Tethered Presidency: Congressional Restraints on Executive Power*, ed. Thomas M. Franck, 153–71. New York: New York University Press.

————, ed. 1981b. *The Tethered Presidency: Congressional Restraints on Executive Power*. New York: New York University Press.

Franck, Thomas M., and Edward Weisband. 1979. *Foreign Policy by Congress*. New York: Oxford University Press.

Friedberg, Aaron L. 1988. *The Weary Titan: Britain and the Experience of Relative Decline, 1895–1905*. Princeton: Princeton University Press.

Friedrich, Carl J. 1941. *Constitutional Government and Democracy: Theory and Practice in Europe and America*. Boston: Little, Brown.

Frye, Alton. 1971. Congress: The virtue of its vices. *Foreign Policy* 3:108–21.

————. 1994. Searching for arms control. In *The President, the Congress, and the Making of Foreign Policy*, ed. Paul E. Peterson, 179–203. Norman: University of Oklahoma Press.

Gardner, Lloyd C., Walter F. LaFeber, and Thomas J. McCormick. 1976. *Creation of the American Empire*. 2d ed. Chicago: Rand McNally.

Geller, Daniel S., and J. David Singer. 1998. *Nations at War: A Scientific Study of International Conflict*. Cambridge: Cambridge University Press.

Gilpin, Robert. 1981. *War and Change in World Politics*. Cambridge: Cambridge University Press.

Ginsberg, Benjamin. 1976. Elections and public policy. *American Political Science Review* 70:41–50.

Glennon, Michael J. 1990. *Constitutional Diplomacy*. Princeton: Princeton University Press.

Gourevitch, Peter. 1978. The second image reversed: The international sources of domestic politics. *International Organization* 32 (autumn): 881–912.

————. 1986. *Politics in Hard Times: Comparative Responses to International Economic Crises*. Ithaca: Cornell University Press.

Gregorian, Hrach. 1984. Assessing congressional involvement in foreign policy: Lessons of the post-Vietnam period. *Review of Politics* 46 (January): 91–112.

Haggard, Stephan. 1988. The institutional foundations of hegemony: Explaining the Reciprocal Trade Agreements Act of 1934. *International Organization* 42 (winter): 91–120.

Hartmann, Frederick H. 1983. *The Relations of Nations*. New York: Macmillan.

Hawley, Ellis W. 1979. *The Great War and the Search for a Modern Order: A History of the American People and Their Institutions, 1917–1933*. New York: St. Martin's.

Hayes, Michael T. 1981. *Lobbyists and Legislators*. New Brunswick, NJ: Rutgers University Press.

Henehan, Marie T. 1981. A data-based evaluation of issue typologies in the comparative study of foreign policy. Paper presented at the annual meeting of the International Studies Association, Philadelphia, March.

Hermann, Charles F. 1978. Foreign policy behavior: That which is to be explained. In

Why Nations Act, ed. Maurice A. East, Stephen A. Salmore, and Charles F. Hermann, 25–47. Beverly Hills, CA: Sage.

Hermann, Charles F., and Roger A. Coate. 1982. Substantive problem areas. In *Describing Foreign Policy Behavior,* ed. Patrick Callahan, Linda P. Brady, and Margaret G. Hermann, 77–114. Beverly Hills, CA: Sage.

Hinckley, Barbara. 1978. *Stability and Change in Congress.* New York: Harper and Row.

———. 1994. *Less Than Meets the Eye: The Myth of the Assertive Congress.* Chicago: University of Chicago Press.

Hintze, Otto. 1975. Military organization and the organization of the state. In *The Historical Essays of Otto Hintze,* ed. Felix Gilbert, 178–215. New York: Oxford University Press.

Hoggard, Gary D. 1974. Differential source coverage in foreign policy analysis. In *Comparing Foreign Policies: Theories, Findings, and Methods,* ed. James N. Rosenau, 353–82. New York: Wiley.

Holmes, Jack E. 1985. *The Mood/Interest Theory of American Foreign Policy.* Lexington: University Press of Kentucky.

Holmes, Jack E., Matthew Ballast, Brian Keisling, and Tom Roodvoets. 1992. Consensus and American foreign policy: A long-term perspective. Paper presented at the annual meeting of the International Studies Association, Atlanta, April.

Holmes, Jack E., and Robert E. Elder. 1983. Classifying presidents and U.S. foreign policy moods. Paper presented at the annual meeting of the International Studies Association, Mexico City, April.

———. 1987. The relationship of introvert/extrovert foreign policy and liberal/conservative political cycles to American foreign policy. Paper presented at the annual meeting of the International Studies Association, Washington, DC, April.

Holsti, Ole R., and James N. Rosenau. 1984. *American Leadership in World Affairs: Vietnam and the Breakdown of Consensus.* Boston: Allen and Unwin.

Huntington, Samuel P. 1961. *The Common Defense: Strategic Problems in National Politics.* New York: Columbia University Press.

———. 1971. Congressional responses to the twentieth century. In *Congress and the President: Allies and Adversaries,* ed. Ronald C. Moe, 7–31. Pacific Palisades, CA: Goodyear.

Janis, Irving L. 1972. *Victims of Groupthink.* Boston: Houghton-Mifflin.

Jentleson, Bruce W. 1990. American diplomacy: Around the world and along Pennsylvania Avenue. In *A Question of Balance: The President, the Congress, and Foreign Policy,* ed. Thomas E. Mann, 146–200. Washington, DC: Brookings Institution.

Jervis, Robert. 1980. The impact of the Korean War on the Cold War. *Journal of Conflict Resolution* 24:563–92.

Johnson, Loch K. 1989. *America's Secret Power: The CIA in a Democratic Society.* New York: Oxford University Press.

———. 1994. Playing hardball with the CIA. In *The President, the Congress, and the Making of Foreign Policy,* ed. Paul E. Peterson, 49–73. Norman: University of Oklahoma Press.

Jones, Charles O. 1995. The pendulum of power. In *Separate but Equal Branches,* ed. Charles O. Jones, 105–27. Chatham, NJ: Chatham House.

Jones, Gordon S., and John A. Marini, eds. 1988. *The Imperial Congress: Crisis in the Separation of Powers.* New York: Pharos.

Jones, Joseph M. 1955. *The Fifteen Weeks.* New York: Harcourt, Brace and World.

Katzmann, Robert A. 1990. War powers: Toward a new accommodation. In *A Question of Balance: The President, the Congress, and Foreign Policy,* ed. Thomas E. Mann, 35–69. Washington, DC: Brookings Institution.

Kegley, Charles W., Jr. 1995. *Controversies in International Relations Theory: Realism and the Neoliberal Challenge.* New York: St. Martin's.

Kennan, George F. ("X"). 1947. The sources of Soviet conduct. *Foreign Affairs* 25:566–82.

Kennedy, Paul. 1987. *The Rise and Fall of the Great Powers: Economic Change and Military Conflict from 1500 to 2000.* New York: Random House.

Keohane, Robert O. 1984. *After Hegemony.* Princeton: Princeton University Press.

Keohane, Robert O., and Joseph Nye Jr. 1977. *Power and Interdependence: World Politics in Transition.* Boston: Little, Brown.

Kesselman, Mark. 1961. Presidential leadership in foreign policy. *Midwest Journal of Political Science* 5 (August): 284–89.

———. 1965. Presidential leadership in Congress on foreign policy: A replication of a hypothesis. *Midwest Journal of Political Science* 9 (November): 401–6.

Key, V. O., Jr. 1955. A theory of critical elections. *Journal of Politics* 17:3–18.

Kingdon, John W. 1989. *Congressmen's Voting Decisions.* 3d ed. Ann Arbor: University of Michigan Press.

Klingberg, Frank L. 1952. The historical alternation of moods in American foreign policy. *World Politics* 4 (January): 239–73.

———. 1983. *Cyclical Trends in American Foreign Policy Moods: The Unfolding of America's World Role.* New York: University Press of America.

Koh, Harold Hongju. 1986. Why the president (almost) always wins in foreign affairs. *Yale Law Journal* 97:1255–1342.

Krasner, Stephen. 1978. *Defending the National Interest: Raw Materials, Investments, and U.S. Foreign Policy.* Princeton: Princeton University Press.

Kugler, Jacek, and A. F. K. Organski. 1989. The power transition: A retrospective and prospective evaluation. In *Handbook of War Studies,* ed. Manus I. Midlarsky, 171–94. Boston: Unwin Hyman. Reprint, Ann Arbor: University of Michigan Press, 1993.

Lazarsfeld, Paul F., Bernard R. Berelson, and Hazel Gaudet. 1944. *The People's Choice.* New York: Columbia University Press.

Lehman, John. 1992. *Making War: The 200-Year-Old Battle between the President and Congress over How America Goes to War.* New York: Scribner's.

LeLoup, Lance T. 1993. The fiscal straitjacket: Budgetary constraints on congressional foreign and defense policy-making. In *Congress Resurgent: Foreign and Defense Policy on Capitol Hill,* ed. Randall B. Ripley and James M. Lindsay, 37–66. Ann Arbor: University of Michigan Press.

LeLoup, Lance T., and Steven A. Shull. 1979. Congress versus the executive: The "two presidencies" reconsidered. *Social Science Quarterly* 59 (March): 704–19.

———. 1999. *The President and Congress: Collaboration and Combat in National Policymaking.* Boston: Allyn and Bacon.

Levy, Jack S. 1983. *War in the Modern Great Power System, 1495–1975.* Lexington: University Press of Kentucky.

Lindblom, Charles E. 1959. The science of muddling through. *Public Administration Review* 19:79–88.

Lindsay, James M. 1987. Congress and defense policy: 1961 to 1986. *Armed Forces and Society* 13 (spring): 371–401.

———. 1993. Congress and diplomacy. In *Congress Resurgent: Foreign and Defense Policy on Capitol Hill*, ed. Randall B. Ripley and James M. Lindsay, 261–81. Ann Arbor: University of Michigan Press.

———. 1994a. Congress, foreign policy, and the new institutionalism. *International Studies Quarterly* 38 (June): 281–304.

———. 1994b. *Congress and the Politics of U.S. Foreign Policy*. Baltimore: Johns Hopkins University Press.

Lindsay, James M., and Randall B. Ripley. 1992. Foreign and defense policy in Congress: A research agenda for the 1990s. *Legislative Studies Quarterly* 17:417–49.

———. 1993. How Congress influences foreign and defense policy. In *Congress Resurgent: Foreign and Defense Policy on Capitol Hill*, ed. Randall B. Ripley and James M. Lindsay, 17–33. Ann Arbor: University of Michigan Press.

Lindsay, James M., and Wayne P. Steger. 1993. The "two presidencies" in future research: Moving beyond roll-call analysis. *Congress and the Presidency* 20 (autumn): 103–17.

Lowi, Theodore. 1964. American business, public policy, case-studies, and political theory. *World Politics* 16:677–715.

———. 1967. Making democracy safe for the world: National politics and foreign policy. In *Domestic Sources of Foreign Policy*, ed. James N. Rosenau, 295–331. New York: Free Press.

———. 1979. *The End of Liberalism*. 2d ed. New York: Norton.

Lumsdaine, David H. 1993. *Moral Vision in International Politics: The Foreign Aid Regime, 1949–1989*. Princeton: Princeton University Press.

Manley, John F. 1971. The rise of Congress in foreign policy-making. *Annals* 397 (September): 60–70.

Mann, Thomas E. 1990a. Making foreign policy: President and Congress. In *A Question of Balance: The President, the Congress, and Foreign Policy*, ed. Thomas E. Mann, 1–34. Washington, DC: Brookings Institution.

———, ed. 1990b. *A Question of Balance: The President, the Congress, and Foreign Policy*. Washington, DC: Brookings Institution.

Manning, Bayless. 1977. The Congress, the executive and intermestic affairs: Three proposals. *Foreign Affairs* 55:306–24.

Mansbach, Richard W., Yale H. Ferguson, and Donald E. Lampert. 1976. *The Web of World Politics*. Englewood Cliffs, NJ: Prentice-Hall.

Mansbach, Richard W., and John A. Vasquez. 1981. *In Search of Theory: A New Paradigm for Global Politics*. New York: Columbia University Press.

McCleary, Richard, and Richard A. Hay Jr., with Erroll E. Meidinger and David McDowall. 1980. *Applied Time Series for the Social Sciences*. Beverly Hills, CA: Sage.

McCormick, James M. 1993. Decision making in the foreign affairs and foreign relations committees. In *Congress Resurgent: Foreign and Defense Policy on Capitol Hill*, ed. Randall B. Ripley and James M. Lindsay, 115–53. Ann Arbor: University of Michigan Press.

McCormick, James M., and Eugene R. Wittkopf. 1989. Bipartisan foreign policy voting in Congress: The effects of issue-area and limited war, 1947–1986. Paper presented at the annual meeting of the Southern Political Science Association, Memphis, November.

———. 1990. Bipartisanship, partisanship, and ideology in congressional-executive foreign policy relations, 1947–1988. *Journal of Politics* 52:1077–1100.

McCormick, James M., Eugene R. Wittkopf, and David M. Danna. 1997. Politics and bipartisanship at the water's edge: A note on Bush and Clinton. *Polity* 30, no. 1: 133–49.

McCubbins, Mathew D. 1985. Legislative design of regulatory structure. *American Journal of Political Science* 29:721–48.

McCubbins, Mathew D., Roger G. Noll, and Barry R. Weingast. 1987. Administrative procedures as instruments of political control. *Journal of Law, Economics, and Organization* 3:243–77.

McCubbins, Mathew D., and Thomas Schwartz. 1984. Congressional oversight overlooked: Police patrols versus fire alarms. *American Journal of Political Science* 28:165–79.

McDowall, David, Richard McCleary, Errol E. Meidinger, and Richard A. Hay Jr. 1980. *Interrupted Time Series Analysis.* Beverly Hills, CA: Sage.

McNamara, Robert S. 1995. *In Retrospect: The Tragedy and Lessons of Vietnam.* New York: Times Books.

Meadows, D. H., D. L. Meadows, J. Randers, and W. W. Behrens III. 1972. *The Limits to Growth.* New York: Universe.

Mezey, Michael L. 1989. *Congress, the President, and Public Policy.* Boulder, CO: Westview.

———. 1991. The legislature, the executive, and public policy: The futile quest for congressional power. In *Divided Democracy: Cooperation and Conflict between the President and Congress,* ed. James A. Thurber, 99–122. Washington, DC: Congressional Quarterly Press.

Miller, Warren E., and Donald E. Stokes. 1963. Constituency influence in Congress. *American Political Science Review* 57:45–56.

Modelski, George. 1978. The long cycle of global politics and the nation-state. *Comparative Studies in Society and History* 20 (April): 214–35.

Modelski, George, and William R. Thompson. 1989. Long cycles and global war. In *Handbook of War Studies,* ed. Manus Midlarsky, 23–54. Boston: Unwin Hyman.

Moe, Ronald C., and Steven C. Teel. 1971. Congress as policy-maker: A necessary reappraisal. In *Congress and the President,* ed. Ronald C. Moe, 32–52. Pacific Palisades, CA: Goodyear.

Moe, Terry M. 1987. An assessment of the positive theory of "congressional dominance." *Legislative Studies Quarterly* 12 (November): 475–520.

Moravcsik, Andrew. 1997. Taking preferences seriously: A liberal theory of international politics. *International Organization* 51 (autumn): 513–53.

Morgenthau, Hans J. 1948. *Politics among Nations: The Struggle for Power and Peace.* New York: Knopf.

Mueller, John E. 1971. Trends in popular support for the wars in Korea and Vietnam. *American Political Science Review* 65:358–75.

Niemi, Richard G., and Herbert F. Weisberg. 1976. *Controversies in American Voting Behavior.* San Francisco: Freeman.

O'Halloran, Sharyn. 1993. Congress and foreign trade policy. In *Congress Resurgent: Foreign and Defense Policy on Capitol Hill,* ed. Randall B. Ripley and James M. Lindsay, 283–303. Ann Arbor: University of Michigan Press.

Oldfield, Duane M., and Aaron B. Wildavsky. 1989. Reconsidering the two presidencies. *Society* 26:54–59.

O'Leary, Michael K. 1976. The role of issues. In *Linkage Politics,* ed. James N. Rosenau, 318–25. New York: Free Press.

Organski, A. F. K., 1958. *World Politics.* New York: Knopf.

Organski, A. F. K., and Jacek Kugler. 1980. *The War Ledger.* Chicago: University of Chicago Press.

Paige, Glenn D. 1968. *The Korean Decision.* New York: Free Press.

Pastor, Robert A. 1980. *Congress and the Politics of U.S. Foreign Economic Policy, 1929–1976.* Berkeley: University of California Press.

———. 1994. Disagreeing on Latin America. In *The President, the Congress, and the Making of Foreign Policy,* ed. Paul E. Peterson, 204–27. Norman: University of Oklahoma Press.

Peppers, Donald A. 1975. The "two presidencies" thesis: Eight years later. In *Perspectives on the Presidency,* ed. Aaron Wildavsky, 462–71. Boston: Little, Brown.

Peterson, Paul E. 1994a. The international system and foreign policy. In *The President, the Congress, and the Making of Foreign Policy,* ed. Paul E. Peterson, 3–22. Norman: University of Oklahoma Press.

———, ed. 1994b. *The President, the Congress, and the Making of Foreign Policy.* Norman: University of Oklahoma Press.

Peterson, Paul E., and Jay P. Greene. 1994a. Questioning by the foreign policy committees. In *The President, the Congress, and the Making of Foreign Policy,* ed. Paul E. Peterson, 74–97. Norman: University of Oklahoma Press.

———. 1994b. Why executive-legislative conflict in the United States is dwindling. *British Journal of Political Science* 24 (January): 33–55.

Polsby, Nelson W. 1971. Strengthening Congress in national policymaking. In *Congressional Behavior,* ed. Nelson W. Polsby, 3–13. New York: Random House.

Poole, Keith T., and Howard Rosenthal. 1997. *Congress: A Political-Economic History of Roll Call Voting.* New York: Oxford University Press.

Posen, Barry R. 1984. *The Sources of Military Doctrine: France, Britain, and Germany between the World Wars.* Ithaca: Cornell University Press.

Pritchard, Anita. 1986. An evaluation of *CQ* presidential support scores: The relationship between presidential election results and congressional voting decisions. *American Journal of Political Science* 30:480–95.

Purvis, Hoyt, and Steven J. Baker, eds. 1984. *Legislating Foreign Policy.* Boulder, CO: Westview.

Putnam, Robert D. 1988. Diplomacy and domestic politics: The logic of two-level games. *International Organization* 42:427–60.

Randle, Robert F. 1987. *Issues in the History of International Relations: The Role of Issues in the Evolution of the State System.* New York: Praeger.

Ransom, Harry Howe. 1970. *The Intelligence Establishment.* Rev. ed. Cambridge, MA: Harvard University Press.

Rasler, Karen A. 1986. War, accommodation, and violence in the United States, 1890–1970. *American Political Science Review* 80 (September): 921–45.

Rasler, Karen A., and William R. Thompson. 1985. War making and state making: Governmental expenditures, tax revenues, and global wars. *American Political Science Review* 79, no. 2 (June): 491–507.

———. 1989. *War and State Making.* Boston: Unwin Hyman.

Rieselbach, Leroy N. 1964. The demography of the congressional vote on foreign aid, 1939–1958. *American Political Science Review* 58 (September): 577–88.

———. 1973. *Congressional Politics.* New York: McGraw-Hill.

Ripley, Randall B. 1969. *Majority Party Leadership in Congress.* Boston: Little, Brown.

———. 1975. *Congress: Process and Policy.* New York: Norton.

Ripley, Randall B., and Grace N. Franklin. 1991. *Congress, the Bureaucracy and Public Policy.* Homewood, IL: Dorsey.

Ripley, Randall B., and James M. Lindsay, eds. 1993a. *Congress Resurgent: Foreign and Defense Policy on Capitol Hill.* Ann Arbor: University of Michigan Press.

———. 1993b. Foreign and defense policy in Congress: An overview and preview. In *Congress Resurgent: Foreign and Defense Policy on Capitol Hill,* ed. Randall B. Ripley and James M. Lindsay, 3–14. Ann Arbor: University of Michigan Press.

Roberts, Chalmers. 1954. The day we didn't go to war. *Reporter* 14 (September): 31–35.

Robinson, James A. 1962. *Congress and Foreign Policy–Making: A Study in Legislative Influence and Initiative.* New York: Dorsey.

Rockman, Bert A. 1979. Constants, cycles, trends and persona in presidential governance: Carter's troubles reviewed. Paper presented at the annual meeting of the American Political Science Association, Washington, DC, August–September.

———. 1994. Presidents, opinion, and institutional leadership. In *The New Politics of American Foreign Policy,* ed. David A. Deese, 59–74. New York: St. Martin's.

Rohde, David W. 1994a. Partisanship, leadership, and congressional assertiveness in foreign and defense policy. In *The New Politics of American Foreign Policy,* ed. David A. Deese, 76–101. New York: St. Martin's.

———. 1994b. Presidential support in the House of Representatives. In *The President, the Congress, and the Making of Foreign Policy,* ed. Paul E. Peterson, 101–28. Norman: University of Oklahoma Press.

Rosati, Jerel A. 1984. Congressional influence in American foreign policy: Addressing the controversy. *Journal of Political and Military Sociology* 12 (fall): 311–33.

Rosecrance, Richard, and Arthur A. Stein. 1993. Beyond realism: The study of grand strategy. In *The Domestic Bases of Grand Strategy,* ed. Richard Rosecrance and Arthur A. Stein, 3–21. Ithaca: Cornell University Press.

Rosenau, James N. 1967. *Domestic Sources of Foreign Policy.* New York: Free Press.

———. 1971a. Foreign policy as an issue area. In *The Scientific Study of Foreign Policy,* ed. James N. Rosenau, 401–40. New York: Free Press.

———. 1971b. Pre-theories and theories of foreign policy. In *The Scientific Study of Foreign Policy,* ed. James N. Rosenau, 95–150. New York: Free Press.

Roskin, Michael. 1974. From Pearl Harbor to Vietnam: Shifting generational paradigms and foreign policy. *Political Science Quarterly* 89:563–88.

Rourke, John T. 1983. *Congress and the Presidency in U.S. Foreign Policymaking: A Study of Interaction and Influence.* Boulder, CO: Westview.

———. 1987. Perception, the two-presidencies thesis, and the Reagan administration. Paper presented at the annual meeting of the Northeast International Studies Association, Philadelphia, November.

———. 1993. *Presidential Wars and American Democracy: Rally 'Round the Chief.* New York: Paragon.

Rourke, John T., and Russell Farnen. 1988. War, presidents, and the Constitution. *Presidential Studies Quarterly* 18:513–22.

Schattschneider, E. E. 1935. *Politics, Pressures, and the Tariff.* Hamden, CT: Archon.

Schlesinger, Arthur M., Jr. 1973. *The Imperial Presidency.* Boston: Houghton Mifflin.

———. 1986. *The Cycles of American History.* Boston: Houghton Mifflin.

Schneider, Jerrold E. 1979. *Ideological Coalitions in Congress.* Westport, CT: Greenwood.

Shepsle, Kenneth A. 1988. Representation and governance: The great legislative trade-off. *Political Science Quarterly* 103, no. 3:461–84.

———. 1992. Congress is a "they" not an "it": Legislative intent as oxymoron. *International Review of Law and Economics* 12 (June): 239–62.

Shull, Steven A. 1997. *Presidential-Congressional Relations: Policy and Time Approaches.* Ann Arbor: The University of Michigan Press.

Shull, Steven A., and Thomas C. Shaw. 1999. *Explaining Congressional Presidential Relations: A Multiple Perspective Approach.* Albany: State University of New York Press.

Sigelman, Lee. 1979. A reassessment of the two-presidencies thesis. *Journal of Politics* 41 (November): 1195–1205.

Silverstein, Gordon. 1994. Judicial enhancement of executive power. In *The President, the Congress, and the Making of Foreign Policy,* ed. Paul E. Peterson, 63–45. Norman: University of Oklahoma Press.

Sinclair, Barbara. 1989. *Transformation of the U.S. Senate.* Baltimore: Johns Hopkins University Press.

———. 1993. Congressional party leaders in the foreign and defense policy arena. In *Congress Resurgent: Foreign and Defense Policy on Capitol Hill,* ed. Randall B. Ripley and James M. Lindsay, 207–31. Ann Arbor: University of Michigan Press.

Singer, J. David, Stuart Bremer, and John Stuckey. 1972. Capability distribution, uncertainty, and major power war, 1820–1965. In *Peace, War, and Numbers,* ed. Bruce M. Russett, 19–48. Beverly Hills, CA: Sage.

Skidmore, David. 1996. *Reversing Course: Carter's Foreign Policy, Domestic Politics, and the Failure of Reform.* Nashville: Vanderbilt University Press.

Small, Melvin, and J. David Singer. 1982. *Resort to Arms: International and Civil Wars, 1816–1980.* Beverly Hills, CA: Sage.

Smist, Frank J., Jr. 1994. *Congress oversees the U.S. Intelligence Community, 1947–94.* 2d ed. Knoxville: University of Tennessee Press.

Smith, Jean E. 1989. *The Constitution and American Foreign Policy.* New York: West.

Smith, Steven S. 1989. *Call to Order: Floor Politics in the House and Senate.* Washington, DC: Brookings Institution.

———. 1994. Congressional party leaders. In *The President, the Congress, and the Making of Foreign Policy,* ed. Paul E. Peterson, 129–57. Norman: University of Oklahoma Press.

Smyrl, Marc E. 1988. *Conflict or Codetermination? Congress, the President, and the Power to Make War.* Cambridge, MA: Ballinger.

Snyder, Jack. 1991. Conclusion. In *Dominoes and Bandwagons: Strategic Beliefs and Great Power Competition in the Eurasian Rimland,* ed. Robert Jervis and Jack Snyder, 276–90. New York: Oxford University Press.

Spitzer, Robert J. 1983. *The Presidency and Public Policy: The Four Arenas of Presidential Power.* University: University of Alabama Press.

———. 1993. *President and Congress: Executive Hegemony at the Crossroads of American Government.* New York: McGraw-Hill.

Stein, Arthur A. 1980. *The Nation at War.* Baltimore: Johns Hopkins University Press.

———. 1993. Domestic constraints, extended deterrence, and the incoherence of grand strategy. In *The Domestic Bases of Grand Strategy*, ed. Richard Rosecrance and Arthur A. Stein, 96–123. Ithaca: Cornell University Press.

Stockton, Paul N. 1993. Congress and defense policy-making for the post–cold war era. In *Congress Resurgent: Foreign and Defense Policy on Capitol Hill*, ed. Randall B. Ripley and James M. Lindsay, 235–59. Ann Arbor: University of Michigan Press.

Sullivan, Terry. 1991. A matter of fact: The "two presidencies" thesis revitalized. In *The Two Presidencies: A Quarter Century Assessment*, ed. Steven A. Shull, 143–57. Chicago: Nelson-Hall.

Sundquist, James L. 1973. *Dynamics of the Party System*. Washington, DC: Brookings Institution.

———. 1981. *The Decline and Resurgence of Congress*. Washington, DC: Brookings Institution.

Tetlock, Philip E., and Aaron Belkin. 1996. *Counterfactual Thought Experiments in World Politics: Logical, Methodological, and Psychological Perspectives*. Princeton: Princeton University Press.

Tickner, J. Ann. 1987. *Self-Reliance versus Power Politics: The American and Indian Experiences in Building Nation States*. New York: Columbia University Press.

Tidmarch, Charles M., and Charles M. Sabatt. 1972. Presidential leadership change and foreign policy roll-call voting in the U.S. Senate. *Western Political Quarterly* 25 (December): 613–25.

Tierney, John T. 1993. Interest group involvement in congressional foreign and defense policy. In *Congress Resurgent: Foreign and Defense Policy on Capitol Hill*, ed. Randall B. Ripley and James M. Lindsay, 89–111. Ann Arbor: University of Michigan Press.

———. 1994. Congressional activism in foreign policy: Its varied forms and stimuli. In *The New Politics of American Foreign Policy*, ed. David A. Deese, 102–30. New York: St. Martin's.

Tilly, Charles. 1975. Reflections on the history of European state-making. In *The Formation of National States in Western Europe*, ed. Charles Tilly, 3–83. Princeton: Princeton University Press.

———. 1990. *Coercion, Capital, and European States, AD 990–1990*. Cambridge, MA: Basil Blackwell.

Treverton, Gregory. 1990. Intelligence: Welcome to the American government. In *A Question of Balance: The President, the Congress, and Foreign Policy*, ed. Thomas E. Mann, 70–108. Washington, DC: Brookings Institution.

Van Doren, Peter M. 1986. The limitations of roll-call vote analysis: An analysis of legislative energy proposals, 1945–1976. Paper presented at the annual meeting of the American Political Science Association, Washington, DC, August.

———. 1990. Can we learn the causes of congressional decisions from roll-call data? *Legislative Studies Quarterly* 15:311–40.

———. 1991. *Politics, Markets, and Congressional Policy Choices*. Ann Arbor: University of Michigan Press.

Vasquez, John A. 1983a. *The Power of Power Politics: A Critique*. New Brunswick, NJ: Rutgers University Press.

———. 1983b. The tangibility of issues and global conflict: A test of Rosenau's issue area typology. *Journal of Peace Research* 20:179–92.

———. 1985. Domestic contention on critical foreign-policy issues: The case of the U.S. *International Organization* 39 (autumn): 643–66.

———. 1993. *The War Puzzle*. Cambridge: Cambridge University Press.

———. 1997. The realist paradigm and degenerative versus progressive research programs: An appraisal of neotraditional research on Waltz's balancing proposition. *American Political Science Review* 91 (December): 899–912.

———. 1998. *The Power of Power Politics: From Classical Realism to Neotraditionalism*. Cambridge: Cambridge University Press.

Vasquez, John A., and Richard W. Mansbach. 1983. The issue cycle: Conceptualizing long-term global political change. *International Organization* 37 (spring): 257–79.

Verba, Sidney, and Norman H. Nie. 1976. The rationality of political activity: A reconsideration. In *Controversies in American Voting Behavior*, ed. Richard G. Niemi and Herbert F. Weisberg, 45–65. San Francisco: Freeman.

Waltz, Kenneth. 1959. *Man, the State, and War*. New York: Columbia University Press.

———. 1979. *Theory of International Politics*. Reading, MA: Addison-Wesley.

Warburg, Gerald Felix. 1989. *Conflict and Consensus: The Struggle between Congress and the President over Foreign Policymaking*. New York: Harper and Row.

Wayman, Frank Weylon. 1984. Bipolarity and war: The role of capability concentration and alliance patterns among major powers, 1816–1965. *Journal of Peace Research* 21, no. 1: 61–78.

———. 1985. Arms control and strategic arms voting in the U.S. Senate: Patterns of change, 1967–1983. *Journal of Conflict Resolution* 29:225–51.

———. 1995. Interest groups, U.S. military spending, and international security. Paper presented at the annual meeting of the International Studies Association, Chicago, February.

Weissman, Stephen R. 1995. *A Culture of Deference: Congress's Failure of Leadership in Foreign Policy*. New York: Basic Books.

Whalen, Charles, Jr. 1982. *The House and Foreign Policy: The Irony of Reform*. Chapel Hill: University of North Carolina Press.

White, Joseph. 1993. Decision making in the appropriations subcommittees on defense and foreign operations. In *Congress Resurgent: Foreign and Defense Policy on Capitol Hill*, ed. Randall B. Ripley and James M. Lindsay, 183–206. Ann Arbor: University of Michigan Press.

Wildavsky, Aaron. 1966. The two presidencies. *Trans-Action* 4:7–14.

———. 1991. *The Beleaguered Presidency*. New Brunswick, NJ: Transaction Books.

Wilkenfeld, Jonathan, G. W. Hopple, P. J. Rossa, and Stephen J. Andriole. 1980. *Foreign Policy Behavior*. Beverly Hills, CA: Sage.

Wilson, Woodrow. 1885. *Congressional Government*. Boston: Houghton Mifflin. Rpt. New York: Meridian Books, 1956.

Wittkopf, Eugene R., and Michael A. Maggiotto. 1983. Elites and masses: A comparative analysis of attitudes toward America's world role. *Journal of Politics* 45:303–34.

Wittkopf, Eugene R., and James M. McCormick. 1998. When Congress supports the president: A multilevel inquiry, 1948–1996. Paper presented at the Third Pan-European International Relations Conference and Joint Meeting with the International Studies Association, Vienna, Austria, September.

Wolfers, Arnold. 1952. "National security" as an ambiguous symbol. *Political Science Quarterly* 67 (December): 481–502.

Wormuth, Francis D., and Edwin Firmage. 1986. *To Chain the Dog of War: The War Powers of Congress in History and Law*. Dallas: Southern Methodist University Press.

Zacher, Mark W., and Richard A. Matthew. 1995. Liberal international theory: Common threads, divergent strands. In *Controversies in International Relations Theory: Realism and the Neoliberal Challenge*, ed. Charles W. Kegley, Jr., 107–50. New York: St. Martin's.

Zimmerman, William. 1973. Issue area and foreign policy process: A research note in search of a general theory. *American Political Science Review* 67:1204–12.

Author Index

Subject Index